To Mya
thanks for
reading in

HARD TIME

2ND EDITION

Jail Stripes
at Orleans

Banged Up Abroad
Raving Arizona

Park School
Dog!

SHAUN ATTWOOD

D1335351

A catalogue record of this book is available from the British Library

ISBN: 978-0-9930215-0-3

Second edition published in Great Britain
by Gadfly Press UK (Shaun Attwood) in 2014

First edition published in Great Britain
by Mainstream Publishing (Random House) in 2010

Cover photo © Derick Attwood 2014
Cover design by Shiv

Printed in Great Britain by Clays Ltd, St Ives plc

MY SOCIAL–MEDIA LINKS

Email: attwood.shaun@hotmail.co.uk
Blog: Jon's Jail Journal
Website: shaunattwood.com
Twitter: @shaunattwood
YouTube: Shaun Attwood
LinkedIn: Shaun Attwood
Goodreads: Shaun Attwood
Facebook pages: Shaun Attwood, Jon's Jail Journal,
T-Bone Appreciation Society

I welcome your questions, comments and
feedback on any of my books:
Party Time
Hard Time
Prison Time
Lessons
Two Tonys (Expected 2015-2016)
We Are Being Lied To (Expected 2015-2016)
T-Bone (Expected 2017)

ACKNOWLEDGEMENTS

A big thank you to my proofreaders: Barbara Attwood,
Penny Kimber, Claire Bishop, Mark Coates,
Ian McClary, Andy Frye, Shiv (cover design)
and Derick Attwood (cover photo)

CHAPTER 1

Sleep deprived and scanning for danger, I enter a dark cell on the second floor of the maximum-security Madison Street jail in Phoenix, Arizona, where guards and gang members are murdering prisoners. Behind me, the metal door slams heavily. Light slants into the cell through oblong gaps in the door, illuminating a prisoner cocooned in a white sheet, snoring lightly on the top bunk about two thirds of the way up the back wall. Relieved there is no immediate threat, I place my mattress on the grimy floor. Desperate to rest, I notice movement on the cement-block walls. *Am I hallucinating?* I blink several times. The walls appear to ripple. Stepping closer, I see the walls are alive with insects. I flinch. So many are swarming, I wonder if they're a colony of ants on the move. To get a better look, I put my eyes right up to them. They are mostly the size of almonds and have antennae. American cockroaches. I've seen them in the holding cells downstairs in smaller numbers, but nothing like this. A chill spreads over my body. I back away.

Something alive falls from the ceiling and bounces off the base of my neck. I jump. With my night vision improving, I spot cockroaches weaving in and out of the base of the fluorescent strip light. Every so often one drops onto the concrete and resumes crawling. Examining the bottom bunk, I realise why my cellmate is sleeping at a higher elevation: cockroaches are pouring from gaps in the decrepit wall at the level of my bunk. The area is thick with them. Placing my mattress on the bottom bunk scatters them. I walk towards the toilet, crunching a few under my shower sandals. I urinate and grab the toilet roll. A cockroach darts from the centre of the roll onto my hand, tickling my fingers. My arm jerks as if it has a mind of its own, losing the cockroach and the toilet roll. Using a towel, I wipe the bulk of them off the bottom bunk, stopping only to shake the odd one off my hand. I unroll my mattress. They begin to regroup and inhabit my mattress. My adrenaline is pumping so much, I lose my fatigue.

Nauseated, I sit on a tiny metal stool bolted to the wall. *How will I sleep? How's my cellmate sleeping through the infestation and my arrival?* Copying his technique, I cocoon myself in a sheet and lie down, crushing more cockroaches. The only way they can access me now is through the breathing hole I've left in the sheet by the lower half of my face. Inhaling their strange musty odour, I close my eyes. I can't sleep. I feel them crawling on the sheet around my feet. *Am I imagining things?* Frightened of them infiltrating my breathing hole, I keep opening my eyes. Cramps cause me to rotate onto my other side. Facing the wall, I'm repulsed by so many of them just inches away. I return to my original side.

The sheet traps the heat of the Sonoran Desert to my body, soaking me in sweat. Sweat tickles my body, tricking my mind into thinking the cockroaches are infiltrating and crawling on me. The trapped heat aggravates my bleeding skin infections and bedsores. I want to scratch myself, but I know better. The outer layers of my skin have turned soggy from sweating constantly in this concrete oven. Squirming on the bunk fails to stop the relentless itchiness of my skin. Eventually, I scratch myself. Clumps of moist skin detach under my nails. Every now and then I become so uncomfortable, I have to open my cocoon to waft the heat out, which allows the cockroaches in. It takes hours to drift to sleep. I only manage a few hours. I awake stuck to the soaked sheet, disgusted by the cockroach carcasses compressed against the mattress.

The cockroaches plague my new home until dawn appears at the dots in the metal grid over a begrimed strip of four-inch-thick bullet-proof glass at the top of the back wall – the cell's only source of outdoor light. They disappear into the cracks in the walls, like vampire mist retreating from sunlight. But not all of them. There were so many on the night shift that even their vastly reduced number is too many to dispose of. And they act like they know it. They roam around my feet with attitude, as if to make it clear that I'm trespassing on their turf.

My next set of challenges will arise not from the insect world, but from my neighbours. I'm the new arrival, subject to scrutiny about my charges just like when I'd run into the Aryan Brotherhood prison gang on my first day at the medium-security Towers jail a year ago. I wish my cellmate would wake up, brief me on the mood of the locals and introduce me to the head of the white gang. No such luck. Chow is announced over a speaker system in a crackly robotic voice, but he doesn't stir.

I emerge into the day room for breakfast. Prisoners in black-and-white bee-striped uniforms gather under the metal-grid stairs and tip dead cockroaches into a trash bin from plastic peanut-butter containers they'd set as traps during the night. All eyes are on me in the chow line. Watching who sits where, I hold my head up, put on a solid stare and pretend to be as at home in this environment as the cockroaches. It's all an act. I'm lonely and afraid. I loathe having to explain myself to the head of the white race, who I assume is the toughest murderer. I've been in jail long enough to know that taking my breakfast to my cell will imply that I have something to hide.

The gang punishes criminals with certain charges. The most serious are sex offenders, who are KOS: Kill On Sight. Other charges are punishable by SOS – Smash On Sight – such as drive-by shootings because women and kids sometimes get killed. It's called convict justice. Gang members are constantly looking for people to beat up because that's how they earn their reputations and tattoos. The most serious acts of violence earn the highest-ranking tattoos. To be a full gang member requires murder. I've observed the body language and techniques inmates trying to integrate employ. An inmate with a spring in his step and an air of confidence is likely to be accepted. A person who avoids eye contact and fails to introduce himself to the gang is likely to be preyed on. Some of the failed attempts I saw ended up with heads getting cracked against toilets, a sound I've grown familiar with. I've seen prisoners being extracted on stretchers who looked dead – one had yellow fluid leaking from his head. The constant violence gives me nightmares, but the reality is that I put myself in here, so I force myself to accept it as a part of my punishment.

It's time to apply my knowledge. With a self-assured stride, I take my breakfast bag to the table of white inmates covered in neo-Nazi tattoos, allowing them to question me.

"Mind if I sit with you guys?" I ask, glad exhaustion has deepened my voice.

"These seats are taken. But you can stand at the corner of the table."

The man who answered is probably the head of the gang. I size him up. Cropped brown hair. A dangerous glint in Nordic-blue eyes. Tiny pupils that suggest he's on heroin. Weightlifter-type veins bulging from a sturdy neck. Political ink on arms crisscrossed with scars. About the same age as me, thirty-three.

"Thanks. I'm Shaun from England." I volunteer my origin to show I'm different from them but not in a way that might get me smashed.

"I'm Bullet, the head of the whites." He offers me his fist to bump. "Where you roll in from, wood?"

Addressing me as wood is a good sign. It's what white gang members on a friendly basis call each other.

"Towers jail. They increased my bond and re-classified me to maximum security."

"What's your bond at?"

"I've got two $750,000 bonds," I say in a monotone. This is no place to brag about bonds.

"How many people you kill, brother?" His eyes drill into mine, checking whether my body language supports my story. My body language so far is spot on.

"None. I threw rave parties. They got us talking about drugs on wiretaps." Discussing drugs on the phone does not warrant a $1.5 million bond. I know and beat him to his next question.

"Here's my charges." I show him my charge sheet, which includes conspiracy and leading a crime syndicate – both from running an Ecstasy ring.

Bullet snatches the paper and scrutinises it. Attempting to pre-empt his verdict, the other whites study his face. On edge, I wait for him to respond. Whatever he says next will determine whether I'll be accepted or victimised.

"Are you some kind of jailhouse attorney?" Bullet asks. "I want someone to read through my case paperwork." During our few minutes of conversation, Bullet has seen through my act and concluded that I'm educated – a possible resource to him.

I appreciate that he'll accept me if I take the time to read his case. "I'm no jailhouse attorney, but I'll look through it and help you however I can."

"Good. I'll stop by your cell later on, wood."

After breakfast, I seal as many of the cracks in the walls as I can with toothpaste. The cell smells minty, but the cockroaches still find their way in. Their day shift appears to be collecting information on the brown paper bags under my bunk, containing a few items of food that I purchased from the commissary; bags that I tied off with rubber bands in the hope of keeping the cockroaches out. Relentlessly, the cockroaches explore the bags for entry points, pausing over and probing the most worn and vulnerable regions. *Will the nightly swarm eat right through the paper?* I read all morning, wondering whether my cellmate has died in his cocoon, his occasional breathing sounds reassuring me.

Bullet stops by late afternoon and drops his case paperwork off. He's been charged with Class 3 felonies and less, not serious crimes, but is facing a double-digit sentence because of his prior convictions and Security Threat Group status in the prison system. The proposed sentencing range seems disproportionate. I'll advise him to reject the plea bargain – on the assumption he already knows to do so, but is just seeking the comfort of a second opinion, like many un-sentenced inmates. When he returns for his paperwork, our conversation disturbs my cellmate – the cocoon shuffles – so we go upstairs to his cell. I tell Bullet what I think. He is excitable, a different man from earlier, his pupils almost non-existent.

"This case ain't shit. But my prosecutor knows I done other shit, all kinds of heavy shit, but can't prove it. I'd do anything to get that sorry bitch off my fucking ass. She's asking for something bad to happen to her. Man, if I ever get bonded out, I'm gonna chop that bitch into pieces. Kill her slowly though. Like to work her over with a blowtorch."

Such talk can get us both charged with conspiring to murder a prosecutor, so I try to steer him elsewhere. "It's crazy how they can catch you doing one thing, yet try to sentence you for all of the things they think you've ever done."

"Done plenty. Shot some dude in the stomach once. Rolled him up in a blanket and threw him in a dumpster."

Discussing past murders is as unsettling as future ones. "So what's all your tattoos mean, Bullet? Like that eagle on your chest?"

"Why you wanna know?" Bullet's eyes probe mine.

My eyes hold their ground. "Just curious."

"It's a war bird. The AB patch."

"AB patch?"

"What the Aryan Brotherhood gives you when you've put enough work in."

"How long does it take to earn a patch?"

"Depends how quickly you put your work in. You have to earn your lightning bolts first."

"Why you got red and black lightning bolts?"

"You get SS bolts for beating someone down or for being an enforcer for the family. Red lightning bolts for killing someone. I was sent down as a youngster. They gave me steel and told me who to handle and I handled it. You don't ask questions. You just get blood on your steel. Dudes who get these tats without putting work in are told to cover them up or leave the yard."

"What if they refuse?"

"They're held down and we carve the ink off them."

Imagining them carving a chunk of flesh to remove a tattoo, I cringe. He's really enjoying telling me this now. His volatile nature is clear and frightening. *He's accepted me too much. He's trying to impress me before making demands.*

At night, I'm unable to sleep. Cocooned in heat, surrounded by cockroaches, I hear the swamp-cooler vent – a metal grid at the top of a wall – hissing out tepid air. Giving up on sleep, I put my earphones on and tune into National Public Radio. Listening to a Vivaldi violin concerto, I close my eyes and press my tailbone down to straighten my back as if I'm doing a yogic relaxation. The playful allegro thrills me, lifting my spirits, but the wistful adagio provokes sad emotions and tears. I open my eyes and gaze into the gloom. Due to lack of sleep, I start hallucinating and hearing voices over the music whispering threats. I'm at breaking point. Although I have accepted that I committed crimes and deserve to be punished, no one should have to live like this. I'm furious at myself for making the series of reckless decisions that put me in here and for losing absolutely everything. As violins crescendo in my ears, I remember what my life used to be like.

CHAPTER 2

Drugs were fun at first. That's why I did them. I have no excuses. No sob story to tell. I was raised by great parents in a loving home. Other than having to eat Brussels sprouts with my Sunday dinner, I suffered no abuse as a child. I excelled at school and dated some of the most popular girls at college. Even when my mother launched her shoes at me for teasing my sister or my father showed my girlfriends naked pictures of me scampering around as a baby, I never had the urge to run away from home. In fact, I enjoyed living there so much I chose the nearest university, Liverpool, so I wouldn't have to move out.

When raving began in England, I went to a club in Manchester called the Thunderdome, and tried Ecstasy and speed for the first time. Before drugs, I was too shy to talk to strangers in clubs and too self-conscious to dance, but on Ecstasy and speed I couldn't stop dancing, smiling and hugging people I didn't know. Studying hard on the weekdays, I lived to rave every weekend. Each time I took drugs, I told myself, *I can quit whenever I want. I can party and still function. I'll never get addicted.* I was oblivious to the downside.

Even though I sat some of my final exams coming down off Ecstasy – with techno beeps and beats resounding in my brain – I scored a 2:1 with honours. Wearing a mortar-board cap over my short Mohawk and a ceremonial robe with what looked like a superhero's cape, I strutted into the Philharmonic Hall in Liverpool. Receiving my BA in Business Studies, I soaked up the admiration from my parents: an insurance salesman and teacher from a chemical-manufacturing town called Widnes.

Long before my graduation, I'd set my career sights on finance. I'd been following the stock market since age 14, and at

16 had doubled my grandmother's money in British Telecom. I read hundreds of books on the subject. Historical accounts of stock-market operators conjured up visions of my own future financial greatness, which elevated the hair on my arms. After university, I applied to be an investment analyst in London. Convinced I'd be hired on the spot because of my passion for the stock market, I ended up going through months of gruelling interviews. Each job rejection crushed my optimism.

Casting around for work elsewhere, I thought of my aunt Mo in America. She lived in Phoenix, Arizona, where she'd earned a reputation for being one of the toughest fraud-busters in the Wild West. She said Phoenix was booming, and from previous visits during my teens – that involved her altering the date of birth in my passport so I was allowed in bars, and introducing me to women as Paul McCartney's nephew – I knew I could go a long way there with just my English accent. My parents supported my decision to move. In 1991, they drove me to the train station. Hugging them, I was sad to leave but excited by the prospect of conquering Wall Street. I planned to make my first million within five years by applying my two favourite mottos:

"Greed is good."
– Gordon Gekko in the movie, *Wall Street*

"It's fuck or be fucked in the business world."
– My aunt Mo

I touched down in Phoenix with a six-month traveller's visa and only student credit cards to survive on. Aunt Mo showed me how to obtain a Social Security number and forge an H-1B work visa using a simple printing set from an office-products store. She coached me on what to say to employers. At job interviews, I felt nervous bluffing about my status in the country, but getting a commission-only stockbroker position was all the proof I needed that it paid to twist the rules.

For the first few months, I cold-called from 6 a.m. to 9 p.m. for no pay, walked to work, and lived off cheese sandwiches and bananas. When my credit cards reached their limits, I feared I'd have to return to England. Seeing I was getting nowhere, the three hardy stockbrokers I shared a table with schooled me in the art of poaching other brokers' clients. I entered a business partnership with another rookie, Matt. We pledged to watch each other's backs.

Exhausted from months of relentless cold-calling, I suggested to Matt that we dumpster-dive other brokerages for sales leads. He dismissed the idea as insane until I stuck my hand in our trash and extracted paperwork with our clients' names, addresses and telephone numbers.

We bought garbage gloves, trash bags and box cutters. We targeted a rival firm because two of their brokers had threatened to blow up Matt's car over a mutual client. Matt drove us to the brokerage. The dumpster was enclosed by three walls and a gate at the front. We grabbed bags and sliced them open. Each bag assaulted us with the odour of coffee-soaked paperwork and leftovers putrefying in the desert heat. Eventually, we found stacks of account paperwork, which we loaded into Matt's car. Dumpster-diving boosted my commission. The branch manager started cutting me in on the distributions of accounts from brokers who had quit. That's how I rose up the ranks in the first two years.

Matt became addicted to crystal meth. He lost his job, fiancée and health. Having run up a drug debt with the wrong people, he fled Arizona. I never heard from him again.

I broke the record for the most new accounts opened. My commissions started to climb. Convinced the meaning of life was making money, I had become a piranha among the sharks.

Five years later, I was the top producer in the office, grossing over $500,000 a year. I had my own secretary and cold callers. I won awards and was sent to luxury hotels and a skiing holiday in Colorado. But I'd worked so hard, I had what the stockbrokers called BOBS: Burnt Out Broker Syndrome. To counter my stress,

I returned to partying on the weekends like I'd done at university.

The first time I took Ecstasy in America was at the Silver Dollar Club, a gay bar frequented by ravers in Phoenix's run-down warehouse district. Hovering around the bar, I waited for my high to arrive. It took about thirty minutes for my knees to buckle. The sides of my head tingled as a warmth inched in. The warmth swept my face, the nape of my neck and travelled down my spine. My diaphragm and chest moved in harmony as my breathing slowed down. Each exhale released more tension. I grew hot but relaxed. Unable to stop smiling, I drifted over to the dance floor in the dark room. The dancers on a platform grabbed my arms and pulled me up. Inhibitions gone, I moved effortlessly to the music. I closed my eyes and allowed the music to move me. I seemed to float. Rush after rush swept my body like electricity. *Are you ready?* came the vocals. *Jump everybody jump everybody jump…* I leapt from platform to platform. When DJ Sandra Collins played the Prodigy, I thought I was at an English rave. I danced my way to the front of the main stage, dripping sweat, hands in the air, eyeballs rolling towards heaven, hugging the strangers around me, grinning at the throng of freaks below. I felt right at home.

Tired of being a worker ant, I salted money away into technology stocks and retired from stockbroking in 1997. With no office to attend or boss to answer to, I decided to make a career out of partying. It began with house parties that went on for days, fuelled by drugs I bought for my friends.

The first time I bought twenty Ecstasy pills in America, I was terrified. I had to wait in my car outside of an apartment while Acid Joey – a stocky Native American high on ketamine – went inside with my $400. Stuck to the seat by my sweat, I convinced myself that the Feds were going to jump out of nowhere with guns and surround my vehicle. I imagined Acid Joey getting robbed or running off with my money. Even when he returned with twenty Eurodollar Ecstasy pills, I drove away certain of being pulled over. But when I didn't get robbed or caught or run into any of the other scenarios I'd seen on TV, I started to believe I could get away with anything.

I wanted my American friends to enjoy the rave atmosphere I'd experienced in England, so we mostly did Ecstasy. Giving drugs away for free increased the number of my friends fast. When the local dealers could no longer supply my needs, I found out who their main supplier was in LA – a surfer gangster called Sol – and arranged to buy 500 hits from him.

Two carloads of us drove for five hours to a house in West Hollywood. Annoyingly, Sol wasn't home at the prearranged time. From a vantage point in a side street, we sat in our cars and waited, our stress rising. Carrying a surfboard, Sol showed up hours later.

"I'll go in now," I said to Wild Man. "If I'm not back out in fifteen minutes, come and rescue me."

Wild Man – my best friend from England – had grown twice my size. When he was a small child, his older brother had special-ised in tormenting him in the cruellest ways, including making him eat dogs' turds. After I took him under my wing, the gang run by his older brother dangled me off a cliff. Hanging out nearly every day after school, we bonded at an early age. To make money, we set up a car wash outside of a hotel. In his later teens, Wild Man honed his fighting skills on nightclub bouncers, scarring all of his knuckles with teeth marks. Worried about him getting into trouble in England, I promised to fly him to America when I had enough money. He ended up in a UK prison for robbing an Ec-stasy dealer. Hoping to get him a job as a wrestler, I flew him to Arizona, but he refused to settle down. I tried to get him various jobs, but he failed the drug tests. Eventually, he refused to do any kind of work, and we both slipped deeper into drugs.

"I'd like to wrap that fucking surfboard around his head," Wild Man said, "seeing as he's kept us waiting this fucking long. Why don't I just kick his door down and take his shit?"

"That's not good business," I said.

"It's not good business him keeping us waiting out here for two hours either!"

"If you rob him, then who're we going to go through?" Turning to Wild Man's cousin, Hammy, I said, "Keep the Wild Man under control, would you?"

"That's like trying to keep a bull from a red rag," Hammy said. "I'll do my best."

I got out and knocked on Sol's door.

"Come in," Sol said.

"I've been here a while." Entering his house, not quite knowing what I was getting into, I braced for someone to jump out and rob me.

"I lost track of time," he said. "I have your 500 Mitsubishis. I'll be right back." He went into another room. For a few seconds, I expected him to reappear with a gun. My heartbeat slowed down when he produced a Ziploc bag with more pills than I'd ever seen.

"How much MDMA's in them?" I asked, feasting my eyes on the quantity.

"One hundred and twenty-five milligrams. From Holland. I don't sell any Made-in-America bunk. Besides, I'm told you can afford a lot more than 500. I'm sick of Arizona ravers coming to my house and buying a hundred here and there. I'd rather sell bulk to one person. It'd be safer for all of us. And the product will be good like these."

"Can I taste one?" I asked.

His eyebrows jumped. "Taste one?"

"I always chew them. They have a distinct taste." I studied his face for hints of deceit.

"Want a chaser?"

"Water, please."

I examined a pill. More dirty white than beige. Speckled like a bird's egg. A press of three diamonds: the Mitsubishi logo. Chewing it, I recognised the sharp chemical taste that precedes an Ecstasy high. "It's a good pill. Here's seven gees. If you want me to buy more, I expect a much better price next time."

The Ecstasy my friends and I didn't eat, we dealt to the local dealers. Making money from them enabled me to increase the scale of things. I threw raves for thousands of people, generating enough profits to give away hundreds of Ecstasy pills every weekend and to squander thousands on lavish after-parties and other drugs like ketamine and crystal meth. The more drugs I fed my friends, the more they pampered me. I was buying popularity, especially with the glitter girls, who spoiled me at the after-parties. Deep in the rave lifestyle, I lost touch with reality. My arrogance was such that I was enjoying every second of it without thinking I'd ever get caught.

The ravers nicknamed me "English Shaun" and "The Bank of England." I was considered one of the wealthiest people in Arizona's rave scene. To avoid getting robbed, I formed my own security team.

One of my bodyguards, G Dog – a tall Mexican American with long hair and prison-tattooed arms – urged me to meet his brother, Raul. He said if Raul and his associates had my back, I'd have few problems in Arizona. With G Dog, I drove to Raul's house in Tempe.

The grenade launcher on top of the biggest TV I'd ever seen belonged to Raul, who was watching a much smaller screen showing the comings and goings on the street outside crowded with lowriders.

"This is the English guy," G Dog said.

Raul, short and plump, tilted his head back. "What's up, homey," he said without smiling.

"Pleased to meet you," I said, shaking his hand. "I like your TV."

"Damn, you talk funny – like an accent – I guess you are from England, homey. Come through to the kitchen. Meet my homies."

Raul introduced me to a gang of gargantuan Mexican Americans. Heavily tattooed, they were standing around a table laden with slabs of crystal meth, cocaine and various weighing scales. They eyed me suspiciously. The biggest swung a spoon with cocaine towards my face. "Snort it." There was danger in his wide and alert eyes.

Concerned, I looked to G Dog for help, but he just nodded back with a stern expression. G Dog hadn't yet told me these men were members of the New Mexican Mafia, the most powerful criminal organisation in Arizona at that time. Or that the man with the spoon was a hit man on a killing spree. Sensing the gravity of the situation, I rolled a hundred-dollar bill, pushed one nostril flat and snorted the cocaine through the other.

The man with the spoon nodded and shook my hand. But he didn't smile. None of them smiled.

"Shaun, let's go talk business." Raul led me into a bedroom. "G Dog tells me you can get this Ecstasy shit and it's all good."

"I can get it," I said, my throat gagging on the numbing aftertaste of the cocaine.

"None of us have ever done that shit. The only thing I do is smoke good weed. Know what I'm saying? I'm having a party at the weekend, some women are coming over and we wanna check your Ecstasy out."

I was present when they all took Ecstasy for the first time. Not only did they smile, it reduced them to overgrown teddy bears who wouldn't stop hugging me. That's how I earned the protection of the New Mexican Mafia. It was a relationship that probably saved my life later on, when, for reasons of their own, they killed some rival gangsters who were about to shoot and rob me.

In the run up to the dot.com bubble, I started day trading and became a millionaire. Now I could really expand my operation. My new main supplier in LA, DJ Mike Hotwheelz, was arrested by the Feds, and the other LA suppliers like Sol couldn't fill my increasingly large orders, so I imported bulk Ecstasy from Amsterdam. At the peak of things, I had my own rave clothing/music store and LSD chemist. At the Little White Chapel on the Las Vegas Strip, I married Amy – a political science student at the University of Arizona who was also a topless dancer doing lesbian Internet porn. We moved into a million-dollar mountainside home in Sin Vacas, Tucson. I had run-ins with gangsters such as Sammy the Bull, my main competitor in the Ecstasy market.

The first time I discussed business with members of Sammy the Bull's crew, I brought one of the notorious Rossetti Brothers, who also worked security for me. Outside of the meeting place, Heart 5, a bar in Tucson, I drank some GHB, which made me fearless. I said to Rossetti, "While I talk to Spaniard, make sure you're always somewhere you can pull your gun in case they try to kidnap me. I'm not going to start any shit, but who knows how big a crew he's with or what might happen."

"No problem. If they try anything, I'll open up on the motherfuckers."

I was at the bar when a six-and-a-half-foot man with dark spiky hair and biceps as broad as my neck tapped me on the shoulder. "I'm Mark, Spaniard's partner. He wants to see you in the VIP area."

"OK, Mark." I shook his hand and followed him.

"Glad you came, English Shaun," said Spaniard, a well-groomed Hispanic. "Mark, clear that sofa."

Mark yelled, "You need to move, so we can sit down!" The people on the sofa jumped up.

To the side of us, Rossetti slipped into the VIP area.

As I sat between them, the GHB jolted my brain. It made me playful and crazy. Just like my grandfather used to do to me, I squeezed their legs above the knee. "So what's this all about?"

They were taken aback for a few seconds, until Spaniard laughed and said in a friendly voice, "Look, we know you're doing your own thing. You've got a lot of people working for you. As do we. It would be best if we worked together rather than be enemies."

"What're you proposing?"

"We're getting a lot of pills and we figure we can give you a better price than what you're paying."

"You don't know what I'm paying. I'm familiar with your pills. I don't think the quality is there. I'm getting European pills. None of the coloured pills you guys are getting."

"Who the fuck do you think you are talking shit about our

pills?" Mark yelled.

Due to the GHB, Mark didn't scare me. I viewed him as a funny monster with a little brain.

"Hey, Mark, calm down," Spaniard said.

"Do you have any idea who Jimmy Moran is?" Mark said, fuming.

"No," I said.

"Sammy the Bull," Mark said. "That's who we work for. One call to him and we can have you taken out to the desert."

I was aware of Sammy the Bull from the news. He'd been a hit man for the Gambino Crime Family – one of the five Italian Mafia families that dominated organised crime in America – run by John Gotti, aka "the Teflon Don." Later on, Sammy the Bull became an FBI informant, confessed to killing nineteen people, and helped the Feds put the Teflon Don away for life. Still, looking at Spaniard and Mark in shiny animal-print polyester shirts, I assumed they didn't have as much power in Arizona as my associates in the New Mexican Mafia. I glanced at Rossetti. The look on his face said, *Should I shoot that lunkhead or what?*

Almost imperceptibly, I shook my head at Rossetti.

"There's no need to say all that," Spaniard said. "Forgive Mark, Shaun. He gets upset real easy. He's a bit of a hothead."

"I have no problems with you guys, but I really don't care who you work for. You just moved in. Over the years, I've made friends with a lot of locals."

"I hear you," Spaniard said, implying he knew of my connections. "But what if we can get you a better price on pills, would you be interested?"

"I appreciate the offer, guys, but no thanks. And here's why: before you guys moved into Ecstasy, the police pretty much ignored us. Now your runners are going around bragging they're the biggest Ecstasy barons in the world. That's brought considerable heat to the scene. And I'm not saying this to put you guys down, but to give you a heads-up on what's happening. Every weekend at the raves, we've got undercover cops and vehicles hanging around. We've got undercover vehicles taping who's going in and out of the raves and driving through the parking lots taping licence plates. It's no coincidence that the police moved in shortly after you guys. It's not each other's crews we need to beware of, it's the cops."

"What about your security team?" Spaniard asked.

"What about it?" I asked.

"Will our runners have problems with your guys jacking their pills?"

"I don't want to start a war with you guys. If my security grab someone and we find out they're part of your crew, we'll let them go. Ecstasy's so hard to get and the demand so high, there's enough of a market for us to coexist. But if I tell my security not to jack your runners, I don't expect any problems from you guys for my runners in the Scottsdale scene."

"Sounds like a good agreement." Spaniard shook my hand.

The peace didn't last long. Sammy the Bull's thugs knocked the teeth out of my top Ecstasy salesperson and offered a reward to anyone who could lead them to me.

Hoping for a peaceful night out in the last place any rivals would try to find me, I went to a gay club called the Crow Bar in downtown Phoenix. High on Ecstasy and relaxing with my friends, I was soon enjoying the friendly atmosphere and the house music pumping from giant black speakers. The floor was packed with topless muscular men, some in yellow construction hats, dancing under flickering strobe lights. I dared any of my friends to dance topless with a construction hat. With a wide grin, Wild Man got on the floor and grooved his big body, surrounded by hip-grinding hunks.

A strip-tease dancer partying in the Crow Bar recognised me and called Sammy the Bull's crew – which I was unaware of until Sammy the Bull's son told me years later. Sammy the Bull dispatched his son as the head of an armed team with instructions to kidnap me from the Crow Bar. They were going to hold me for ransom, and if the ransom wasn't paid, they were going to take me out to the desert to eliminate their competition. Fortunately, Wild Man got into a scuffle and we had to leave the Crow Bar in a hurry. The Gravano crew arrived too late.

The meltdown of my business interests came on fast. The NAS-DAQ, where I'd invested most of my money, crashed in late 2000. Some of my smugglers were arrested at airports around the world. Most of my crew were doing so much crystal meth they were growing paranoid and scheming against each other. My top sales-man firebombed Wild Man's fiancée's apartment, almost setting Wild Woman ablaze, and he tried to rob my LSD chemist, result-ing in a shootout that made headline news. I could no longer af-ford my mountainside home and the $20,000-plus-a-month bills for that home and multiple cars and apartments. My wife, Amy, was arrested in a grocery store, high on Mexican pharmaceuticals, walking around barefoot, babbling to herself, with shotgun shells in her handbag. Later on, she bought a one-way ticket to Egypt to commit suicide. She ended up slashing her wrists and overdosing on prescription pills in her hotel room, where she was rescued by staff. With us both too messed-up to sustain our relationship, it fell apart, like everything else in our lives.

Drugs had scrambled my mind. I reacted to the disasters by trying to numb myself with more drugs, accelerating my down-fall. Through bad choices, I lost almost everything. All of the fun, glitz and glamour were gone. I was no longer swanning into raves with my entourage, getting hugged and thanked left and right by partiers high on my Ecstasy. I was hiding out in an apartment, fearing the police or rival criminals were coming to get me, hav-ing to take Xanax to fall asleep. The meltdown put an end to my large-scale criminal activity.

Towards the end of it all, an attorney I used whenever one of my associates was arrested called me into his office.

"How're you doing, Ray?" I said, shaking his hand.

"I'm good. It's you I'm worried about."

"Why?" I asked, alarmed.

"My sources at the Drug Enforcement Agency tell me it's

time for you to get the hell out of Arizona."

"Since the stock market crashed, I've not been doing much anyway."

"You shouldn't be doing anything at all! You've had a good run. Now's the time to get out. You're an intelligent guy. You've got your whole life ahead of you. If you continue on, there's only one way this is going to end."

I knew he was right, but I couldn't kick my habit. The person who encouraged me to sober up was Claudia, a tall Scandinavian blonde. I met her at a friend's apartment. She mocked me for being a raver – which I couldn't help but admire, not to mention the desire it kindled – so I asked her out. She said no – further inflaming my desire – so I obtained her number and pursued her for months. It paid off. I won the heart of one of the most caring people I'd ever met. Thanks to her, I'd quit dealing, ditched the English Shaun persona, returned to online stock trading and enrolled in Scottsdale Community College to study Spanish. She didn't approve of my raver friends, so I didn't let them know where we lived. As my mind started to clear, I grew more afraid of the consequences of hanging out with the people I used to lead. Knowing the police were onto me, I mostly stayed at home on my computer. We were saving up to start new lives in LA, where she wanted to be an actress and I planned to do a Masters in finance.

CHAPTER 3

"Tempe Police Department! We have a warrant! Open the door!"

I leap up from my computer table. My insides clench. I rush to the door. The peephole's blacked out. Feeling the threat flare up from the other side, I flinch back. Through a window, I see police positioned behind cars and marksmen aiming rifles. Afraid of getting shot, I duck. *Get the hell out!* Blood surges to my head. *Hide in the ceiling? Jump off the balcony? Nowhere to go! I'm trapped!* Boots thud up the outdoor stairs to our apartment.

Bang, bang, bang, bang!

Wearing only boxer shorts, I run to the bedroom. "Claudia, wake up! It's the cops!"

"Tempe Police Department! Open the door!"

Claudia scrambles from the bed. "What should we do?" she asks, anxiously fixing her pink pyjamas.

Bang, bang, bang, bang, bang, bang, bang!

"Open the door!"

We search each other's faces.

"Better open it," I say, but before I can make it to the door – *boom!* – it leaps off its hinges.

Big men in black fatigues and ballistic armour blitz through the doorframe, aiming guns at us. I freeze. I gape as they hem us in with a wall of Plexiglas shields. Fear of getting shot paralyses me. My chest seizes up.

"Tempe Police Department! Get on the fucking ground now!"

"Police! Police! On your bellies now!"

"Hands above your heads!"

"Don't fucking move!"

As I drop, they fall upon me. There is a beating in my chest as if I have more than one heart. Crushed by hands, elbows, knees and boots, I can barely breathe. Cold steel snaps around my wrists. I'm hoisted like a puppet onto my feet. As they yank Claudia up by the cuffs, she pinches her eyes shut; when she opens them, tears spill out.

"I'm Detective Reid," says a tall burly man with thick dark hair. "English Shaun, you're a big name from the rave scene. I'm sure this raid will justify the charges." There is a self-satisfied edge in his voice, as if he is savouring a moment of triumph.

In shock, intimidated, I fumble around for an appropriate response. "There's nothing illegal in here."

He smirks knowingly and reads my Miranda and consular rights.

I want to put my arms around Claudia to stop her trembling. "Don't worry, love. Everything's going to be all right," I say, trying to hide my fear.

"Don't fucking talk to her! You're going outside!" Detective Reid takes a dirty T-shirt from a hamper and slaps it on my shoulder. "Take this with you!"

"I'm exercising my right to remain silent, love!" I keep yelling as they push me outside.

"Shut the fuck up!" Detective Reid growls.

"We told you not to fucking talk to her!"

Yelling over each other, they shove me down the stairs. They briefly remove my cuffs, so I can slip the T-shirt on.

"Stand by the stairs and keep fucking quiet!" Detective Reid leaves me guarded by a policeman.

The heat of the sun rising over Phoenix adds to my daze. Detective Reid escorts Claudia out and locks her in the back of a white Crown Victoria. It speeds off with my fiancée of one-and-a-half years. Police in state uniforms, federal uniforms and plain clothes swarm our place. Every so often, Detective Reid and a short bespectacled lady confer. Neighbours assemble, fascinated. Sweat trickles from my armpits and crotch. I think about Claudia. *What will they do to her? Will she be charged?*

Detective Reid stomps down the stairs, scowling. "Tell us

where the drugs are, Attwood. It'll make things much easier for you in the long run. They in the safe?"

"In the safe's just a coin collection and stuff like my birth certificate."

"You're full of shit, Attwood! Where's the key for the safe? You might as well just give the drugs up at this point."

"The key's on my key chain, but it needs a combination as well as a key."

"What drugs are in it?"

"None."

"Don't play games with us, Attwood. Don't force me to call a locksmith."

"I'm telling the truth."

"We'll soon see about that." He sounds desperate.

I'm about to volunteer the combination, but he pulls out a cell phone and dials a locksmith.

"Get in the back of that car over there," says an officer in a dark-blue uniform, forty-something, with a rugged face. He looks the type who likes to take a detour on the way to the station to teach certain criminals a lesson. New to manoeuvring in handcuffs, I fall sideways onto the back seat. I straighten myself up. He throws a pair of jeans on my lap. He gets in the car, mouths a stick of gum and turns on 98 KUPD Arizona's Real Rock. He bobs his head to the music as he drives. Every now and then he looks over his shoulder, and I see two tiny distorted images of me on the lenses of his reflective aviator sunglasses.

He parks by Tempe police station. "Looks like we're gonna be waiting outside."

Sealed in the Crown Victoria, cuffed, cramped, sweaty, I know my life will never be the same. *The price has finally come for my crimes.*

"Bring him in," someone radios.

The driver parks by a mobile police unit. He uncuffs me, tells me to put my jeans on and escorts me to a man sitting at a desk.

"Fill this out."

NAME, DATE OF BIRTH, SOCIAL SECURITY NUM-
BER, HOME ADDRESS, OCCUPATION, WORK AD-
DRESS...

"I'm exercising my right to remain silent," I say.

"You must fill this out, or else we'll book you in as a John Doe,
and you don't want that."

After complying, I'm escorted into the police station. "What
about my right to make a call?" I ask, desperate to notify Ray the
attorney.

"Not now. Straight to a cell." He deposits me in a small cell,
clean and air-conditioned. It has two bunks and a stainless-steel
toilet with a built-in water fountain. The smell of bleach is rising
from the recently mopped floor.

The police put Cody, the head of my security team, in the cell
opposite. Close to average height and weight, he isn't intimidating. I'd put him in charge due to his knack for staying sober while
the rest of us were high. I'd initially disliked this quirky character
who sported a blond crew cut and preppy clothes, but he proved
to be trustworthy and a methodical smuggler. That's how he became my right-hand man.

I rush to the front of the cell. We exchange nervous smiles, like
kids caught smoking.

"Where they get you?" Cody asks.

"Knocked my door down. And you?" I ask.

"I was out and about, taking care of bills and shit, driving from
place to place, and I noticed a helicopter above me. I watched it
for a while and it didn't go away. So I drove to the other side of
town, and there it was, still above me. I thought I was losing my
mind. I thought of *Goodfellas*, how the helicopter was above him
every time he looked out of his car. No matter where I went, it
stayed with me, but I still wasn't 100 per cent sure. So, to see if I
was just sketching, I decided to speed back over to the other side
of town. I got on the freeway and headed east. I'm in the fast lane.
I notice the helicopter's still above me, to the side. I'm cruising
along wishing the helicopter would go off in another direction,

and I notice a bunch of cop motorcycles in the traffic behind me. I slowed down expecting them to overtake me, but they surrounded my car – four of them! – and signalled for me to get off the freeway. There was nothing I could do. I parked and they arrested me."

"Helicopters and biker cops! My God! At least my arrest wasn't quite as dramatic as yours. SWAT knocked our door down. They yelled and pointed big guns at us. They sure spent a lot of money on these arrests. Not a good sign. They catch you with anything?"

"Nothing for them to catch me with."

"Same here. They tore my pad apart looking for drugs. Took my computer and everything. We should be able to get bonded out when they don't find anything," I say, hoping it to be true.

"Come out, Attwood!" A young policeman escorts me to a room full of electronic equipment.

"Mug shot. Get against that wall," he says.

"Is this good?" I ask, in no mood to smile at a camera.

"Where's that accent from?"

"England."

"I'm from England, too. Which part?"

"Widnes, Cheshire."

"Rugby-league town, eh?"

"Yes."

"How'd you end up in here?"

"They knocked my door down."

"If they knocked your door down, you must be in a lot of trouble. Stay still right there." He takes my photograph. "Well, nice to have met you. Good luck with your charges. Maybe they'll ship you back to England."

If only, I think, dwelling on how much trouble I'm in.

"Get in the strip-search room," says a large black guard.

The room is tiny, cold, bare.

"Take everything off."

I undress. The day's events have retracted my penis. I shield it with my hands to minimise my embarrassment.

"Now raise your arms. Good. Open your mouth. Raise your tongue. Good. Lift your nutsack. Good. Pull your foreskin back."

"What?"

"Pull your foreskin back. You could have drugs in there."

The request is too much for my penis. It wants to hide inside my body and die of shame. Reluctantly, I draw back my foreskin.

"Good. Now turn around. Bend over and spread 'em."

Spreading, I feel vulnerable. I tell myself it's no different from the mooning I did as a child. Just when I think the worst is over, he says, "Spread 'em wider." It's beyond mooning now. More of a visual raping. "Good. Let me see the bottoms of your feet."

Relieved the strip search is over, I'm escorted back to my cell and served a hot meal. Salisbury steak. Mash. Gravy. It tastes like second-class airline food. I pick at it, but I'm too nervous to eat.

It's night when two transportation officers carrying boxes of steel restraints extract us from our cells to take us to Sheriff Joe Arpaio's jail system, where new arrestees are housed. They cuff my hands and tether the cuffs to my torso with a belly chain. The heavy leg cuffs cut into my ankles. I can only shuffle out of the jail.

"Watch your heads getting into the van!"

I bundle myself into the van, surprised to see more of my party friends, including Wild Man and Wild Woman. Galvanised by the day's events, everyone tries to talk at once.

"Where's Claudia?" I ask.

"They let her go," says Wild Woman – who'd flown over two years ago to be with Wild Man. She is in her forties, blond and tiny, but tougher than most men. Armed with a bar stool during a pub fight, she had put multiple people in hospital. We'd nicknamed her and Wild Man the Wild Ones. Out of all of the arrestees, I trust the Wild Ones and Cody the most.

"Thank God for that," I say.

"I was outside the room they were questioning her in," Wild Man says. "She was crying 'cause they said they'd found some prescription pills without written prescriptions in your apartment, and she was facing some very serious charges. So I yelled, 'Serious fucking charges my arse,' and they tried getting crazy with me. Daft pig bastards."

"Our attorney friend probably knows we've been arrested by now," I say, hoping he has. "He'll be doing all he can to find out what's going on. Any of you get caught with drugs?"

They say no.

"If they didn't find any drugs," I say, "I don't see how they can hold us for very long."

"Where they taking us?" Cody asks.

"The Horseshoe," Wild Man says. "We'll be stuck in filthy holding cells for days while they process us."

"Why they call it The Horseshoe?" Cody asks.

"'Cause you go in at one end and work your way round the cells in a horseshoe shape," Wild Man says. "They kept me in there for almost a week one time 'cause I wouldn't tell them my name."

The van parks in a subterranean lot. A transportation officer allows the women out first. The thirty or so male arrestees waiting to go inside the jail stop heckling the prostitutes in the line and focus on my friends:

"Ooh, babies!"

"Nice ass!"

"Show us your titties!"

"Come and play with the bad boys!"

"This way, honey!"

"With those boobs, I'm surprised you ain't got two black eyes!"

Shuffling towards the men, the women cower. The last woman out of the van is Wild Woman.

From inside the van, Wild Man watches his fiancée. Other than an eyebrow reacting – one shoots up and stays up, while the other doesn't budge – he seems unperturbed. But I know that particular eyebrow formation means he is about to do something in character with his name.

In a Liverpudlian accent that sounds as if she is hawking phlegm, Wild Woman scolds the men, who respond by turning up the volume of their chant, "Show us your boobs!"

"Get out of the van!" a transportation officer yells.

Wild Man stoops out, stops on the top step and unfurls the physique of a bear. He cocks his head back, targeting the men over his Viking's beard. "If you don't pack it in and leave my woman alone, I'll have any of you when we get inside those cells." He nods at The Horseshoe and grins. "If you think I won't, just keep it up and see what happens." Wild Man laughs in a way that says he really knows how to hurt someone. Most of the men shut up.

CHAPTER 4

"Any pain, bleeding, fever, skin problems, lice, scabies, open sores?"

"No," I say into the speak holes of a Plexiglas window in the crowded pre-intake room at the Madison Street jail.

The old lady fires more screening questions and grimaces at my answers as if my voice hurts her. The Tempe transportation officers remove our chains and leave us in the custody of Sheriff Joe Arpaio's deputies.

"Take your shoes off, put your hands up against the wall and spread your legs!" yells a drill sergeant of a guard in the admissions' hallway.

Guards pat us down, examine our shoes and confiscate our shoelaces.

"Step through there," yells a female, pointing at a walk-through metal detector.

On both sides of the corridor, the inmates in the intake holding cells are banging on the Plexiglas windows. Outside of the cells, the guards are shouting surnames, slamming doors and cursing the inmates.

"You, this way!" a guard yells at me.

I walk by a Mexican woman in a black restraint chair, limbs shackled, chest strapped. The drool string dangling from her chin swings like a pendulum as she wriggles in the tilted-back seat. When a guard hides her head in a spit hood, she howls like a cat on fire.

"I'm Attwood."

"Get in there!" The guard points at one of the first holding cells in The Horseshoe.

My heart pistons as I enter a cell containing dozens of men huddled on the floor in a variety of uncomfortable positions.

Swastikas and gang graffiti – South Side Posse Bloods, Aryan Brotherhood, South Side Phoeniquera – loom down from the walls. I gag on the plague-like stench. "Excuse me," I say, pushing through the men clustered around the door yelling at the guards. At either side of the room, rows of men on steel double bunks form shelves of humans. Manoeuvring over the patchwork of limbs and bodies, I find a space with a urinous odour by the toilet. Resting against the filthy back wall, I slide down. I'm congratulating myself on finding a place to sit until I notice cockroaches darting on the floor. I flick one off my sneaker and rise fast. My feet brush the surrounding ranks of them away. Some scale the ankles of a hobo sleeping under a bunk and disappear into his trousers. I've never been surrounded by so many people and felt so lonely. Everyone looks agitated. I soon lapse into the same state. Every five minutes or so, the cell door swings open and a guard orders someone in or out. Desperate for relief from the suffocating atmosphere, I hope my name is called.

"Fuck you! Get up!" says an old hobo, rising unsteadily; his ravaged face belongs on a shrunken head in a jar. The top of his grimy beard sinks into his mouth as he slurs a string of insults.

Grumbling, his rival rises. The cell hushes as if the curtains have opened for a violent comedy show. His rival swings, misses and falls on a gang member.

"Don't fucking fall on me, you drunk-ass motherfucker," the gang member says, pushing a hobo into the other.

Ranting, the hobos fall as one, tied together by their bluster until they twist apart.

The disappointment in the lack of bloodshed is palpable until a black man, roused by the antics of the hobos, yells, "Why you look at me?" at the man sitting next to him.

"What're you talking about?" The man sidles away.

"He's a crazy Cuban," someone says.

On his feet now, the Cuban ranges the room like a time bomb. Watching him confront people, I fear I'll be the one he explodes on. He is gravitating towards me when the door opens.

"Attwood, get out here! Stand over there!" a guard yells, pointing at a ledge down the corridor.

"Sign here," says a woman behind a Plexiglas window.

"What am I signing for?"

"Charges."

"Good. It's about time I found out my charges." I sign. She slides me a form:

CONSPIRACY BOND 750000.00 CASH ONLY
LEAD/ASSIST CRIM SYN
ILL CONT OF ENTER-EM
USE ELEC COM DRG TRN
ILL CONT OF ENTERPR...

"What's all this mean?" I ask, stunned by the size of the bond.

"You need to go up there," she snaps.

"Where?"

"See the guard at that cell?"

"Hold on. I've no clue what this means."

"What?"

"These charges. It says my bond's $750,000 cash only."

"Let me see."

I give it to her.

"Must be a computer error," she says. "It can't be that high. It's probably seventy-five thousand."

"I hope so," I say, easing up a bit but still dazed by the number.

"Go over there. The next cell."

Sweat and grime gnaw my skin as I urinate. I perch myself on the end of a top bunk. The cell fills fast. The bewilderment on the faces of the new arrivals dwindles as they share arrest and crime stories heavy on police brutality.

A tiny Mexican enters, his dilated eyes darting haphazardly. Yelling, he bangs on the Plexiglas at such a rate that the other bangers stop to admire his ability. Hyperventilating, he cups his left pectoral and looks over his shoulder as if anticipating an attack. *He must be the guy who swallowed the drugs when the cops came.*

A big bald man in a black T-shirt swaggers in, addressing the cell as if he knows us all. "I was on my way to Disneyland with my little daughter. They pulled me over for speeding. But giving me a speeding ticket would have been too easy for this motherfucker. He ran my name, and a warrant came up. Thank fucking God I called her mom. He arrests me in front of my kid – now that's fucking child abuse if you ask me! I'm supposed to be at my other kid's birthday this weekend. I'll be pissed if I miss her fucking birthday party. I hope this only takes two days. Awww fuck! I love my kids. Awww fuck!"

An even bigger man with a pirate's beard comes in and says to the bald man, "Hey, Chad, they're gonna try and ship me back to New Mexico. They've got a body, but they can't link me to it. They've got nothing on me. Motherfuckers!"

Much to my relief, Cody arrives. I climb down. We hug and discuss our bonds.

Chad interrupts our conversation. "You've got a cool accent, man. Did you say you've got a $750,000 cash-only bond?"

"Yes, but they said it's a mistake," I say, turning to Cody for support.

"Let me see your paperwork."

"Here you go."

"That ain't no mistake, buddy," Chad says.

"What do you mean? She just told me it is." I feel dizzy.

"Conspiracy. Crime syndicate. Were you guys whacking people or what?" Chad asks.

"No. They raided my apartment. There were no drugs found."

"Well, you've got drug charges."

Having distributed drugs for years, I don't know which transactions I'm accused of. With most of my money squandered, I have no hope of raising $750,000.

From outside, Wild Man bangs on the Plexiglas and mouths, "What's your bond?"

"It says three-quarters of a mill! What's yours?" I yell.

"Half a fucking mill!"

His response torpedoes my hope of us bonding out. "Aw shit!" I say, agonising over having to tell my parents. One of my biggest fears is them learning about my crimes. They'll be devastated 5000 miles away in England. I almost retch.

"Get in this cell! Do you hear me?" A guard grabs Wild Man.

"I've got it," Chad says. "You're part of Sammy the Bull's crew."

"I'm nothing to do with him," I say, not wanting to admit to any criminal relationships. "I did throw raves years ago."

"That's it. Raves. Ecstasy," Chad says. "With a bond like that, you might be on the news."

"I hope not," I say, worried members of my family in Arizona will see it and contact my parents.

A guard slides a large plastic bag into the doorway. "Who's hungry?" The prisoners shift towards him, like ducks on a pond to someone with bread. He throws brown paper bags at them.

"They're Ladmo bags," Chad says. "Green-baloney sandwiches."

Food is far from my mind. Curious, I peer in my Ladmo bag. A grapefruit. Bread dotted with blue mould. Slices of processed cheese leaking an orange oil. Green baloney – slimy cuts of meat, iridescent, but with an underlying greenish shine.

Baloney consists of various low-grade meats, fat, flavourings and preservatives. Sheriff Joe Arpaio introduced it in an attempt to get the cost of feeding each inmate down to forty cents a day. Arpaio boasted to the media that it costs more to feed his police dogs than his inmates. Green baloney is unfit for commercial sale due to oxidation. It is sometimes delivered to the jail in bags labelled "Not For Human Consumption." Stolen by inmates, some of the bags ended up in the offices of attorneys suing Arpaio. The term Ladmo bag comes from the children's television programme *The Wallace and Ladmo Show*. Ladmo gave kids paper bags with food and toy gifts. The bags had a surprise element, but they became skimpier over time, hence the comparison.

To distance myself from the rank smell of decaying flesh, I

off-load my Ladmo bag on the men casting around for leftovers. Trying to refresh my mouth, I eat a grapefruit.

"Attwood! Come on! Hurry up!" yells a female guard.

"Right here!" I scramble to my feet, relieved to be on the move.

"See her in that room in the corner."

The room is full of electronic equipment, like a photocopy store.

"Who're you?" a woman asks.

"Attwood."

"Wash your hands and come here," she says, addressing me like a piece of property. She grabs my arm, spreads my fingers onto a scanner and rolls each finger. Each print appears on a screen with the words: PRINT SUCCESSFUL. She prints sections of my hand. "You're done with me. See her."

"Put this ink on your hands!" yells a female. "Good. Now give me your hand." She grabs my hand, separates and presses my fingers down. "Relax! Relax! What's wrong with you?" I seethe. She pushes my hand onto an inkpad and my palm onto a print card.

"Wipe the ink off your hands with this." At arm's length, she gives me a paper towel. It disintegrates. I wipe my hands on my jeans. "See him next."

"Stand on that line. Look up at the camera. OK. Good."

The camera flashes.

"Put your head in there," he says, pointing at a metal box. "Put your eye up against that part." He pushes a button and my retina appears on a screen.

In the next cell, I perch on the end of a top bunk, feeling somewhat safer above the mass of testy men, cockroaches and drunken hobos. An ache spreads throughout my body. It must be the small hours because I'm exhausted from sleep deprivation, almost a day since my arrest.

"Everyone pee who needs to pee! You're going to court!" a female yells.

The sleepy group rises and forms a line for the toilet. Men air their hopes of getting their bonds reduced, raising mine.

The guard yells names to the tune of urine splashing, water flushing and bursts of farts.

"Attwood!"

Thirsting for fresh air, I step into the corridor.

"Go sit in that booth, Attwood!"

A lady in a booth slides out a form. The young woman hovering behind her is the one who had conferred with Detective Reid outside of my Scottsdale apartment on the day of the raid. She has timid mousy features and curly brown hair.

On the form, I put the Tucson address I'm using for my green-card application. Sensing something underhand, I list the Scottsdale apartment as a second home. I explain that I have two addresses. The lady insists a note has been made on the computer. The woman behind her snickers and walks away. I feel uneasy.

"Finished? Go through that door into the courtroom!" a guard yells.

Joining the fatigued captives on rows of plastic chairs in the large white courtroom, I gulp down the cool air. Over to my right, sitting at a desk by the bar is the familiar woman from the raid. Everyone is waiting for the judge. I cling to the possibility of a bond reduction.

The clerk of the court is sitting at a desk next to the judge's bench. She stands and clears her throat. "When your name is called, line up at this desk and the judge will call you one at a time. He will ask you some questions, and when he is finished with you, you will step to the desk at the other side of the judge's bench where you will sign your court papers. You will then proceed back to your seat. Does everybody understand?"

There are a few murmurs of assent. The judge enters.

"All rise. Judge Powell's court is now in session."

Judge Powell trudges to his bench like an overweight clergyman, his face grotesquely impassive, as if he's under the influence of a dental drug heavy on cocaine.

"Garcia! Watkins! Snyder! Vasquez! Castillo! Johnston!

Lynch!" the clerk shouts.

The first group jumps like a team of firefighters responding to an emergency call. In an apathetic voice, Judge Powell chastises them, one by one, for committing petty crimes.

"Walker! Ramirez! Brooks! Wright! Lopez! Washington! Attwood!"

Judge Powell reads my charges. When he quotes my bond, the crowd gasps. "Do you have anything to say on your own behalf?" he asks, impatience in his voice and slitty eyes.

"Your Honour, I was arrested yesterday morning, told the raid would vindicate the charges, but no drugs were found. I trade stocks for a living and have an investment in a clothing store, but there's no way I can pay this bond. I'm–"

"Enough!" Judge Powell's head swivels towards the familiar woman.

She rises. Her face animates around large glasses as she launches into her statement. "Judge, I'm Gloria Olivia Davis, prosecutor for the Organised Crime Division of the Attorney General's Office. About six years ago, Tempe Police Department began receiving reports of an Englishman involved in throwing raves and distributing drugs in and around the Phoenix and Tempe area. Surveillance was set up, but the Englishman moved around a lot, eluding earlier investigations. He used numerous aliases; so many we couldn't even list them all in his indictment. Detectives only discovered Mr Attwood's real name this year and were finally able to capture him. It is the allegation of the State that Mr Attwood is the head of a drugs organisation and that he has been operating a continuous criminal enterprise in Arizona for at least six years. The Attwood Organisation specialises in the distribution of club drugs, including the drug he is most well-known for: Ecstasy. Mr Attwood is a citizen of England and poses a considerable flight risk if he were bonded out. Mr Attwood is also a liar, Judge. He lied to your staff here today, stating that he lives in Tucson, when he in fact lives in Scottsdale. He also put that he works at a store, in sales – maybe he meant drug sales? The State requests his bond remains the same."

"Bond remains the same. Next!"

His words are like a kick to the testes. I want to throw up. I have to steady my hands to sign the court papers. Back in my seat, I brood on the impossibility of bonding out and having to tell my parents. *How much longer can I stay awake before my mind snaps?*

"Everyone who's seen the judge," the bailiff yells, "go through that door and get back into the jail right now!"

Apprehensively, I return to The Horseshoe. Seeing the amount of men sardined in the next cell, I sigh. I wedge myself in past the tiny Mexican from earlier who is still hyperventilating. I spot another familiar face: the Cuban. He's stood next to the Mexican, staring blankly, like a wind-up toy waiting for someone to turn the key in his back.

I work my way to the toilet and unbutton my pants. Urinating, I wince at the sour smell. I cup water in my hand and lean forward. My eyes slam shut as I splash my face. The water cools my skin, washing away some of the grime and tiredness. Removing my T-shirt releases the odour of stale sweat mixed with yesterday's deodorant. I wet the T-shirt and wipe my face and armpits. I put the T-shirt back on. It clings to my body, cooling it down. My mouth tastes foul. Gargling water fails to stop the burning in my throat. I pick the coating of white scum off my lips in tiny clumps and strings. Sitting down against a wall, I can feel the filth in the air reattaching itself to my skin. A headache sets in. I drift in and out of consciousness. Worries take on surreal dimensions in my semi-dream state. Every time I feel too itchy, I revisit the sink and repeat my bathing ritual.

Except for the Mexican and Cuban, everyone seems exhausted. The Cuban has been staring at the wall for a while, his eyeballs bulging slightly more than the Mexican's. Every ten minutes or so, he reanimates and yells at someone. Inevitably, my turn comes. "Why you look at me?" He stares at me hard.

I'm tense enough, yet my stress elevates. My alertness returns. "I wasn't looking at you. My friend, are you OK?" *Try and calm him down. Do a good deed.*

"You fuckin' no-no look at me!" His head convulses as if demons are trying to burst through his crown.

Maintaining eye contact, I rise. My stress surges into anger at him. What I'm feeling is wrong, but a force is pushing me to fight him. Expecting to be the one he finally attacks, I raise my arms and shift my left side forward.

"Take no notice," a wizened Mexican American says. "He's crazy."

Shouldn't be fighting a crazy. No backing down either. With everyone watching, I can't display weakness.

"Why you look at me? Why you fuckin' look at me?"

He's testing me. Respond like the other prisoners. "Shut the fuck up!" The severity in my voice surprises me.

The Cuban shuffles away, pivots like a robot and heads for the tiny Mexican. He stops next to the Mexican and gazes out of the window. Even men who were nodding off fixate on the twosome. The Cuban settles into a trance. Just when the spectators are losing interest, the Cuban mutters and trembles.

"Who look at me no-no look at me!" he screams at the Plexiglas, as if imaginary people in the corridor are eyeballing him.

The Mexican jumps like a startled animal and thunders on the Plexiglas with both fists.

The Cuban whirls towards the Mexican. "Why you fuckin' look at me?"

Pounding on the Plexiglas, the Mexican howls for someone to save him.

The Cuban wags his finger in the Mexican's face. "You fuckin' look at me! No-no look at me!"

They feed off each other's hysteria until a hillbilly guard the size of a buffalo swings the door open and says in a bumpkin voice, "What in the Sam Hill's going on in here?"

When the Cuban yells, "Why you fuckin' look at me?" at the guard, the Mexican ducks under the guard's arm and sprints down the corridor.

"Hell's bells!" The guard slams the door and radios for backup.

I can't resist vying for viewing room at the Plexiglas. Side by side, two guards are marching towards the Mexican, driving him back towards the hillbilly who is blocking the corridor. The Mexican feints to the left. The hillbilly lurches in that direction. The Mexican veers to the right and zigzags around the guard.

"This little fella's quicker than a bob cat!" the hillbilly says.

Keys jingling and a staccato of radio interference announce the arrival of groups of guards at both ends of the corridor, snapping on rubber gloves, marching with menace in their stride. The Mexican skids into a U-turn and heads back towards the hillbilly. Within seconds, he has nowhere to go. He swivels his head wildly, appraising the situation like a lamb aware of its slaughter. Boots squeal as the guards fall upon him. He resists briefly, kicking and yelping, but curls into a ball. He is pinned down, picked up and thrown into a restraint chair. As they strap him in, his tiny body pants as if his chest is going to explode. As they slide the chair down the corridor, his wails fade out of earshot.

The hillbilly extracts the Cuban and places him in a cell opposite. We watch the Cuban shout at a man. A large figure rises from the floor at the back of the cell as if roused from sleep. Approaching the Cuban, the figure knocks people out of the way. It's Wild Man. He comes up behind the Cuban and applies a chokehold. The Cuban's arms windmill and flop down. Wild Man drops the Cuban to the floor like a sack and grins at us.

Other than the heat rising and falling, I have no sense of night or day. The heat is up again when a guard extracts me to see a nurse at a desk in the corridor. She jokes about my accent, takes my blood pressure and sticks a needle in my arm.

"I fucking hate needles. I'm refusing this shit," Wild Man says, sitting next to me opposite a nurse. "How're you?"

"Shattered. I need sleep. Hungry. I can't eat green baloney."

"You ready?" the nurse asks Wild Man.

"I told you, I'm refusing."

"It's for your own good."

"I'm fucking refusing." Wild Man laughs.

"How can you refuse?" I ask.

"I just did."

"I didn't know that," I say.

"They got you good didn't they?"

"I guess."

"If you're refusing, get back to your cell!"

"See you," Wild Man says.

"See you," I say.

As the nurse applies a Band-Aid to my arm, Wild Woman and my female friends arrive. Prisoners leer and bang on the Plexiglas.

"How're you doing?" I ask.

"It's terrible," one of my friends says. "But Wild Woman's taking care of us."

"What do you mean?" I ask.

"I already twatted one fucking daft bitch for picking on my mates," Wild Woman says.

"She head-butted some chick and boxed her down."

"They know better than to fuck with me now," Wild Woman says. "I'm in no fucking mood. I hope another daft cunt talks some shit. I'm looking for some fucker to take my fucking anger out on."

"You! Stop talking to the females! In fact, come with me!" A guard leads me to a cell on the third corridor.

"It's the $750,000-bond man!" Chad yells.

"What's up, brother!" Cody explains he's been discussing our prospects with Chad and Tony the pirate-looking murderer.

"If you haven't got any priors," Tony says, "the worst they can give you is five years on a Class 2 felony."

"What's priors?" I ask.

"Prior felony convictions."

"I've got no prior felonies."

"You're looking at five years max."

"Five years!" It seems like the rest of my life.

"Five's a walk in the park. You're also eligible for probation."

"I'd sign for probation right now just to get out of here," I say.

"If you're a first-time non-dangerous drug offender, you're eligible for probation. Take no notice of that bond. It's just a scare tactic and so you can't bond out and prepare a good defence. Just make sure your crew keep their mouths shut when they try to scare them into snitching. 'Cooperate or you'll never see the light of day,'" Tony says in a high-pitched mock voice. "It's all bullshit. If no drugs or money were found, then they fucked up. You're gonna have to be careful 'cause they spent a lot of money on this case, so they're gonna be looking to justify it. Get a real good defence attorney and you'll be all right. Don't sign the first plea bargain they offer you unless it's for less than five years."

The door swings open. The hillbilly tosses Ladmo bags at us. "It's like feeding a pack of javelinas. Y'all smell about the same."

Hunched over Ladmo bags, the men barter food as volubly as traders on the New York Stock Exchange. A line forms for the toilet. The stench of bowel movements dominates the other odours our bodies are letting loose. Chad and Tony amuse themselves by throwing grapefruit peel at anyone who dares, accidentally or otherwise, to fall asleep.

The door swings open. "Attwood, come with me!"

I arrive at a massive cell at the end of The Horseshoe. It has multiple bunk beds on two opposite walls and a toilet at the back. Some of the inmates are in street clothes, others in jail attire: black-and-white bee-striped pyjamas, pink boxer shorts, orange shower sandals.

Nervously, I search for the courage to ask my aunt Ann (my aunt Mo's older sister) to notify my parents. On the wall by the cell door is a collect-call phone. To dial, I have to stoop – the phones have short cords to prevent suicides. I'm so disgusted with what I'm about to do that hanging myself seems an easier option. I half hope no one answers, but Ann does. Surprised by the news, she reassures me that she'll tell my parents as gently as possible. Dazed, nauseated, I hang up. *I've sent a bomb over the Atlantic Ocean aimed at my parents' home.* I sit on my own, imagining their reactions, the devastation I've caused such gentle and loving people.

The door opens every few hours and a guard yells the names of the inmates being transported to one of Arpaio's local jails.

Wild Man introduces me to an old-timer who killed his wife in Florida and has been classified to the Madison Street jail's maximum-security quarters. He was shipped from a Florida prison to face charges of stealing a Renaissance-era painting from a wealthy Arizonan. With my male co-defendants present, I ask him for advice.

"What they'll do next is try and play you all off against one another, so they can build cases against whoever they want to portray as the big players. They'll assign you all scumbag attorneys who are on the payroll of the State and the attorneys will try and frighten everyone into signing plea bargains, so they don't have to do any real work, like defending you at trial. The sooner you sign a plea bargain, the sooner they get their fee and they can move onto their next victim."

"No shit!" Cody says.

"Yes. Your best bet is to form a united front. Have a highly-paid attorney act as the lead attorney for the whole case. The prosecutor is relying on the domino theory in a case like this. If one of you falls, you all will."

In tones of solidarity, we pledge a united front. If the police have no drugs, no evidence, there is no case, and no need for anyone to cooperate. Or so I think.

Hours later, my name is called. A guard escorts a group of us to a changing room. We are instructed to strip naked, deposit our clothes in garbage bags and put on the jail uniform. I return to the cell dressed like a chain-gang con.

After the next delivery of Ladmo bags, I scour the area for fruit and eat a few oranges and grapefruits. My eyes sting as I watch men nod off, fall on their neighbours, wake up and repeat the cycle. But I am beyond tired and entering a kind of madness. I desperately need to do something for my skin – it feels as if lice are burrowing into it – so I march to the water fountain with some grapefruit peel, rip my top off and splash water on my upper body. Attempting to reduce the onion stink in my armpits, I squeeze grapefruit peel below them.

"Does that work?" a skinhead yells. "Give me a piece!"

I throw him some. Smelling my left armpit, I watch the skinhead squeeze the grapefruit peel. The onion smell has gone, replaced by the stink of a chemistry-class experiment gone wrong. I splash more water onto my armpits. Pacing the cell, I feel the rush of a trapped animal. My mind starts to slide. Thoughts of never being free again are rising, hovering and flitting, as if my skull is full of hummingbirds. I want to explode, thump a wall, project my anger onto something. Anything. I feel a primeval rage.

I'm distracted by an inmate at the front of the cell announcing the names on the new batch of IDs on the guard's desk: "Attwood, your ID's white. Medium security. You're off to Towers jail." My journey through The Horseshoe is over. Now that I've been booked in and seen by a judge, I'm to be housed in one of Arpaio's jails in accordance with my security classification. Wild Man and I are medium-security inmates. The rest of my co-defendants are minimum, so they'll be housed at Durango jail.

A guard calls my name, but not Wild Man's. Disappointed that he's not coming with me, I'm chained to four other inmates. A hippy. A lanky black guy. A middle-aged bespectacled man. A prisoner resembling a homeless version of Jack Nicholson. Anxiously, I yell goodbye to my co-defendants. Craving sleep, I pray my next destination is softer on my soul than The Horseshoe.

CHAPTER 5

Sunlight bears down on my head and glistens off the transportation guard's Terminator sunglasses as we wait outside Towers jail – a complex of beige buildings, including six identical towers, surrounded by chain-link fences, razor wire and palm trees on the outskirts of Central Phoenix. With less than thirty officers guarding close to 1000 un-sentenced prisoners, the jail is dangerously overcrowded and understaffed.

The entrance door buzzes open. "Everyone get inside. Wait for the interior door to open!"

Chained together, we shuffle into a bare room.

A young guard unlocks the interior door. "Line up in the corridor!" He has spiky blond hair and is wearing the standard beige uniform with black boots and a utility belt.

Inmates in the holding cells rap on the Plexiglas and heckle us.

"Turn and face the wall! First in line, raise one leg and lift your foot toward me!" The transportation guard removes our cuffs and chains. "This lot are all yours now. I'm out of here."

"What's up, Kohl!" the Jack Nicholson-looking inmate says to the young guard.

"Not you again!" Officer Kohl says, frowning.

"'Fraid so."

"What's your name?"

"Boyd."

"Smoking crack again were we, Boyd?"

Boyd smiles, displaying the remains of his teeth. "Any chance of Ladmo bags? We haven't eaten all day."

"Any Ladmo bags left?" Officer Kohl shouts.

At the reception station, a guard sighs, slams down *The Arizo-*

na Republic newspaper, opens the refrigerator, grabs some Ladmo bags and chucks them at us.

Folding green-baloney sandwiches, my companions shower the floor with breadcrumbs.

"I need you all in this cell. Show me your IDs as you enter!" Officer Kohl says.

Less filthy than The Horseshoe, the empty cell has three sets of double bunks and a toilet in the corner with no privacy divide. I sit on a bottom bunk. The bespectacled prisoner sits apart from the other three who chat like regulars at a social club.

"I gotta take a crap," Boyd says.

"Me, too. But you called it first," the hippy says.

"This chow always sends me straight to the shitter," the black inmate says.

With no privacy, they go about their business as casually as kids pick their noses. The toilet flushes louder than on an airplane. I wonder why they push the button as soon as they sit down and keep flushing.

For days, all I've eaten is fruit. Desperate to freshen my mouth, I unpeel an orange and eat a slice. The juice soothes my mouth. Minutes later, stomach cramps spread to my bowels. I've reached such a low in my life it is now necessary to go on the toilet in front of four strangers. That three went before me offers little comfort. Searching for something appropriate to say, I play around with, "Hey, guys, I need to take a dump." But I can't get the words out. Instead, I adopt a diversion strategy: I give them my Ladmo bag. As they argue over the food, I rush to the toilet, push my pants and boxers down and try my best to act like someone who's been going on the toilet in front of strangers all of his life. The seatless steel chills my behind. Straining in vain, I regret attempting the toilet. Convinced I need to go, but I'm too nervous, I take deep breaths. Eventually, something happens, but not much.

My deposit is barely underwater when Boyd says, "Goddam, put some water on that to kill the smell, dog!"

It dawns why they flushed so much. Blushing, I press the button. The toilet flushes, spraying water on my backside like an out of control bidet. I want to get off the toilet, but I have to wipe. I pick up the institutional toilet paper, course and thin. Seated with a buttock raised, I wipe. All done, I run water over my hands, dry them on my pants and return to the bunk. In the foetal position, I drift in and out of consciousness for hours, aching all over, the metal surface adding to my discomfort.

Officer Kohl's voice rouses me. "Line up in the corridor!"

We shuffle out of the cell.

"I need to pat you down! Turn around, put your hands against the wall and spread your legs! I hope for your sakes, none of you have any weapons or drugs keystered!" I'm unaware that keystered means anything stored in the rectal cavity, that most inmates are involved in keystering tobacco, drugs and paraphernalia.

Kohl pats me down. I've lost count of the men in uniform who've karate-chopped my crotch in recent days. Officer Kohl puts on wraparound sunglasses and escorts us down a series of corridors. "Right! Stop there!"

A hibernating bear of a Mexican is curled up and snoring on the floor of an adjoining corridor.

"Wake the hell up, trusty!"

The trusty blinks a few times. A pained expression materialises. Reluctantly, he rises.

"They need mattresses and bedding!"

The trusty fetches us blankets, sheets and towels. We help ourselves to torn thin mattresses leaking black soot. My companions coil their mattresses around their belongings. I copy them.

"Keep walking! We're going to Tower 2!"

Shouldering our mattresses, we exit into a breezeway with a metal roof. We pass two recreation pens surrounded by chain-link fence and razor wire. Due to the weight of my belongings and the heat, sweat is streaming into my eyes by the time Kohl buzzes us into Tower 2.

As we walk down the cement-block corridor, tattooed men in bee stripes bang on the Plexiglas at either side of us like zoo animals yearning to attack their visitors. Unnerved by the rows of hard faces, I want to look straight ahead, but my eyes instinctively jump to the loudest banging. Some of them mime smoking, their way of asking if we are smuggling in cigarettes.

"Stop below the bubble," Officer Kohl says.

We stop in the middle of the building, all Plexiglas, metal and concrete. In the centre are spiral stairs leading up to the control tower – a giant fishbowl in the air giving the guards a view of the four identical pods A, B, C and D. Separated by cement-block walkways with Plexiglas windows, each pod takes up almost a quarter of the space below the control tower and has its own electronically-activated sliding door. Walking in a circle in the control tower is a guard struggling to keep an eye on almost forty-five men in each pod. The other guard is watching surveillance screens. He occasionally presses a button on the control panel to open a sliding door to allow an inmate in or out of a pod. At the back of each pod are two storeys of cells facing the day room and the control tower. Each pod has stairs running from the middle of the upper tier down to about six feet before the sliding door at the front of the pod. The stairs are metal grid, so the guards can see through them. Most of the inmates in the pods are sizing us up. I brace to join the overcrowded population of sweaty hungry violent men. A guard descends the control-tower stairs and orders us to wait further down the corridor. Officer Kohl disappears. We sit on our rolled-up mattresses. The men in the pods talk to us in sign language.

"He's swindowing you," Boyd says, pointing at a skinhead with a swastika and skulls on his chest.

"Swindowing?" I ask.

"Talking through the windows," Boyd says.

"What's he want?"

"To know if you're affiliated."

"Affiliated?"

"With the gangs. Probably 'cause your head's shaved."

"I'm not. Can you tell him it's my first time?"

"Sure." Boyd raises his right arm to almost head height, hand horizontal, palm down and shakes his head and hand in sync.

"Thanks," I say.

The skinhead waves his arms.

"Now he wants to know if you're bringing dope in."

"No dope, no smokes."

The inmates keep harassing us for contraband. I'm starting to regret not being a smoker. I wish I had something to throw to the wolves other than just myself.

A guard descends from the control tower and directs the black inmate and the hippy to D pod, the rest of us to cell 12 in A pod.

The sliding door burrs open, unleashing the stink of smoke and body odour. As I enter the pod, the heavy atmosphere weighs on my lungs. In the day room are four steel tables bolted to the floor: two at either side of the metal-grid stairs. The inmates at the tables stop playing cards and watching the small TV fixed on a wall to check us out. I feel their eyes follow me up the stairs and along the balcony.

Boyd bolts ahead to A12 and claims the bottom bunk. David, the quiet bespectacled man, quickly puts his mattress on the middle bunk, leaving me the top, the smallest slab of space. The cell is the size of a bus-stop shelter. The floor is concrete, greasy black with grime. The walls are stained brown. On one side of the cell are our three bunks separated from a steel combination toilet and sink by a thin wall. The other side consists of just enough floor space to do push-ups on and a tiny steel table and stool bolted to the wall. The toilet at the front of the cell reeks of sewage. The front wall is metal grid – the guards and prisoners outside can see right in – so there is no privacy for the toilet. At the far end of the cell, a tiny barred window provides a glimpse of the desert, chain-link fences and razor wire. On the top bunk, there is hardly enough room to raise my head without it hitting the ceiling, which it does as I arrange my mattress and bedding.

"I can't believe they put three people in these," I say.

"They were originally designed for one man," Boyd says.

"Rather than build more cells, they double-bunked them. After they got away with that, they triple-bunked them. Now you've got forty-five men living in a pod designed for fifteen."

"When're they going to start putting four in a cell?" I ask.

"They already do," Boyd says. "There's just enough floor space for a mattress, so the fourth guy sleeps on the floor."

My cellmates urinate. They are soon snoring, shrouded in white sheets like corpses awaiting burial.

For a few hours, I try to sleep, but my heart refuses to settle down and my mind is all over the place. Afflicted by the shock of the newly incarcerated, I begin hallucinating. I hear my name whispered in the day room – *English Shaun. Yeah him. English Shaun. That's him. Let's get him.* I see men line up on the balcony, preparing to give me a heart check.

I know about heart checks from one of my bouncers. He said gang members attack new arrivals to see if they show heart by fighting back, which earns respect. Those who don't fight back are considered weak and open to getting extorted and raped.

I must fight back or even better attack them first to show heart. I visualise moves I learned in kickboxing. I see myself punching, kicking, mowing my attackers down. No problem. In theory. I am psyched up until my mind swerves to concern for my teeth. I've invested a lot in American dentistry. Fighting multiple assailants will expose my investment to unnecessary risk. I might even have to write off a tooth or two. But if I don't fight now, I will lose more teeth in the long run fending off extortionists and rapists.

"If you don't stand up for yourself during a heart check, everyone'll punk you," my bouncer friend had said.

Teeth be damned! I jump off the top bunk and charge from the cell. "Come on, motherfuckers!" I get slapped in the face by silence. There is no one on the balcony. I almost laugh aloud.

The day room has emptied, except for four blacks slamming dominoes down with excessive force. They frown at me in a way that says, *Just another crazy white boy wigging out on drugs again.*

Out of the cell now, I figure I'd best do something appropriate. With an air of purpose, I march down the stairs. I try one of the phones bolted to the wall, but it doesn't accept telephone numbers. *I need instructions.* The blacks are really hurting their dominoes. I think twice before interrupting them. "Any of you guys know how these phones work?"

One takes me aside. "Are you on drugs, man?"

"No," I say.

"You look paranoid."

"I've been up for days in The Horseshoe."

"Where you from, man?"

"England."

"No shit. That's cool. Look, man, I'll give you a heads-up 'cause you're new here. You be running round all paranoid and shit, motherfuckers'll be thinking you got something to hide, and you'll get your ass smashed double quick. Get some sleep, man, and settle down."

"I will after I make a call."

He picks up the phone. "Look, tell me the number. I'll put you through."

I thank him and give him my aunt Ann's number. He dials it, speaks his name into the phone a few times and passes it to me. Desperate to hear how my parents have reacted to the news of my arrest, I listen to her phone ring. When she answers, a computerised female voice tells her it is a collect call from the jail and asks her to press 0 to accept the charges.

"Shaun, are you OK?" Ann asks.

"Yes. Did you get through to England?"

"I spoke to your mum. As you can imagine, she's pretty devastated. Your dad is at work. Fortunately, Karen was there with your mum," she says, referring to my twenty-eight-year-old sister, a trainee journalist living with my parents. "I think she was in a state of shock 'cause after I told her, she started talking to me as if nothing had happened. She said, 'How's your family?' which I thought was strange."

Oh my God. What have I done to my mum?

"She said for you to call them as soon as you can, any time day or night."

"I'd better do it right away. Look, I don't know how much these calls are costing, so I'm going to hang up and call England."

"OK. They'll be glad to hear your voice."

Trembling, I put the phone down.

The black inmate puts me through to England and returns to his buddies.

An enormous sense of guilt about the way I've treated my family makes me shudder. I desperately don't want to break their hearts. As their phone rings, my stomach clenches and churns. Ashamed of where I am, I pray they'll be supportive. Karen answers and accepts the collect call. Fighting the urge to retch, I greet my sister in a weak uncertain voice.

"Shaun's on the phone!" Karen yells. "What have you done? Mum and Dad are in a proper state. They're worried sick."

"Look, it's not as bad as it sounds," I say.

"God, I hope not. For Mum and Dad's sake. They don't deserve this, Shaun."

"You'd better let me speak to them," I say, bracing myself.

"Anyway, I hope you're OK in there. It must be a nightmare. Here's Dad. Bye! Love you."

"Love you, too." Speaking to Karen reinforces my guilt. *She's right. My parents don't deserve any of this.*

"Are you OK?" Dad asks.

The strain in his voice devastates me. I imagine my mum taking it the worst. "I'm in trouble, but I'm fine," I say, trying to sound reassuring.

"Well, we'll do whatever it takes to help you."

I'm relieved. "I have a list of charges, but no clue what they mean. My bond's $750,000. None of us has that kind of money."

"I know about the bond. I rang the jail. It sounds pretty serious. I was on the automated line for about forty-five minutes, going around in a loop – press 1, press 2, press 3 – putting your booking number in at different stages, and all of a sudden a voice popped up. I explained the situation to her. As soon as I said, 'I'm calling from England about my son who's been arrested,' she immediately wanted to help me. The English accent has its advantages."

"It does. It's helping me in here. What did she say?"

"I said, 'I can't understand what's happened. I can't believe what's going on or why he's been arrested.' She said, 'Give me his booking number and I'll find out what I can for you.' She gave me the charges – which I didn't really understand – and she said, 'The bond is $750,000. This looks pretty serious.'"

Panic sets in again. "Oh dear. I'm so sorry. Mum must be worried sick."

"She's bearing up."

"I'd better speak to her."

"Here she is."

"Shaun, are you safe in there?" Mum is crying.

To prevent inmates from noticing how upset I am, I pretend to wipe sweat from my face while using my fingers to flick off tears. "Yes, I'm all right, Mum," I say, not wanting to add to her worries.

"What's all this about?"

"I can't really say much on these phones, Mum. I was raided, but no drugs were found. My bond's so big, it doesn't look like I'll be going anywhere anytime soon."

"I can't believe this has happened," she says.

"I know. I'm so sorry. I've got money in some accounts. I'm going to have to get a lawyer." I'm unaware that the police hacked my computer with a NetBus Trojan horse and are in the process of seizing the investments I'd made in the names of UK citizens I'd flown over.

Her voice calms somewhat as she says firmly, "We'll do what we can to help you." I know they'll be there for me no matter what. "Is Claudia OK?"

"She was arrested, but they released her. You should give her a call."

The female computerised voice says, "You have thirty seconds remaining."

"It's going to hang up, Mum."

"We love you very very much. We'll do what we can."

"Love you, too. So sorry about all–"

The line goes dead. They are billed $80 for the call – part of the collect-call exploitation of prisoners' families.

As soon as I hang up, the black prisoner returns with questions about England. I sit with him at a vacant table, but the hurt I've caused my family makes it impossible to concentrate. The strain in my family's voices is haunting me.

About five minutes later, the black prisoner grows uneasy and says in a loud voice, "You'd better go talk to your people."

"What do you mean?" *What's going on?*

"You stick with your own kind in here. Your people might not like you talking to me. Now go on now." He nods at a corner of the pod, stands and walks away.

Lingering in the doorway of the corner cell are three skinheads. Young. Tattooed. Waiting.

Forcing a smile they fail to return, I join them. "I just got here," I say, aware of the fear in my voice.

"You need to come inside the cell, dog, so we can have a little chat."

"OK," I say.

"Go in there."

I walk into the cell, stop by the window and turn around. Gazing at them, I notice my left eyelid is twitching. One of them blocks the doorway. Another leans an arm adorned with a Valknut – three interconnected triangles found in early-medieval Germanic inscriptions – against the wall, forming a barrier.

"Where you from?"

"England."

"What the fuck you doing out here?"

"I was a stockbroker who threw raves."

"So what they arrest you doing?"

"I'm not quite sure. They didn't actually arrest me doing anything. I was just–"

Raising his forearms, the biggest steps forward, fists clenched. "What the fuck you mean, you're not quite sure?"

All of my muscles tighten.

"How the fuck don't you know your charges?"

I'll try to push my way through them and escape.

"I do but–"

"Every motherfucker knows his charges! What're you hiding from us?"

Got to push through them. If I fight against the wall they'll just close in on me.

"He's bullshitting us!" The third closes the door to almost locked.

I'm screwed. Charge and hope for the best.

"If you've got sex offences, you'd better tell us now 'cause we will find out!"

"I don't have sex offences. What I mean is, I don't understand my charges: conspiracy, crime syndicate. I'm new to this. The cops just raided me and nobody's explained what evidence they have. I thought they'd let me go when they didn't find any drugs. I don't know what's going on."

"Where's your paperwork?"

"Right here." I fish it from my top pocket.

"Let me see." The biggest skinhead snatches the charge sheet. "Goddam, dog! $750,000 cash-only bond! You some kind of Mafia dude or what?"

"No. I threw raves. We did drugs. Everyone had a good time."

Are my charges acceptable to them?

"I shot someone in the chest at a rave," the mid-sized one says in a disturbing matter-of-fact tone. "I'm getting ten for attempted murder."

A raver or doesn't like ravers?

"I'm here for drugs, too. Name's Rob," the biggest says. "Stand up and hold your fist out."

Heart check? I raise both fists, drop my chin and try to squint in a tough way.

They laugh. "Not like that! Just hold a fist out like this." Rob holds his right fist out horizontally. I copy him. He bumps his fist into mine. "That's how we shake hands in here."

I laugh and they join in. My tension falls like a firework plummeting to earth.

"It's to avoid catching diseases from people's fingers. There's a lot of sick motherfuckers up in this joint."

"My mouth's killing me. How do I get a toothbrush?" I ask.

"I'll grab you one," Rob says. "I'm the head of the whites for this pod. Used to be in the Marines." He holds out a tiny toothbrush, splayed and stained.

"Thanks, Rob. Why's the toothbrush so small?"

"So we can't make shanks out of them."

"Shanks?"

"Knives. You've got a lot to learn."

"Got any toothpaste?"

"Here you go." Rob smears the toothbrush with AmerFresh, a brand made in China that Sheriff Joe Arpaio provides – five years later, the Food and Drug Administration find AmerFresh to be contaminated with diethylene glycol (DEG), a toxic chemical used in antifreeze and as a solvent.

"Do you mind if I brush my teeth at your sink?"

"Nah, go ahead," Rob says.

I shuffle past them. The AmerFresh puts out the fire in my mouth.

"You need to take a shower, too," Rob says.

I think of all the shower scenes I've seen in prison movies. Usually a skinny guy gets thrown in with big tattooed men who brutalise him. *I hope that doesn't happen to me.*

"Everyone coming from The Horseshoe fucking stinks. You're making our race look bad going around smelling like that. We don't want to have to smash you for bad hygiene."

"No problem. Where's the showers at?" I ask, still brushing my teeth.

"In the corner, next to this cell," Rob says, pointing at the wall.

"Better get in there before they call lockdown," the mid-sized one says.

"What time's that at?"

"Ten thirty."

"All right, I'm off to the shower." I rinse my mouth with water cupped in my hand and step towards the door, relieved to get away from them.

Rob blocks me. I flinch. "Not so fast. We ain't finished with you yet."

His statement crushes me. "What is it?"

Rob cocks his head back, narrows his eyes. "What do you know about your cellies?" Accusation is back in his voice.

"Cellies?"

"Cellmates."

"Not much. Boyd seems OK. David has barely said a word."

"Yeah, we know all about crackhead Boyd. What about the other one? Any idea what his charges are?"

Rob trains such a gaze on me, I gulp. "No idea."

"We think he's a mo."

"Mo?"

"A chomo. A child molester."

"Uh oh."

"You can get smashed in here for having a celly who's a chomo."

"What should I do?" I ask, worn down by the questions.

"Usually, we'd tell you to tell him to roll up, but we're gonna handle it for you."

"OK. Thanks," I say, unsure why I thanked them. "I'd better go and get my shower then."

"You do that. And don't go in the shower barefoot. Jailhouse foot rot ain't nothing nice."

I return to A12 for my towel. In the day room, I strip to my boxers and place my clothes on a vacant table. I'm relieved the shower area is tiny, and not a big communal affair. Out of the two showers barely separated by a small divide, I choose the one furthest in as it provides more reaction time against an attack. Tiny black flies bother my face as I balance my boxers and towel on the showerhead. I step into a puddle of scum and pubic hair that swirls around my feet when I turn the water on. I find a piece of soap in the puddle, rinse it off and apply it to my armpits and genitals. Feeling vulnerable, I shower fast and get dressed in the day room.

Figuring the skinheads have told David to leave by now, I'm surprised to see I still have two cellmates. I climb up to my bunk, mindful not to bump my head. There are no pillows. The thin mattress is uncomfortable. Trying to sleep with my head so close to the ceiling and my nose to the wall is like being in a coffin. My body aches. Rotating from side to side only provides temporary relief. My pulse remains fast, but I eventually pass out from exhaustion.

CHAPTER 6

High-pitched static ringing in my ears rouses me from a night-mare. Roughness itches my skin: an old blanket. *Where am I?* Inches from my face is a cement-block wall. Raising myself in a hurry, I hit my head on the ceiling. *Ouch!* Sweeping my vision across the room, I'm struck all over again by the shock of the environment. My heart is beating so fast I doubt it ever slowed down. Toilets flush and roar.

More static assaults my ears, followed by a voice crackling out of the public address system: "Chow's in the house! Line up at the sliding door! Fully dressed with your IDs!"

Boyd springs from his bunk, urinates, throws his clothes on, dashes out.

"It's breakfast time." David puts on his bee stripes.

"Not more green baloney," I say, dreading going another day without food.

About forty men are out, yawning, rubbing their eyes, cursing the place. Apprehensively, I tread down the metal-grid stairs and join the queue. The sliding door opens. Holding a clipboard, Officer Kohl checks IDs while a trusty dispenses Ladmo bags and tiny cartons of milk. As each inmate takes a Ladmo bag, he yells what he wants to trade.

"Meat for peanut butter!"

"Jellies for cheese!"

"Who said meat for peanut butter?"

"Over here, dog!"

"I've got cheese. Who's got jelly?"

"I've got jelly!"

"Over here!"

"No! Take mine, dog!"

"Milk for tonight's dinner juice!"

"I'll take it, dog!"

Each race occupies an octagonal steel table. The blacks call themselves kinfolk. The whites: woods. The Mexican Americans: Chicanos. The Mexicans: paisas. In the scramble for table space, the senior members of each race quickly take ownership of the four stools bolted to each table. Some prisoners take their Ladmo bags back to their cells.

I return to A12. David is on the stool, Boyd the bottom bunk.

"Park your ass there," Boyd says, nodding at the toilet. "The best seat in the house."

Staring at the toilet, I shake my head.

"Here, put this over it." Boyd throws me a rag. "It'll reduce the smell."

Using the rag, I sit down on the toilet. Inspecting the contents of my Ladmo bag, I regret lacking the nerve to yell what I want to trade. I devour a few crackers.

"I'm lactose intolerant. Anyone want another milk?" David says.

I'm on the letter Y of the word yes when Boyd's arm strikes out like a rattlesnake.

"I'll break bread," Boyd says, smiling at me.

"Break bread?" I say.

"Split the milk with you."

"You're all right. Keep it."

Wolfing his down, Boyd eyes my food. "You gonna eat that?"

"I can't eat this crap."

"I'll handle it for you."

"Mouldy bread! How can you eat it?"

"You just scratch the mould off. You'll be doing the same soon enough. Eating green baloney just like the rest of us."

"Here you go." I hand it to Boyd.

"Good looking out, dog!"

I sip milk. A12 is towards the middle of the upper tier. There is an iron-railing balcony in front and the top of the stairs to one side. My view is almost as good as that from the control tower. I sit there intrigued by the inmates downstairs using sign language to communicate with those in adjacent pods. When the guards aren't watching, the trusties pass items from pod to pod by pushing them under the sliding doors. Two guards cannot monitor all four pods at once, so contraband moves unnoticed.

"What're they passing?" I ask.

"Dope. Tobacco," Boyd says. "There's usually only one syringe in each tower, so everyone has to share."

"What about catching diseases from sharing?" I ask.

"Most of them have hepatitis C anyway. Why'd you reckon that guy's yelling at the guard for bleach?"

"To clean his cell?"

"Nope. So the fellas can bleach the needle before shooting up."

"So after green baloney everyone just moves onto drugs?"

"Pretty much. There's more drugs in here than anywhere in the world."

His answer surprises me.

David grabs his towel and starts to leave the cell.

"Where're you going?" Boyd asks with accusation.

"Take a shower." David exits.

"Boyd, can you show me how to use the phones? I must call my fiancée." Downstairs, I follow Boyd's instructions. I enter my booking number and say my name multiple times for the PIN-LOCK Speaker Verification Service. Claudia answers. My spirits rise to her voice. "You OK, love?"

"I miss you," Claudia says.

"I miss you loads," I say, pressing the phone to my ear to make her presence nearer.

"I sleep at my mom's or on the floor in the sweaty T-shirt you wore for kickboxing with my foot touching the door 'cause I'm afraid someone's gonna bust it in again."

"I'm so sorry, love. I just…I wish I was there with you."

"I'm gonna visit you–"

"Yes, visit me! Please visit me! I must see you. This place is–"

"It must be horrible. You OK?"

"I'm fine so far. Well, kind of. Just stressed. It's crazy in here. I don't know where to begin." Not wanting to burden her, I change the subject. "When are you visiting?"

"Tomorrow."

"Great! Oh God, you don't understand how much I really need to see you right now. What happened to you with the cops?"

"That Detective Reid told me I was going to jail for a long time, and that you're never getting out, and–"

I squeeze the phone handle as if it's a stress ball. "Never getting out! Why?"

"'Cause you've got so many charges. He said, 'It's OK to talk about him 'cause he's never getting out.' He really tried to threaten me to turn and talk. That time we went to your dentist in Tucson, he said we didn't go the dentist, we picked up drugs."

"That's crazy!" *Is he bluffing her? Is he out to put me away forever?* "How long were you there?"

"Close to dinner time. Ten to twelve hours. They kept telling me my mom was calling the jail asking if they'd fed me my vegetarian food."

I smile sadly. "That's funny."

"She sent my brother to pick me up with bean burritos from Taco Bell. What's gonna happen, Shaun?"

"Don't worry, love. They didn't find any drugs, so they shouldn't be able to hold me too much longer. The problem is my bond."

Cries for help and thuds stop the chatter in the day room.

"Hold on," I say, craning my neck.

The commotion is in the shower area, about fifteen feet behind me. Skinheads are attacking a naked figure on the floor. Inmates stop what they are doing, gravitate towards the showers and form a sinister audience.

"What is it?" Claudia asks.

"Looks like…er…some kind of disturbance."

"What? What's wrong? You all right?" she says, her voice starting to crack.

"Sure…er…I'm fine. It doesn't involve me," I say, distracted by the violence and proximity of the growing crowd.

The naked man raises his head. *It's David.* There is a plea for help in his eyes as they meet mine – a look that freezes me against the wall.

"Er…I might need to get off the phone here soon."

"Die, you sick child molester!" Rob yells, dropping his heel on David's temple.

"*Arghhhhhhhhhhhhhh…*"

"What's going on? Are you OK?" Claudia asks, her voice hitting high notes.

The skinheads vie for stomping room. David arches his back in agony.

"Yes. I'm fine," I say, struggling not to relay my fear. "It just gets crazy in here. That's all."

The blows silence David. Blood streams from his nose.

"I have to go now. I love you," I say, not wanting to worry her any further.

"Love you, too. Every time I go to my mom's, I take your sweaty T-shirt and Floppy." Floppy is a Build-A-Bear that plays my voice saying, "Happy Valentine's Day. I love you, Bungle Bee."

A skinhead jumps up and down on David. I think I hear his ribs snap. I scrunch my face in revulsion of the cracking sound.

"I can't wait to see you tomorrow. Bye, love." I hang up.

The spectators have adopted the safety-in-numbers strategy of the wildebeest. None of them dare venture from the herd. Mesmerised by the violence, they watch from a safe distance. Gripped by the same instinct, I join the back of the herd.

As if they've exhausted their supply of aggression on David, the skinheads stop the beating and march away. David is a whimpering heaving mound of flesh, blood pooling around his head.

What kind of world am I in? This stuff really happens. It could have been me last night. How will I survive?

Just when the violence seems to be over, a rhinoceros of a man with spider webs tattooed on his thick neck approaches the skinheads. "How come we can still hear the little bitch?"

"We fucked the chomo up good," Rob says.

"Not good enough." The man approaches the shower with the casual gait of someone going to the shop to buy a bottle of milk, grabs David's neck and starts slamming David's skull against the concrete as if he's trying to break open a coconut. *Crack-crack-crack...*

I'm revolted but compelled to watch. The big man has increased the stakes. The code of these people probably includes killing anyone who interferes or flags down a guard. Even walking away will be a show of disapproval, an invitation to be attacked next. I'm too scared to move.

David's body convulses. His eyes close. Stillness. Silence. *Is he dead?* He remains on the floor while the prisoners resume their activity as if nothing happened. Eager to distance myself from what looks like a corpse, I return to my cell.

Ten minutes later, a guard enters the pod to do a security walk. When he arrives at the shower, he yells, "Everybody, lockdown! Lockdown right now!"

Shouting at the guard, the prisoners return to their cells, slamming doors behind them. Guards rush into the day room. Having never seen violence at this level before, I press myself to the cell door to assess David. I watch them remove him on a stretcher. There is fluid other than blood leaking from his head. A yellowish fluid.

CHAPTER 7

"Cells A5, A7, A12, roll up!" announces the control-tower guard.

"What's he mean, roll up?" I ask.

"They're moving a bunch of us out," Boyd says. "Roll your mattress around your property. We've got to go downstairs."

"But we only just got here!" I'd arrived at Towers jail hoping for relief from the mayhem, but seeing David get attacked has frightened me more than the violence at The Horseshoe. Images of him on a stretcher, possibly dead, are replaying in my mind.

"They roll people up all the time. They might think we had something to do with what happened to David 'cause he was our celly. We might be going to lockdown."

Great. Now I'm a murder suspect. And what the bloody hell's lockdown? Are there places worse than this? Afraid of what Boyd might say, I don't ask. *Wherever I end up, I'll just tough it out when I get there.* I coil my mattress around my bedding and carry my belongings onto the iron-railing balcony.

"Where you moving us to?" yells a black prisoner on the metal-grid stairs, windmilling his arms at the guards in the control tower. Lugging my mattress, I stop behind him, hoping he moves on. The guards ignore him. He waves again. His short sleeves fall back, revealing triceps protruding like thick horseshoes. When he gives up on the guards, I follow him down the stairs. I place my rolled-up mattress by the sliding door that allows us in and out of the pod.

"Where you from?" I ask.

"Jamaica," he says, greeting me with a raised fist.

"I'm Shaun from England." I bump his fist.

"Just call me Jamaica, Shaun," he says in a friendly Caribbean voice.

"How'd you end up in Arizona?" I ask, feeling a bond with this fellow foreigner.

"Got busted at Sky Harbor Airport. Should have never got off the plane. Was going from LA to New York. The plane stopped in Phoenix, so I figured I'd take a look around. They stopped me before I got back on, found $100,000 cash in me carry-on. They took the money and arrested me."

Unjust and perhaps racially motivated. Is he telling the truth? He doesn't look the criminal type. I believe him but decide not to ask why he had so much money. *Too personal. It was probably drug-related.* "They robbed you."

"Yeah, man. They ran my name, figured out I wasn't a citizen, took the money and now they've started deportation proceedings against me, so I'll never be able to get the money back. It's kind of my fault for getting off the plane. I never knew Arizona was this bad. This state's the worst, Shaun. New York and LA don't fuck with you like that. I'm telling you."

Bringing Ecstasy into Arizona wasn't one of my brightest ideas either. "You can't get your money back?"

"That's the thing: it's not my money," he says, shaking his head.

"Oh no." *Is he a smuggler for a yardie gang?*

Arms sleeved in white-supremacy tattoos throw a mattress next to mine. "What's up, wood!" They belong to a stocky man with cropped ginger hair and an all-American square jaw, a few inches shorter than me, with a freckly face, a bulbous red nose and a collection of red marks on his forehead and cheeks that could be acne or small lesions.

"I'm Shaun." I bump his fist. "From England."

"I'm Carter. Us woods have got to stick together in here." He squints at Jamaica. "Know what I'm saying?"

I don't appreciate being told who I can talk to, but I don't want to make enemies either. *Better play on my ignorance.* "I'm new here," I say in a light-hearted way.

Carter leans towards me, gazing without blinking. "Well, learn fast if you don't wanna get smashed."

Talking to Jamaica was distracting me from the dangers of the environment, but Carter has restored my fear. I don't know what to say. *Is he giving me advice or threatening me?* Sweat trickles down my armpit hairs.

I'm glad when an announcement interrupts our conversation: "Pill nurse in the house! Come to the sliding door with your IDs and a cup of water."

The sick and mentally ill emerge from their cells, bearing paper cups of water. They crowd our area, changing the dynamic of the day room. There is too much going on for Carter to bother me now.

A few seconds of static are followed by the guard's voice. "Get away from the day-room door! Form one straight line!"

The sick line up. The door slides open.

A Bulgarian shot-putter of a nurse steps inside the day room and scowls at the men. "Name?" she yells at the first in line.

Holding up his ID, he replies, "Fiori."

"Here's your lithium, your Prozac." She watches him mouth the pills and drink water. "I hope to God you swallowed them!"

"Yeah," the man says, rubbing his left eye.

The nurse is furious. "I don't believe you! Open your mouth. Raise your tongue. OK. Next!"

Each prisoner receives the same treatment. As soon as she leaves, those who pretended to swallow their medication offer them for sale:

"Drugs for thugs!"

"Seroquel for one item!"

"Who wants Thorazine?"

"Give me the Thorazine, dog!"

"The best sleeping pills over here."

The day room bustles like a marketplace. I'm admiring the barter, trying to decipher the terminology, when the control guard hits the button to activate the sliding door. I pick up my mattress and walk out. Being on the move again raises my pulse.

A plump middle-aged guard with a blond flat-top streaks

down the corridor. "Pick your shit up! You're going to *my* tower – Tower 6!" he yells, leaning into his stride as if he can't wait to take control of us. He spots Boyd and shakes his head. "Oh no! Not you again!"

"Why Tower 6, Officer Alston? 'Cause that's where lockdown is?" Boyd asks.

Lockdown. David's dead or dying. We're going to lockdown. I did nothing to save him. I'll be charged with murder. It might even get pinned on me by the skinheads. If I say it wasn't me they'll kill me too. Must stop thinking about David and the way he looked at me.

"None of your beeswax," Officer Alston says. "All that matters is you troublemakers behave in *my* tower. That includes not lying to me. Ever! I detest liars. So if you wanna stay off my shit list, don't lie to me. Now head down that corridor!"

I've only just got here and I'm classified with the troublemakers. Or is this guard crazy? Some kind of military nut? Bracing to deal with a pod full of troublemakers, I shoulder my curled-up mattress and set off.

"Mordhorst still your shift partner?" Boyd asks.

"Yeah. I bet he just can't wait to see you again."

Why's Boyd so cheerful? He knows where we're going. Maybe it's not so bad.

"Mordhorst ain't nothing nice," Boyd says. "He just loves his job. He's the most grieved guard at Towers."

"And he's proud of it," Officer Alston says. "He collects inmate grievance forms. Wallpapers his home with them."

As we walk down the cement-block corridor, the Tower 6 inmates mob the Plexiglas at either side of us. Afraid to stare directly at them, I flick my eyes from left to right. Some of the whites nod at Carter. *A bad sign.* In the control tower is Officer Mordhorst, a squat man with a round ruddy face, a bulldog eager to bite someone for no reason. *Stay out of his way.*

"C's lockdown. B's max security," Boyd says, pointing at those pods. "We must be going to D or A."

Not lockdown? Relief distracts me until I realise I'm about to be plunged into a new mob and who knows what danger. I'm as jittery as when I first stepped onto a roller coaster. *Will I be accepted? Will I be smashed?* We stop at the foot of the control tower. Tower 6 is identical to Tower 2, except in C pod the inmates are all locked down for violating jail rules. I notice a group of prisoners in D pod staring at me. *What's going on? Have I lost it again or are they looking at me? Yes, they are. I must be a target.* One of them points at me. My body heats up. He is a buff hippy and looks familiar. *Friend or someone I've crossed in the drug world? Maybe an enemy from Sammy the Bull's crew.*

Officer Alston reads our cell assignments – mine is upstairs – and radios Officer Mordhorst to activate D pod's sliding door. Taking deep breaths, I plan to rush to my cell and take it from there like yesterday. Hope for the best. Boyd dashes in first theatrically. *Good old Boyd. My guinea pig.*

"Look who it is, everyone!" someone yells in the day room. "Jack Nicholson's back!"

Boyd draws their attention. Good. He bows. They laugh. Even better. That's exactly what I want to hear: laughter. Not the sound of someone getting smashed in the shower. *Keep them laughing, Boyd, at least for the ten seconds it'll take me to get to my cell.* I step onto the metal-grid stairs. Seven seconds. Six. I'm almost at the top, a mere three or four seconds away from my cell, when someone comes up behind me. Fast. My back muscles clench.

"Shaun! English Shaun!"

I crane my neck but keep going. It's the buff hippy. *What does he want?*

"It's Billy! Remember?"

"You look familiar, but I don't remember." I try to search my memory bank. Nothing registers. My mind is too congested with fear of the present to travel to the past.

"I'm Billy," he says, tapping his broad chest. "I was in your limo with you outside the Icehouse that night you got Larry the Limo Driver so high he had to call out another limo driver. You stole my glitter girls, Samantha and Aubrey."

I stop at the top of the stairs. *Billy! Fellow raver!* Relief gushes. *I actually know someone in here. Surely this will help.* "No shit! It is you. But you've doubled in size." I want to hug him.

"Fellas, this is English Shaun!" he announces to the day room. "I know him from the streets. He's a good fucking dude."

Members of all four racial groups clustered around their separate tables look over. A few actually nod and smile. I can't believe it. *These men are smiling. They don't want to kill me.* I'd shown Billy a good time and never expected to see him again. I walk along the balcony feeling slightly safer. He follows me into D10 and closes the door to almost-shut.

D10 is to the left of the top of the stairs, at the same height as the control tower it faces. It is a standard Towers' cell: six-by-nine foot, triple-bunked. There is a mixture of unclean smells hanging in the hot air. The toilet stinks as if tomcats have marked their territory on it. The short podgy man perched on the bottom bunk is giving off body odour with a vinegary tang. Scrutinising me with amused curiosity, he looks like a pocket-sized Henry VIII. He has Henry's features, but his long unkempt beard makes him seem deranged. "What's up, dog! I'm Troll. One of your new cellies."

"I'm Shaun, Troll." I place my mattress down and we bump fists. There is something endearing about him. I want to get more acquainted, but the door swings open and bangs against the wall, making me jump.

A topless man with WHITE PRIDE across his midsection barges past Billy. Everything about him screams king of the jungle. Size. Aura. Blond mane. "What's up, dog! I'm Outlaw, the head of the whites."

"I'm Shaun, a friend of Billy's."

"Hey, you need any hygiene products, anything like stamps, envelopes?" Outlaw asks.

People are actually being nice to me.

"I'll sort him out," Troll says.

"Hey, you wanna go smoke, dude?" Billy asks.

"I don't smoke." Being offered kindness and saying no feels

awkward. I'm tempted to start smoking just to bond.

"Everyone in here smokes," Billy says. "The more you get to smoke, the more important you are."

Troll cackles like a fantasy-book creature. "Good looking out on not smoking, dog. We're trying to keep this a smoke-free cell. There's not many in here who don't smoke."

I'm relieved Troll doesn't smoke.

"Are you sure you don't wanna jump in the car?" Billy says.

"The car?" I ask, confused.

"Come smoke with us."

"Thanks, but I'll pass."

Billy and Outlaw dart out.

"I guess I'm on the top bunk," I say.

Troll stands. "You start at the top and work your way down as your cellies leave," he says with a schoolteacher's tone of authority. "Look, I've got to go play spades. Catch you later."

I'm surprised he leaves so fast. Everyone seems to be rushing off to somewhere in this place that goes nowhere. Strange. After making my bed, I sit on the stool and try to unwind. Impossible. I've seen and been through so much, my nervous system won't settle down. Although glad of the move to Tower 6 and Billy vouching for me, I still expect someone to attack me at any moment. I can't take my eyes off the doorway. *They allowed David to settle in before pouncing on him. That could easily happen to me. Will my heartbeat ever return to normal?*

I'm happy to see Billy return. He sits on the toilet. "So they finally caught up with you?"

I tell him about the raid and my charges. "How about you?"

"I was on the news about six months ago. I reported a burglary at my house. The cops came out and got suspicious. A few days later, they sent SWAT to arrest me."

"You called them out and they ended up arresting you?" A mosquito whines by my ear.

"I refused to be arrested. I was in a standoff for hours. I've been here ever since. Haven't even done a crime."

"That's outrageous! You shouldn't be here. I hope they let you out soon." *He's suffered even more injustice than Jamaica. I need information.* "What's it like in here?" I want to make sense of the violence, so I won't fall foul.

His expression darkens. "You've got to be very careful, Shaun. Watch what you say to people. Don't let anyone bulldog you, 'cause if anyone gets anything out of you, it opens the door for everyone else. If anyone calls you out – like says you're a punk-ass bitch – you must fight or else you automatically get smashed by your own race. Fights break out all the time over stupid shit. I've seen people get smashed over an orange or a brownie. I had nine fights in my first three months, so I quit doing meth, started working out and I gained sixty pounds."

Nine fights in three months! I need to get bigger. "How can you possibly gain weight eating this chow?"

"Have your people put money on your books."

Claudia. Must call her again.

"There's a store list you can shop from once a week. Had red death yet?"

"What's that?"

"The evening meal. Slop with mystery meat in it."

"Oh no! Sounds worse than green baloney." I'm hungry for information on greater threats than food. "What's all this head-of-the-race stuff about?"

"Each race has a head. Mexicans. Chicanos or Mexican Americans. Blacks and whites. Each head has torpedoes – usually youngsters looking to prove themselves – who smash people for their head, no questions asked. If the head of your race holds a meeting, you must go or else you get smashed for failing to represent your race. The head of the whites is usually some Aryan Brotherhood dude here from prison. Outlaw is our head. So far we've had no race riots under his rule. That's good. There's always someone getting smashed, but just try and stay away from the drugs, drama and politics, and you'll be all right."

"OK," I say, worriedly trying to digest his advice.

"I'm glad I'm off meth. Now I just smoke weed and do these pills called Pac-Mans. Some guy who has seizures sells them to me. Hopefully, I'll be out of here soon and not have to deal with this bullshit. There's a lot of meth in the pod right now. Some of them have been up for days. So just be careful 'cause when they've been up like this they start sketching out on each other and shit gets crazy. You'll be all right in this cell, though. Troll's a good celly and so is Schwartz."

"Schwartz?" I ask, imagining a neo-Nazi.

"Yeah, but don't be fooled by the name. Schwartz is a Chicano, a youngster, a cool little dude. And Troll spends a lot at the store every week. He's a rich kid from Cali. Anyway, man, you're trying to settle in, so I'll leave you alone. If you need anything just come down to D14."

"Thanks, Billy," I say, comforted.

I wait almost an hour to get on a phone in the day room.

"I'm glad you called again," Claudia says. "It sounded so crazy in there last time."

"I'm much better. They moved me," I say. "I met someone I know and it's much safer where I am. How about you?"

"Not good." She starts to cry.

"What's the matter?"

"What do you think's the matter? You've been arrested!"

"Look, I'm all right. You've got to be strong. We've both got to be strong."

"I feel so scared for you in the jail, especially after that last call."

"I'm OK. What happened didn't affect me." I see an image of David on a stretcher, his head leaking yellow fluid. "How're you?"

"I can't sleep properly since they knocked our door down. One night, I was lying in my mom's bed with Floppy and – remember how I used to bother you to hold your hand while we were sleeping? – I did that to my mom. At first she thought it was OK 'cause she was half asleep, but then later on, I held her hand so tight she jumped up and threw my arm away. It really scared her. I don't know exactly what she said, but it was something along the lines of, 'What the fuck are you doing? You're weird! Stop snuggling me!'"

Imagining her short tough beer-loving mum saying such things, I cackle and snort. Claudia joins in. "What time are you visiting?"

"I'm gonna get there for 9 a.m. 'cause that's when they open."

"How'd you find that out?"

"I called the phone number. It gave the visitation schedule and all that stuff. What do you think I should wear?"

"Anything. I just need to see you."

"I can't wear sexy clothes."

We laugh.

"It doesn't matter. I just need to see you. And please find out how to put money on my books before I starve."

"Are we going to be able to hug each other, hold hands, kiss?"

"I don't know. I'll have to ask my cellmates. I hope so. I really need to hug and kiss you right now."

After calling Claudia, I lie on my bunk, my mind bobbing around on the swirl of events. Staring at the ceiling a few inches from my head, I wonder how much of the brown splatter is blood and whose blood will be up there next. Every now and then I slap away a mosquito with its landing gear out. I start hearing voices again, rising from the chatter downstairs, insisting I get smashed. Other voices join in, led by Billy's, defending me. Concluding it's a rerun of yesterday when I'd charged onto the balcony for no reason, I take no action. But I continue to hear voices, one minute getting frightened and convinced they are real; the next, telling myself I'm going crazy and shrugging them off.

Troll enters with a baby-faced Mexican American. "Here's our other celly, Schwartz."

Glad of Schwartz's warm eyes and smile, I lean onto my side and dangle my fist for him to bump.

"Viddy well, little brother. Viddy well," Schwartz says, imitating a working-class English accent. "I heard you're from England."

"That's a great *Clockwork Orange* impression," I say, looking down at him from near the ceiling.

"We were all feeling a bit shagged and fagged and fashed, it being a night of no small expenditure."

"That's the best I've ever heard an American do it," I say. "How the bloody hell did you learn all that?"

Shwartz sits on the stool. Troll takes the bottom bunk, so I'm looking down at the top of his head.

"I watch it all the time. It's one of my favourite movies. I practise Alex's lines at home."

I'm thankful for all things English that are novelties abroad. *Maybe my Englishness will continue to help me.*

"Aren't you wondering how you ended up in a cell with a Chicano called Schwartz?" Troll asks.

"Yes," I say.

"Got a Mexican mom," Schwartz says. "Pop's American. His parents are German."

"Then we're fellow Europeans," I say.

We discuss our charges. Troll has Class 2 felonies, including fraudulent schemes and artifices; Schwartz, a petty drug possession.

Schwartz demands I climb down from my bunk, so he can demonstrate something. On the tiny steel table, he places a black pawn on a chessboard. "I'm getting bonded out soon, but I'll be right back. Compared to you two, I'm just this little guy." He points at the pawn. "In the real world, this is how people like me get pushed around." He knocks the pawn over with a white castle and surrounds the castle with black pawns. "The only way the little people like me can push back against the big people with power and money is when we gang up like this." He moves the pawns closer to the castle. "But when we push back, they call the big guns in, and we can never ever win." He circles the black pawns with the larger white pieces and knocks the pawns down with a white knight and bishop.

I laugh at how well Schwartz summarised a subject I'd struggled to understand in Economics: Karl Marx's theory of class conflict.

"It's the same in jail. They'll do us dirty, and we'll take a stand, flood our cells and shit, but then they send the goon squad in."

"The goon squad?" I ask.

"Sheriff Joe Arpaio's goons," Schwartz says. "Massive dudes who come in, throw us around, make us get naked and blast us with Tasers and shotgun rounds."

"Shotgun rounds!" *Is he joking?*

"Non-lethal. You'll see them soon enough," Troll says, chilling me even more. "You play chess?"

"Not for about twenty years," I say.

"Let's play." Troll starts setting up the board.

Schwartz stands. "I'm out of here. Later, cellies."

"Whoever draws white or wins a game gets to sit on the stool. The other stands." Troll holds out two fists. "Pick one."

"The left."

He unclenches a black pawn. "Unlucky."

Troll listens to a tiny black radio via earplugs and sings during the opening stage of the game. I'm rusty and it shows. My rustiness lowers his guard. He makes some careless moves and turns the music off too late to stage a comeback. Heckling me into losing concentration doesn't work. I win by a narrow margin. He says, "Ain't that-about-a-bitch," abandons his radio and continues to talk trash, probing for chinks in my psyche as we start the next game. I compliment him on his chess ability, hoping to throw his game off. Playing Troll reveals his crafty side. We end up tied 3-3.

"You've got game," Troll says, returning to his bunk.

I stay on the stool. "You, too. How did someone as intelligent as you get busted?"

Troll rests his elbows on his thighs and steeples his fingertips. "I was going in banks with fake IDs and cashing cheques. I'd take out small amounts, get to know the bank staff, and when I felt comfortable, I'd withdraw a large sum. The crazy thing is on the day I got busted the cops had already let me go."

"What do you mean?"

"The bank called the cops. The cops questioned me. I bullshitted my way out of it. I left the bank and was on my way to my car, when the Feds stopped me. I tried to bullshit the Feds, but they were having none of it." He presses his palms together as if praying to erase his arrest. "That was a year ago. I've been here fighting my case ever since."

"I can't imagine what a year stuck in this hellhole is like," I say, clinging to the hope that I'll be released somehow. "I'd go insane."

"Last year, they offered me five years, and I refused to sign the plea bargain. I'm from Cali. You have to kill someone there to get five years. So what did they offer me next? Eighteen fucking years! This state's the worst to get caught in. Arizona ain't nothing nice." He drops his chin onto his palms and stares at the concrete as if at a funeral.

"So now what?"

His eyes meet mine and sparkle irrationally. "I'm fighting back! I've filed a Rule 11."

"Rule 11?"

"It means you're not competent to stand trial. If you file a Rule 11 and they determine you're crazy, they send you to the nuthouse and let you go after a few years."

"A lot of people must be filing Rule 11's then." I add filing a Rule 11 to my list of legal options.

"They are. But not many get it. It can take years to run all the tests while you sit rotting in here. I've got to act like I'm nuts every time I see the doctors. That's why I don't shave or take care of myself and I look like a troll. Some guys go to see the doctors and eat their own shit. Would you eat your own shit if they'd let you go tomorrow?"

"I don't want to think about it."

Troll grins. "If they said all you had to do was suck off the judge and he'd let you go, would you?"

"You are a Rule 11!"

Cackling, Troll slides a brown paper bag from under his bunk. "Hey, want a candy bar or something?"

"I'm bloody starving," I say, salivating.

"Snickers?"

"Hell, yeah!" I demolish the Snickers in record time, appreciating it more than anything I've ever eaten.

"In here, he who controls the food, controls the prisoners. And I'm talking about store food, not state food like red death. I used to get $500 worth of store a week. They had to bring two trolleys with store on them: one for the rest of the pod and one just for me. Then they decided I was getting extorted, so they changed the rules and now the limit you can spend on store is $100 a week." His eyes latch onto the control tower. "Looks like swing shift's here. The whole atmosphere changes when Mordhorst goes home. We've got Mendoza and Noble."

"What're they like?"

"Mendoza's the Chicano with the glasses on. Stutters a lot. Seems friendly enough, but I've seen him slam motherfuckers to the ground. The youngster's Noble. A cage fighter and military reservist. We've got way more play with these than the other two."

"Play?"

"We can get away with more shit."

Hours later, I'm on my bunk reading Troll's Spanish dictionary when Officer Mendoza announces. "Chow's in the house! L…L…Line up at the sliding door! Fully dressed and with y… your IDs or you will not be s… s…served!"

Troll springs up. "Come on, let's get in line, so we don't have to wait around."

We dash downstairs. The men awaiting red death look as dissatisfied as Russians in a bread queue. The first in line presents his ID to Officer Noble and takes a tray from the trusty. Noble ticks each name off his clipboard, so no one can claim a second tray.

When Troll receives his, he turns to me. "I don't eat red death.

I donate it." He gives his tray to a gaunt man hovering around him and hurries up the stairs.

A trusty hands me a large brown plastic tray. The slop – red death – looks like carroty vomit blended with blood with blobs of oil floating on it. Meat, bones and gristle in assorted shapes, shades and sizes are protruding from the sauce. Gagging on the sulphurous smell, I place the tray on the nearest table and sit down. As I'm one of the first to get served, the races haven't mobbed the tables yet, so I've forgotten about the segregation.

Seconds later, a cannonball of a Mexican taps me on the shoulder. "You can't sit here!" He has a shaved head, deep-set eyes and long eyelashes.

Dozens of men focus on us. I maintain eye contact.

The Mexican puts his hands on his hips. Raising his voice, he says, "This table paisas' table!"

Mexicans surround me. None smiling. It was foolish to think I was safe due to Billy's introduction. *Maybe I'm safe from the whites, but what about the other races? Where are all these Mexicans coming from? I've got to get out of here, but not in a cowardly way.* "No problem," I say in a deep voice, trying to sound tough. Standing up, I look around.

Troll flies down the stairs. "England, you can't sit there!" Turning to the Mexican who tapped me on the shoulder, he says, "Hey, Carlo, this is England, your new neighbour. England say hello to Carlo, the head of the paisas."

The atmosphere turns friendly as fast as it had soured. *I can't get over this place. The Mexicans aren't going to smash me now. We're all going to be friends.* I bump fists with Carlo, greeting him with the limited Spanish I know. He seems to appreciate my effort.

"Come over here!" Billy yells.

The whites are laughing at what I thought was a dangerous situation. *Have I blown it out of proportion?* I think of the skinheads' words in Tower 2: *You've got a lot to learn.* It's standing room only at the whites' table.

"Give him some room on the corner," Outlaw says.

The whites are shovelling down slop, chatting, gnawing on mystery meat. Some eyeball my tray.

With my stomach hurting as if it's trying to digest its own walls, I'm in a hurry to eat. I dunk my plastic Spork – a cross between a spoon and fork – into the red death and fish out a chunk of potato. I raise my Spork, salivating in the way Englishmen are conditioned to do at the prospect of a good spud. I'm about to devour it when I spot the lesions, large, brown, deeply engrained. My Spork stops short of my lower lip. I drop the potato in the slop. From the potatoes, I detach some long white hairs and the sections that are rotten or dirt-encrusted, and eat what's left. Sifting through the meat, I eliminate the slimy grey, green and brown pieces I suspect are spoiled. I find a clump of long pale strands. *Chicken?* I attempt to chew the clump, but it turns into straw in my mouth. I swallow it. A dark chunk of meat feels sticky in my mouth and requires lots of chewing but it eventually goes down. Eating the two slices of bread that don't have mould on them dries my mouth up. What I've salvaged only teases my hunger.

"Any of you guys want this?" I ask.

Their eyes crowd my tray.

"I'll take care of that." Outlaw says.

I slide my tray to him. "It's all yours."

"Good looking out, dog!" He divides the red death among the whites.

Now they've classified me as a food source, they are slightly warmer towards me. I take advantage of the tiny elevation in their mood to excuse myself from the table. With a sickly taste in my mouth and my stomach starting to react to the red death, I trudge home and find Troll munching commissary.

"A month from now, you'll be eating all your red death just like the rest of them," Troll says.

"I won't eat that shit again even if it's the last meal on earth. I don't see you eating it either!"

"I can give you another Snickers, but you're gonna have to get me back on store day."

"No problem."

I play chess with Troll until 10:30 when Officer Mendoza announces, "Lockdown! Lockdown! Ki…Ki…Kiss each other good night and return to your cells!"

Whooping and yelling erupt in the day room.

"We ain't locking down!"

"Fuck you!"

"Come make us lockdown!"

Prisoners pelt the Plexiglas with grapefruits. The more hyperactive chase each other around, cackling like children on a playground. Reluctantly, they drift back to their cells and slam their doors. They taunt young Officer Noble, walking cell to cell with a headcount clipboard. When Noble leaves, the obscene banter grows louder. Mexicans sing in Spanish. Men chat through the vent system. Others exchange threats and swear they'll fight when the doors reopen. Every now and then everyone hushes to listen to a dirty joke. It's hours before the only sounds left are snoring, the fan rattling on the day-room wall and water dripping from the shower as steadily as my life seems to be leaking away.

CHAPTER 8

After experiencing mild diarrhoea and taking a shower, I'm sitting on the toilet watching *Jerry Springer* through my doorway – cell D10 has one of the best views of the day-room TV – when an announcement comes: "D10, Attwood, you have a regular visit!"

I jump up, giddy and excited, grab my anti-shank toothbrush, smear it with AmerFresh, and lean over the sink – a steel basin above the toilet caked in toothpaste spit and chin shavings. Pushing a metal button makes water dribble from a tiny faucet. Attempting to get rid of the foul breath caused by the vapours rising from my constantly empty stomach, I brush until my gums bleed.

"D10, Attwood, turn out for your visit!"

Prisoners in the day room parrot the announcement. Some come to my door.

"C'mon, dog! You've got a visit!"

"Get your ass out there, dog!"

"I'm coming! I'm coming!" I yell, applying state deodorant to my armpits. The previous layer had trickled down the sides of my body, washed away by my constant sweat. The deodorant bubbles and fizzes and settles into foam with a disinfectant smell. I don't yet know that the prisoners shun the state deodorant, that most of them use the ladies stick from the commissary. I throw my shirt on, attach my ID to the upper left side and rush from the cell. I bound down the metal-grid stairs as joyful as a dog fetching its first stick of the day, harangued by men yelling, "Who's coming to see you?"

"The missus!" I say proudly and wave at the guard.

The control guard spots me and presses the button to open the sliding door. "Do you know where Visitation is?" he asks over the speaker system.

Gazing up at him in the Plexiglas bubble, I shake my head.

"You!" He points at another prisoner in the corridor. "Show him where Visitation is!"

"What's up, dog!" the prisoner in the corridor says.

Beaming at the prospect of seeing Claudia, I say. "All right, dog!" Starting with dog, I've been adding jail slang to my vocabulary in the hope of fitting in. Every other sentence in here seems to end with the word dog pronounced dawg.

Smiling back, he says, "Follow me."

We exit the building. The sun blinds me for a few seconds. We take a short path down the breezeway and turn right into Visitation.

"Stay in there until the visitors are all seated." Overweight Officer Green points at a Plexiglas holding tank overlooking the visitation room. Behind rectangular spectacles, his beady eyes are full of suspicion. He is struggling to keep an eye on everything going on: prisoners arriving, prisoners in the holding tank, electronically-activated doors opening and closing to allow guards in and out.

The visitation room is the size of a small warehouse. It consists of a guard station – two officers sitting at a raised desk – overlooking rows of small wooden tables and blue plastic chairs bolted to the floor. In the corners of the room are old security cameras that creak as they rotate. There are no vending machines or toilets. The visitors have to wait outside, sometimes for hours, while the prisoners summoned for visits are packed into the holding tank. Almost an hour into my wait, the visitation-room security door opens with a tremendous grinding sound. Seeing the first batch of visitors, we scramble to our feet. Fights almost break out when the biggest inmates shoulder-barge their way to the front of the holding tank. To our visitors, we probably look like a display of wild animals. The attention from our visitors soon switches the mood back to friendly. There is much waving of hands and blowing of kisses. In the next batch of visitors, I see Claudia's long golden hair, pale narrow face and big eyes. My heart flutters. She spots me and waves. Smiling, I long to hug her. I hope Officer

Green lets us out of the tank soon. Everything in my life has been taken away, and I'm grateful to have something so precious back, even if only for a short while. On the tips of my toes, I smile and wave as she sits down. She looks nervous, until she flashes her long-toothed smile.

Officer Green mans the guard station as if stood on a stage, a no-nonsense look on his face. "In a moment, I'm going to allow the inmates in." He speaks slowly and precisely. "I do expect you to obey the rules at all times. Posted on the wall are the rules." Everyone's heads swivel. He pauses for a few seconds. "If you do not follow the rules, your visit will be ended. You will not get a second chance! There will be no passing items. Anyone that gets caught passing items will have their future visits cancelled and may possibly be charged with promoting prison contraband. There will be no hanky-panky." He puckers his face at the few visitors snickering. "Anyone caught kissing will lose their visit. You may hold hands. If your hands slip below the table at any time, you will lose your visit. Do you understand me, ladies and gentlemen?"

The crowd murmurs acknowledgement.

"Enjoy your visits then. Officer Gonzales, please let the inmates in."

Officer Gonzales is a slim new recruit in his early twenties. He opens the door that allows us into the visitation room. "Form a straight line. Roll down your pants' cuffs. Have your IDs ready as you enter the room."

We show him our IDs and form a line at the guard station. Officer Green ticks our names off his list and instructs us to specific tables. "Attwood, table 9."

Rushing to Claudia, I yell, "I'm so glad you're here!" She's crying. "I know. It's crazy isn't it? I think I'm still in shock, too." I sit down, pick up her thin hands and lean into the musky floral scent of her perfume, filling myself with as much of her smell as I can in one loud inhalation.

"I love you," she says, her hands trembling within mine.

"I love you, too. I wish I could show you my pink boxers."

She manages a chuckle. "Pink's my favourite colour."

"I know," I say, smiling. "So you all right or what?"

"I'm OK if you're OK," she says, brightening up.

"I'm doing fine. It was a bit rough at first, but so far I'm not having problems. It's just the conditions."

"Like what?"

"The A/C barely works. There's mosquitoes everywhere. The heat's the worst though. Everyone's got itchy skin infections and rashes because of the heat. I can barely sleep. I'm basically lying in a pool of sweat all day and night."

"The food must be terrible," she says, shaking her head.

"Most nights it's red death! That's what these guys call it. Slop on rotten potatoes that have long white strands of human hair in them. We only get one cooked meal a day, and it's mostly inedible. Other than red death, there's a meal I haven't had yet that the inmates call Kibbles 'n Bits because it resembles dog food. Breakfast's raw green baloney and mouldy bread. I've barely eaten anything since I got here, and what I did eat gave me the runs. I got off lucky though. Some guys have food poisoning so severe they are retching and crapping throughout the day and night, and the guards won't do anything to help them. I'm told you have to be almost dead to see a doctor."

"Well, I've put some money on your inmate account."

"Thanks so much!" I say, gently squeezing her hands. "Now I can buy peanuts or something to stop my hunger pains. Some of the inmates spend the day rummaging for food. I see them going through the trash. I got lucky: my celly, Troll, gets store, so he's hooked me up with Snickers. Most people are begging him for store. Thanks for the money. It'll go a long way in here."

"What's the people you live with like?"

"My cellmates are nice, but they've got three of us squeezed into a tiny cell designed for one person. I was in Tower 2 at first. I didn't like it. I didn't know anyone, and the skinheads were running wild. I was so nervous. But now I'm in Tower 6, it's better."

"That's good."

"I sat at the wrong dining table though."

"What do you mean?"

I explain the racial segregation.

"It sounds creepy."

"The heads decide who gets smashed and who gets to smoke and get high."

"Cigarettes and drugs in here! How?"

"They keyster them in. That means they stick them in their behinds. Visitors bring them in balloons and condoms. When the guards aren't looking, they pass them, and the inmates stick them in their behinds."

"That's disgusting!"

"They put all kinds of things in there. Lighters. Needles. Knives. Nearly everyone's getting high."

We are avowing our eternal love when Officer Green announces, "Visits are over! Visitors please say your goodbyes. Inmates remain seated."

Our thirty minutes are up. It's hard to let go of her hands and watch her slip away. The feeling of being alone again overwhelms me. Most of the visitors, including Claudia, group by the security door. A few remain, crying, staring tenderly at the prisoners they are visiting. Claudia keeps waving and blowing kisses. I struggle to appear strong.

"Visits are over! Did you not hear me? You all need to leave the room or else I will suspend your visitation privileges. Do you hear me, table 21? Leave now!"

When all of the visitors are clustered in front of the security door, it groans open. They depart, waving sadly, some, including Claudia, are crying. They leave behind an atmosphere redolent of over-perfumed women and soiled nappies.

"Inmates, stand up and enter that room." Officer Green points at the door of the strip-search room, tiny and windowless. We cram in. He locks the door and abandons us.

There is barely any air flowing into the room. By the end of the first hour, my clothes are soaked. Dizzy, I fear I'm going to suffocate. Most of us had showered before our visits, but now we are stinking again. Every time we hear the jingle of keys, we stop panting and focus on the doors. When the jingling fades, we curse Officer Green and return to wallowing in our claustrophobia. He leaves us in there for about two hours. By the time he opens the door, I'm dazed from a heat headache. I wonder if leaving us in there is a unique form of torture he's devised for those of us lucky enough to have visits. If so, it is effective: as much as I want to see Claudia again, I'm dreading spending hours in this room.

"Strip down to your boxers, gentlemen. I'm going to let you out one at a time." His slow steady voice contains a trace of delight in what he's done to us. "As you exit the room, hand me your clothes. While I search your clothes, I want you to drop your boxers, lift up your ball sack, spin around, bend over and spread your cheeks."

The stench is bad enough before the liberation of our crotch odour. In a hurry to escape the room, the men who've wisely disrobed the fastest are ploughing their way towards Officer Green. I don't fancy my chances against the mass of big tattooed men, so I hang near the back. Everyone's boxers are patterned with sweat stains.

"Drop and spin," Officer Green says to each inmate.

Eventually, I step forward and hand him my stripes.

He feels my stripes for contraband. "Drop and spin."

I drop my boxers to my ankles, grab my scrotum and raise it.

"Good. Spin around."

I turn, bend over and spread my behind.

"OK. Get dressed." He returns my clothes. I join the men dressing in the corridor. When everyone is done, he says, "Go back to your houses."

I'm permitted three visits per week. Claudia visits twice on the weekdays, and my aunt Ann joins her on the weekends. Claudia does everything she possibly can for me under the circumstances. Her devotion is my lifeline. She sends letters daily. I reply with equal frequency. Writing to her puts me in a zone that transcends the jail's walls. Outside of visits, mail call is the most exciting time of the day. A guard places our letters on a table in the day room. We mob around him. He yells the name on each letter. The prisoners are happy or sad depending on whether they receive any.

May-June 2002

Hey now, Claudia!

Just got your first letter and thank you very much. Glad to read you're occupying your time and in good spirits.

You asked about this making our love stronger, and I think that anything that does not break us up will make our love stronger. I just regret that my mess is taking your life away from you when you should be out having the time of your life. I am so sorry that you are being put through this punishment as well.

Today, I'm just doing the usual, playing chess, reading a Spanish dictionary and living off mouldy bread and oranges.

One of my cellmates, Troll, just got back from a legal visit. They're still offering him 18 years so he's bumming. He's such a nice guy. It sucks how their lives are taken away so easily.

My new celly, OG, is teaching me about shanks. He said a shank will save you when some "big mothers come for ya," but he added that shanks always get him in trouble. I think I'll stay away from shanks. I'll tell you how he carries a shank around in a later letter.

Keep writing to me as much as you can. Your letter really brightened my day up. I can't wait to see you on Saturday.

Love,

Shaun

ps) It sucks writing with these golf pencils. They constantly go blunt and I have to sharpen them on the walls.

Hello my love,

Thanks so much for all of your love and support. Without your help I would be mental right now. I love you loads and my whole family think you are great for supporting me. I have found "a good girlfriend finally" that's what my mum said.

Thanks also for putting money on my books. I won't go hungry this week. Whoopee! Isn't it pretty sad when the highlight of my week is eating a Snickers? Thinking about Snickers is making my stomach rumble. Chow should be coming around soon. I've requested a veggie diet as the meat is atrocious. If you ever get arrested remember to tell them you're a veggie straight away otherwise weeks of red death will kill you!

It's so boring in here. It's like an insane asylum, but ah well, there's little I can do but grin and bear it. I read the dictionary for 2-3 hours a day, work out, play chess, eat the usual crap. I'm doing 500 push-ups a day with Sniper, a La Victoria gang member downstairs.

There is an ol' prison tale circulating that they put stuff in the orange drink to reduce our aggressiveness and a side effect is it is harder to get erections. In the shower there is a button on the wall that you either have to press every 10 seconds or keep it pressed the whole time to keep the water running. I think they designed this to make it hard to concentrate on jacking off. There is no privacy in the shower just skilful towel work. Sandals are essential, as you can imagine with 40 guys a day jacking off. I've heard stories of gangrene, swollen feet and toes getting cut off.

It's official. I'm the in-house chess champion. 23 games undefeated. One of the guys I play is in cell 8. Right next to his bunk there is an ant breakout. He wakes up with them in his sheets, crawling all over him, proper third world style. I feel sorry for him.

After chow:

I traded the whole evening meal for tomorrow morning's fruit. I'm going to load up on Kit Kats and Snickers. Crap never tasted so good.

There was a fight. A guy got bloodied and his arm broke.

Signing out for now,

Love,

Shaun XXX

Hey my love,

It's 2am. I can't sleep and just jumped out of bed because I have to write and tell you how special you are to me. It is your strength and love that have really helped me to cope with this situation. I am experiencing all kinds of emotions. I feel like I have let my family down and I am worthless. When I first got to Tower

2, I was hearing voices of people wanting to kill me, and I think I had a nervous breakdown that night. But after speaking to you I turned a corner. Talking to you gave me hope and meaning. You have proven to be my guardian angel.

It's now too hot to work out or do anything other than lie down. I hate being treated like an animal. I constantly see other inmates cracking up mentally and being taken away. Troll tells me that now my first month is up time goes really fast.

The food has been absolutely shit for over a week now. The mashed potatoes today tasted like bleach and looked like come. I am wasting away.

Playing chess with my celly Troll I put your pic next to the board for good luck and I won! Now we're all plugged into 104.7, and when a good song comes on OG and Troll insist we all dance. I'm getting good at dancing to rap.

I love you!
Goodnight.
Shaun XXX

My incarceration brings us so close, I propose to Claudia at Visitation. She says yes, and mails me pictures of wedding dresses she likes. I stick pictures of Claudia under the bunk above me. I admire them throughout the day and draw strength from them whenever the sadness of our separation overwhelms me.

CHAPTER 9

Phoenix is the hottest big city in America. It's against federal law for a jail to use heat as a punishment or a health threat. To get around this, Towers uses a swamp cooler that barely works. It is supposed to blow water-cooled air through a vent system into our cells, but the little air we receive is as warm as our breath. In June, it stops blowing. Outdoor temperatures exceed 110 °F, making us dizzy, ill and delirious. So many heatstroke victims are taken to hospital on stretchers, lockdowns are constant. At night my skin itches, keeping me awake. In the day, I pass out while reading.

"Due to temperatures rising to over one-hundred-and-ten degrees, you're now authorised to wear only your boxers in the day room!" Officer Alston announces.

Cheering at this miniscule concession, we strip on the spot: in our cells, on the balcony, in the day room. We parade around in pink boxers and orange shower sandals, comparing the rashes patterning our bodies like the mould on our bread. Troll's skid marks attract mockery. He says he doesn't care. Four men strip naked, fill the mop bucket and take turns throwing water on each other, creating a gay-porn scene.

Sheriff Joe Arpaio introduced pink boxers in 1995 because prisoners were stealing the white boxers with MCSO (Maricopa County Sheriff's Office) stencilled on the rear and selling them for up to $10 in Phoenix. When laundry staff reported $48,000 worth of the white boxers missing, Arpaio had the boxers dyed pink. Arpaio said theft plummeted because the pink boxers are too noticeable to smuggle out of the jail. His opponents claimed the pink boxers were introduced as a moneymaking scheme and pointed out that Arpaio quickly offered them for sale worldwide, raising $400,000 within months. "I guess I should thank the inmates for stealing the shorts," Arpaio said. "Their crime was the birth of a great idea."

Prisoners are constantly on the move. We can be rehoused within the jail at any time. Sentenced prisoners are sent to the prison system to serve the balance of their sentences – in America jails mostly hold un-sentenced prisoners. Federal marshals collect illegal aliens awaiting deportation. Some prisoners bond out. Schwartz is among the latter. Sorry to see him go, I move to the middle bunk.

The top bunk goes to OG, an intimidating Mexican American in jail for trying to shank (stab with a homemade knife) someone in the prison system. OG has a Freddie Mercury moustache and no front teeth due to his love of fighting prisoners. He snaps at random and credits decades of heroin addiction for his paranoid delusions. His behaviour towards Troll and me ranges from threatening to shank us in our sleep because we are conspiring against him, to singing and dancing with us on Saturday nights when we tune our radios into live deejay sets from Club Freedom. Not that he doesn't threaten to kill anyone on Saturday nights – he does gleefully. He threatens those complaining our revelry is keeping them awake. As most of the inmates are out of their minds on drugs, only a minority speak up.

CHAPTER 10

Partying for years, I never saw such devotion to getting high as in my new neighbours. I had no idea society rounded up people with addiction issues and dumped them in a place full of the hardest drugs. The Mexicans are smuggling in ounces of crystal meth at Visitation. Troll trades commissary for a quarter of an ounce. The dealers give OG some for protection. As he doesn't do meth, OG trades it for commissary to buy heroin with. Troll and OG transform D10 into a drug den. No forewarning. No board meeting. We receive constant visitors, about two-thirds of the pod, wanting to snort, smoke and inject crystal meth in our cell.

Choosing to do drugs put me in jail, so taking drugs now is inconceivable. *How will I survive or fight my case if drugs are scrambling my mind?* While the traffic flows in and out of our cell, I lie on my bunk doing exercises from a Spanish textbook, but it's hard to concentrate. The visitors frown on my sobriety. Cell visiting is prohibited. I fear the guards will search our cell and send us to lockdown. Or even worse: charge me for any drugs found, which could harm my case and extend my stay.

Early one morning, the meth users pile into D10. They've been up all night. Their voices wake me up. OG is snoring on the top bunk. Having not slept, Troll begins the morning ritual of dispensation.

"I'm trying to sleep!" I yell. "Can't you guys keep it down?"

"Who the fuck are you telling us to shut up?" Outlaw replies.

Regretting offending the head of the whites, I try to make amends. "Just trying to sleep, fellas," I say in a friendly tone.

They issue threats, unnerving me from dozing off.

Joining the queue for breakfast, I feel I'm being watched. I take my Ladmo bag to my cell and eat quietly with Troll, swilling water in my mouth to get the stale bread down. No moves are made against me, but my sixth sense tells me not to let my guard down.

I've been working out with Sniper for a week. He is the son of a leader in the New Mexican Mafia, a member of the gang La Victoria out of Tempe and the head of the Chicanos. Short, muscular and clean cut, he exercises fanatically. A friendship is blossoming between us. On the day after I yelled at the men in my cell, I'm concerned when I see Sniper pacing the balcony, spying on the table of his fellow Mexican Americans.

Keeping his eyes on the day room, he sidesteps into D10. "Something's up with my people."

"What do you mean, Sniper?" Troll asks from his bunk.

"I heard one of them call me a snitch. Now they're planning on rolling me up."

"No way, Sniper! Who said you was a snitch?" Troll asks.

Sniper returns to the balcony, nods at the Chicano table and looks at Troll.

"Your own people!" Troll says. "Are you sure it's not just the meth making you trip out?"

"Yup."

"Then you'd better go handle your business and put your people in check."

Frowning, Sniper dashes out. He descends the stairs and paces around the day room as if circling prey. Hoping working out with him will distract him from his paranoia, I go down and we start sets of push-ups.

Glistening with sweat and circling the day room is Outlaw. Upon the completion of each lap, he drops down and does a set of push-ups off his knuckles. Every time he passes us, he gives me a funny look. I have no idea what it means. *Probably animosity from the morning I yelled at the men.*

When Sniper leaves to fill his water bottle, Outlaw rushes up to me, quickly joined by Carter.

"What's up, dogs!" I say, expecting them to offer their fists to bump, but they don't.

"You're new here and shit, but do you see any of the other whites working out with the other races?" Outlaw asks.

Carter folds meaty freckled arms and shakes his head.

Looking around, I realise the men are all working out in small groups of their own races. I scratch my scalp. This is my second strike with Outlaw after he scolded me the other morning. I'm afraid to speak in case I make matters worse.

Sniper returns and sees them talking to me.

"What should I do?" I say low enough for Sniper not to hear.

"Finish your workout," Outlaw says. They walk away.

"Everything all right?" Sniper asks.

"It's all good," I say.

"Your people turning on you, too?"

"No one's turning on no one."

Sniper feeds off my agitation. His paranoia returns. He quits the workout to pace the balcony. Afraid of him doing something he might regret, I explain the situation to OG, his fellow Chicano. We spend until lockdown urging Sniper not to fight anyone, insisting he is just high and needs to sleep it off. The next morning, he is our first visitor.

OG climbs down from the top bunk. "You're cut off, Sniper."

Taking the stool, Sniper grins like a repentant child. "It was my first time ever doing meth! What did you expect? I got a few hours' sleep. I'm fine now."

"You slept!" Troll says, perched on the bottom bunk. "I just listened to my radio all night."

Picking sleep from his eyes, OG says, "Sniper, you were about ready to smash someone last night."

"Don't do any more, Sniper," Troll says.

"I can handle my shit!" Sniper folds his arms.

"Don't do it, Sniper," I say, fearing for Sniper. I hope the cell empties so I can get off my bunk and use the toilet without all of them stood around arguing.

Sniper tilts his head back. "Hell, I've done all kinds of other drugs."

"Come on, Sniper, don't do it," OG says, hands on hips.

"I'm gonna prove to you guys I can handle my shit."

We urge him not to.

Sniper unfolds his arms and displays his palms. "Fuck it! Just give me a fucking line!"

"OK! If you think you can handle it," Troll says, shaking his head. "Sniper, let me sit there and you keep point."

On the toilet, Sniper watches for guards.

Troll tips white powder onto the table and snorts a line through rolled paper. "OK, your turn." Troll hands Sniper the paper.

Less than an hour later, Sniper returns. "Homey thinks I'm a fucking snitch! I'm gonna handle my business this time!" He runs downstairs and circles the day room.

Outlaw rushes in, glazed in perspiration as usual. "You want a line, dog?" he asks me.

"No thanks," I say, hoping Carter doesn't arrive.

He squints as if I've failed a test, unsettling me. "You want to smoke some then?"

"I'm good thanks."

Outlaw squats, whips out a lighter, sprinkles white crystals onto tinfoil and heats it from underneath. He inhales the acrid fumes with a cardboard funnel, bounces up and leaves without saying goodbye.

"He's pissed at you," Troll says.

"At me! Why?" *For working out with Sniper?*

"It's disrespectful to refuse drugs from the head of the whites. Sometimes people want to see you do drugs, so they know they can trust you. Like you're not a cop."

"How was I supposed to know that?" *Was that my third strike? Are Outlaw and Carter planning on smashing me now?*

"You do now."

"Sure do." *Should I tell Troll about my problems with Outlaw? I could do with his advice. But he might tell others and make things worse. I can't take the chance.*

Most of the men have been awake for three days. I remember Billy the Hippy's advice: *Be careful 'cause when they've been up like this they start sketching out on each other and shit gets crazy.* The day room is more boisterous. Men I've never seen talking to each other before or who rarely come out of their cells are chatting about all sorts.

The first to lose it completely is a Mexican. He dashes around the day room ranting in Spanish about his arresting officer who he swears is undercover in the pod and about to re-arrest him. A formation of Mexicans tries to prevent him from sparking a race riot by surrounding him, shadowing his movements, but every so often he breaks free from their net, hurls himself at a random person and yells himself to tears. He is on his knees sobbing when I notice Sniper pacing the balcony again.

From the cell table, I call to Sniper, "What's going on out there?"

Sniper comes in, tight-lipped. "My cellies are gonna do something to me."

"What?" *He's gone mad.*

"I can't tell you, but they're gonna do it after lockdown," he says, his eyes sad and dilated.

"Maybe you should–"

He slips out to patrol the balcony.

Carter arrives next. "Outlaw wants to see you in his cell."

My luck has finally run out. It's come to this. I'm through. "All right." I get off my bunk, hoping he doesn't notice I'm trembling. "Everything all right?"

"You can talk to him."

Tensing up, I follow Carter downstairs, into Outlaw's.

Outlaw is gazing out of the tiny window at rows of military tents housing female prisoners. Hearing us, he wheels around. "What's up, dog!"

Carter brushes past me and guards the door. Having a man to my front and rear is intimidating, but I appreciate Outlaw bumping my fist. *Maybe things aren't so bad? Or are they just settling me so I drop my guard?* "What's going on?"

"We see you've not been working out with the other races, and we appreciate that." Outlaw is stood about two feet in front of me, heaving his topless chest. His muscles and long blond hair bring to mind Thor.

Do they know Sniper has lost his mind and is in no condition to be working out? Say nothing and take the credit. "No problem."

"Look, we know what you were doing on the streets. You've got a lot of connections. We've got no white boys bringing dope in. The Mexicans have got us by the balls. If a wood was hooking us up from the streets, we wouldn't have to deal with the other races."

This is heading in a bad direction. Say nothing. Just nod and listen.

"Why don't you use your connections, so we can step on the Mexicans? We'll pay you."

Dealing drugs while in jail on drug charges is the last thing in the world I want to do. But safety is my priority. I can't just refuse and risk insulting the two most powerful whites in our pod. Flustered by the pressure they are applying, I struggle to respond. *Decline in a way that doesn't invite violence.* "I have no way to do it." Realising I've opened a door for them, I regret my answer. I brace for their reply.

"Yes, you do," Carter says from behind, causing me to swivel. "Your chick's visiting you all the time. She can bring it in."

What a nerve! Due to my involvement in drugs, I deserve them asking me to commit crimes, but not Claudia. *How long have they been planning this behind my back?* Concealing my anger, I try to bluff them. "I'll have to ask her." *I can pretend to ask her and tell them she said no, so it will look like I tried.*

"We'd appreciate that, wood."

I'm a wood now, not merely a dog. All they care about is dope, and they'd put Claudia at risk to get it. "I can't talk to her about it on the recorded phone lines, so I'll ask her at Visitation." *I've just bought a few days.*

"All right, good looking out, wood." There is a con-artist's tone in Outlaw's voice. But I prefer him trying to bend me to his will by manipulation rather than violence.

A dealer becomes so paranoid he gives his last ounce to OG in case it's found and used as evidence against him. The users top up in our cell. But their euphoria is short-lived. They've been wired for so long they turn suspicious of each other. They share conspiracy theories and organise witch hunts. Some go from group to group and cell to cell insisting the groups and cells they've just broke off from are plotting against them. The day room is explosive. Leaving my cell to use the phone, I fear getting lynched for being sober.

Troll believes the guards know he is high and it is only a matter of time before they demand a urine sample. He thinks his best strategy is to avoid them. He hides on his bunk and sends packing anyone who asks him to play cards. "The guards know I'm always out playing spades," Troll says, his voice shaky. "They know why I'm hiding out." After surveying the guards in the control tower for hours, Troll bangs on the bottom of my bunk. "I see the dogs! I see the dogs! I see the dogs!"

His knocking reverberates right through me. "What're you talking about?"

"The sniffer dogs are in the fishbowl!"

Concerned the goon squad has arrived, I lean off the middle bunk. "There's no dogs, dog," I say, squinting down at him.

"They're bringing the dogs! Oh fuck, dog! I'm a bust!" he says, slapping his temples.

"There's no dogs, Troll. You're sketching."

"I see them," he says, poking his cheeks with his fingertips.

"Troll, there's no dogs!" I say, shaking my head. "And if they do come, it's 'cause of the way you're behaving right now."

"Look at my pupils. Am I a bust?" he says, pointing at his eyes.

His pupils are little black ponds. The whites of his eyes are strewn with red squiggles as if his capillaries are about to burst. I don't want to panic him. "Take it easy, Troll."

He gazes at the control tower. "Are you sure there's no dogs, dog?"

"I thought you didn't sketch, Troll. How come you're sketching?"

"I don't sketch! I was just kidding about the dogs," he says in a fake-relaxed voice. He rolls over on his bunk, out of sight.

I return to my Spanish book.

Five minutes later: "Dog! Dog! Do you see the dogs?" This goes on all day.

Before breakfast the next day, guards converge on Sniper's cell. They handcuff and escort him to lockdown.

Troll reveals what happened to Sniper. "A guard caught Sniper on his bunk with his fingers in his ass."

"What?" I ask, shocked.

"They asked him what he was doing. He said, 'I got raped by my cellies and I'm checking the damage.'"

"What'll happen to him?" I ask.

"They'll send him for a psych evaluation," Troll says. "There's no way the guards'll believe his two skinny-ass cellies raped that buff dude." Convinced the guards are going to do something bad to him, Troll still hasn't slept.

Officer Mordhorst appears at our door, pointing at Troll. "You're my chow server this morning." He marches away.

"Ain't that-about-a-bitch." Troll rocks on his bunk. "He's never asked me to serve chow before. Oh fuck! He's onto me. I'm a bust. How big are my eyes?"

They are still helter-skelter. I must be honest in case Mordhorst notices them. "Still big."

"Fuck!"

Ten minutes later, Mordhorst summons Troll.

"I'm fucked! Mordhorst's gonna see my eyes and bust me," Troll says, "and I can't refuse 'cause then he'll know something's up and bust me anyway, so I've got to do it and risk getting busted."

"Look, you don't know for sure he's onto you. Just try and act normal." *Mordhorst's probably onto him. Troll will end the day in lockdown. I'll lose a good cellmate and get a bad one.*

"I haven't slept in five days! How can I act fucking normal?" Troll says, clenching and unclenching his hands.

"Just try."

Joining the queue for breakfast, I study Troll stood next to Officer Mordhorst. He has a hair net on. His face is trembling as he hands out Ladmo bags and milks to inmates hounding him for extra food he dare not give. His lips are pursed, his eyes darting as if seeking a way out of the situation.

When he's done serving chow, Troll returns to D10, stunned and shaking. "Why me? Why'd he pick me? I've never served chow. He saw my pupils. I know he did. I'm a bust. They're gonna call me for a piss test any second. The dogs were at Tower 5 yesterday. They'll be here soon. Oh fuck! Shaun! Shaun! Check out the fishbowl for me. Do you see the dogs?"

"Still no dogs," I say.

"They'll be here soon with the goon squad."

Fear ripples through me. *The goon squad is coming to extract a price for all of the people going berserk on drugs.*

After chow, the Mexican who is convinced his arresting officer is undercover in the pod runs around the day room yelling in Spanish. He gives the Mexicans shadowing his movements the slip and charges at people of all races, almost stirring up a race riot. The Mexicans grab him and try to drag him into a cell. This inflames him more. He runs from them screaming, dashes into his cell, bangs around and re-emerges with his mattress rolled up. He rushes to the sliding door and pounds on the Plexiglas to get the attention of the guards. He keeps looking over his shoulders as if expecting the undercover cop – the star of his delusions – to re-arrest him. When the sliding door opens, he dashes down the corridor. Guards chase him out of sight.

The pod is extremely dangerous now. Everywhere, someone is acting up on drugs. I stay on my bunk, flinching every time I hear a head clang against a steel toilet or a body slam onto the concrete. Following these noises, a bleeding and disorientated inmate usually vacates the pod.

During my party years, I thought drugs were glamorous. Now constant exposure to round-the-clock drug users is crushing that viewpoint out of me. Surrounded by the chaos and destruction that drugs cause, I feel guilty for putting people on the road of drug use. *I'll never deal or do drugs again.*

Our water is off the following morning. Anticipating a raid, the majority hide contraband in their behinds. Having heard so many descriptions of the goon squad, I dwell on terrible images of them, dreading a bunch of armed commando types storming our living quarters, stripping us naked and tearing through our belongings. Our tension rises. Will they come or not? Is the water simply turned off for maintenance? Why won't the guards tell us anything? Surely that means they're coming. A collection of us on the balcony discuss these things like village elders, our eyes wide and faces pinched.

"Check this out!" Troll yells from the cell.

I go inside. "What?"

Troll points at his bunk. I laugh at the giant smiley face he's made by placing brownies next to each other.

"Any food the state gave us, the goon squad are gonna trash." Troll picks up a legal folder. "I hid two brownies in here."

"Here they come!" everyone yells.

We rush to the front of the cell. A group of big men in black shank-proof armour and protective goggles charges down the corridor. It is the Strategic Response Team (goon squad). They are even bigger and fiercer-looking than the men who raided my apartment. As they approach the middle of the tower, the prisoners downstairs start to flee to their cells. First to charge into the day room is a white man with massive tattooed biceps. He raises a shotgun and fires a thundershot distraction round that delivers a flash of light and a deafening bang that make my eyelids slam shut.

"Put your hands on your heads! No one fucking move!"

OG bolts into the cell. "What a bunch of fucking assholes!"

Yelling at the few prisoners who haven't made it back to their cells, the squad members spread out in the day room, sharing the same cold expression, as if they've come to kill us all without a scintilla of remorse.

"You do not move unless we tell you to move! You do not talk to us unless we tell you to talk to us!" Some storm up the stairs.

"Aw, fuck. They're about to hit our cell," Troll says.

"Fuck 'em!" OG says.

OG and Troll press their palms up high on the cement-block wall. I copy them, my adrenaline surging as I relive the morning of my arrest.

A Hispanic goon-squad guard slams our door open. "Strip now!"

We get naked.

"You, turn around, bend over and spread 'em," he says to OG. After OG complies, he says, "Put your boxers back on and go downstairs." Troll and I do likewise.

I'm descending the stairs with my hands on my head when the K9 unit arrives. The dogs bark wildly, no doubt picking up the scent of drugs everywhere.

"Keep your hands on your fucking heads as you line up against the day room wall!"

I join the line. Jamaica emerges from his cell, his arms at his sides.

A guard shoves him from behind. "Put your hands on your fucking head now!"

Jamaica spins around, raising his arms as if to defend himself. "Don't touch me like that, man."

The urge to attack the guards flares up on the faces of the inmates. It grips me, too. Jamaica is a good guy. If he can be victimised, any of us can. Sensing a riot is about to ignite, the guards form a row, facing us, intimidating us into thinking twice.

Behind the wall of guards, things are deteriorating for Jamaica. His arms are half up as if he fears being hit again and doesn't want to leave his midsection exposed. Watching the guard who shoved him, he fails to notice the guard behind him draw a Taser. The guard he is facing says, "Do as you're told! Put your hands on your fucking head!" The Taser crackles before he can comply. The electroshock jackknifes Jamaica. The guards throw him on the concrete, twist his arms behind his back and handcuff him. We jeer as they drag him from the pod. I expect violence, but this adds a terrifying new dimension.

The guards order us to leave the pod and throw our filthy boxers into a cart. We are herded, naked and humiliated, down a corridor that dead-ends. Through the Plexiglas, we watch them search our cells. They rifle through our belongings. They drop our bedding on the floor and trample on it as they examine our mattresses. They fling stationery and books on the floor. They tear open our brown paper commissary bags. They confiscate our state food: fruit, bread, peanut butter, brownies (including the two Troll hid)… They check every hiding spot with search mirrors and probe sticks, but no drugs are found as they were keystered. They find hooch. The brewer and his cellmates are identified, cuffed and escorted to lockdown. I'm worried they might find a syringe or a shank belonging to OG, but they don't as he keystered his metal. They march away with plastic bags full mostly of extra towels, bedding and clothes – our sole means of remaining somewhat clean. When they are almost out of earshot, OG yells something about a prisoner fornicating with the girlfriend of the Hispanic goon-squad guard. They hear him, stop and turn around, eager to put the heckler out of his misery. As their eyes roam over us, we cling onto silence. Unable to determine who yelled, they glance at each other and move on.

CHAPTER 11

"Got an attorney?" Troll asks, eating breakfast in our cell in June.

"No," I say, sitting cross-legged on my bunk eating crackers.

OG is making a green-baloney sandwich on the table. "It's gonna cost you, homey. You'd better have a lot of money stashed."

"They seized all my money."

"Ain't that-about-a-bitch!" Troll says.

"You're fucked then, homey!" OG says.

"You're fucked," Troll says. "With your charges, you must get a private lawyer. They've took your money so you can't get a good attorney or bond out. Now they can really bend you over and stick it to you."

"What should I do?" I ask, starting to worry. Every time I ponder a long prison sentence, I feel ill. It's my biggest concern after staying alive. I'm usually good at thinking up ways out of situations, but the more I contemplate this, the more trapped I feel. Nightly, I terrify myself with it for hours. *How will I get through years of this?* During the day, I try to block it out, so I can concentrate on survival. But deep down, I know I need to deal with my legal situation in order to get the best possible plea bargain. Trials are rare, defendants winning even rarer. Those who lose at trial are punished with headline-making sentences designed to deter others from exercising their right to a trial.

"My private attorney cost $30,000," Troll says. "So far he hasn't done shit for me. I'd like to fire his ass. You've got to be real careful."

"One of my security guys, G Dog, told me if I ever get into trouble, the best attorney to call is Alan Simpson," I say. "He's supposed to know all the loopholes."

"He represents a lot of Mexican Mafia," OG says, nodding.

"I've heard of him, too," Troll says. "He's good. You should call him up. Maybe he'll take over my case."

"But I've got no money."

"You'd better find some," OG says.

"My grandpa's paying for my attorney," Troll says. "Can your folks raise any cash? If this guy can slip you through the cracks in the system, it'll save you years."

I call Alan Simpson's office and give his secretary my booking number and some brief information about my case. She assures me he will look at my charges and visit me. I ask about the cost of representation. She says every case is different and Alan will tell me in person. I dread having to turn to my parents for a large sum of money, burdening them on top of the shock they are going through.

Entering Visitation, Alan Simpson is treated like royalty. The staff and attorneys stop what they are doing to nod and smile at him. Some of the attorneys even rise from their tables to shake his hand and congratulate him on recently saving an innocent man, Ray Krone, from death row. The State of Arizona had paid an expert witness $50,000 to lie in court and say that Ray's teeth matched the bite mark on a murder victim. They hid DNA evidence found at the scene that proved Ray's innocence. Through legal action, Alan forced the State of Arizona to release the DNA. A crime-lab worker ran the DNA through a database and uncovered the identity of the murderer. Having been on death row for ten years, Ray was almost executed multiple times.

"Alan Simpson's your attorney," Officer Green gasps and politely takes us to a private room.

Alan is fifty-something with a charismatic face, clean cut except for a greying moustache. He smiles a lot, displaying braces. His charm puts me at ease. He slaps paperwork down on the table. "Here's your grand jury indictment."

"What's that mean?"

"It's a list of criminal offences the prosecutor presented to a grand jury to get you indicted before you were arrested."

It probably contains every crime I ever committed and then some. "I see. How bad is it?"

"To be honest, I've read it, and it seems they barely have a case against you."

Am I hearing right? Barely a case against me? Am I getting out of here? "I'm not sure what you mean."

"They've had wiretaps set up since the beginning of the year–"

"And I've been in college, concentrating on stock trading, pretty much laying low over that time," I say, starting to twig on.

"Detective Reid even admits that you never talk on the phone, in emails, or have people at your home. That you're beyond surveillance. They're using the gist of the conversations of the co-defendants as the main evidence against you. The prosecutor's trying to say the lack of evidence against you proves you're a criminal mastermind, too clever to be detected. So the lack of evidence against you is actually evidence against you, which is ridiculous!" He laughs irresistibly and I join in. "What crimes did you actually do?" he says, his voice serious.

"Starting in the late nineties, I threw raves and invested in club drugs, especially Ecstasy. It started out small, but by the time everything peaked we were bringing tens of thousands of hits in from Amsterdam. I had a lot of money in the stock market around the time of the dot.com bubble in 1999 to 2000, but when that collapsed, so did the size of my criminal activity." *Now he's going to say I'm looking at serious time.*

"Were you bringing drugs in from Amsterdam this year?"

"No."

"Then they've missed the boat. Are you telling me the truth? I must know what we're up against."

"I've seriously spent this year getting back to stock trading."

"And apparently your stock-trading data overloaded the police computers that were spying on your computer. They had to fly software engineers in from Washington." Alan breaks into laughter. "This is a very flimsy case."

I smile. "So what am I looking at?"

"Anywhere from probation to five years is the norm for a first-time offender with these types of drug charges."

I'll take probation.

"You'll be better able to help me if I get you out of this hellhole."

My smile broadens. "How?"

"Well, your bond is a steep $750,000. I think I can get it down to $100,000. Can you mange that?"

"They seized my money."

"You'd only need to put ten percent down with a bond company."

"I think I can manage that."

"If you're going to retain me, one of the first things I'll do is file for a bond reduction."

"How much will it cost to retain you?"

"My retainer's $50,000."

I gulp.

"It could cost more, but I imagine they'll offer you a decent plea bargain within six months. I can't see them wanting to drag this out and waste even more money on a flimsy case like this."

The words *flimsy case* tickle me inside. "I'll have to discuss it with my parents. If it's a flimsy case, why does everyone in here I show my bond and charges to get all worked up?"

"I wouldn't pay too much attention to anyone in here. The prosecutor's overcharged you on purpose. The more mud she throws, the more she hopes will stick. This gives her plea-bargaining power. I respond by attacking the case with motions. Because the case looks so weak, you should be offered a decent plea bargain everyone is happy with."

"How soon do you think I can get my bond reduced?"

"I can get a hearing within the next couple of months."

Goodbye Towers jail! I beam at him.

"Your next court appearance is a preliminary hearing."

"What's that?"

"The prosecutor has to show probable cause to be holding you."

"She slammed me at the first hearing."

"She's about to slam you again, and I won't be saying anything till we see if there's any more evidence we're up against."

"If you can get me out in a couple of months that would be wonderful." I see myself back at the apartment with Claudia, eating Indian food together, going to the gym, making love…

"Can you cope with this place for a few more months?"

"I'll try." *It'll be a lot easier now I'm getting out.*

After the visit, I call Claudia. She relays the news to my parents. We are all thrilled.

June 2002

Dear Mum, Dad & Karen,

Hope you are all doing good in the free world. I guess I'm over the initial shock of the situation and am settling down to the daily routine of being an un-sentenced inmate. I play chess most of the day, watch TV and read. The people in my cell and pod are real nice and I have had no problems.

Regarding my situation, I figured being involved with the rave scene would eventually get me in trouble. So here I am rounded up in a dawn raid style sweep with a bunch of other people from the rave scene including Wild Man and Wild Woman. Although no stash of drugs was found, they are charging me with conspiracy, which means I was involved with a group of individuals (co-conspirators) in kind of a crime family way, and they've pegged me as the leader. Unfortunately we all get charged with each other's crimes. It is like we are all one unit and it's a serious charge.

The police must have thought I was big time because of the money spent, the serious nature of the charges and the $3/4 million bond. However all they have rounded up is a ramshackle group of people with no money and very little drugs. They are livid. They froze my retirement account, which has $20K in it and my bank accounts and took my SUV.

They don't have much of a case, but still I'm scared because they slapped so many high felony charges on me. From probation to 5 years seems a predicted time for these types of crimes, as a first offender. Kingpins get 25 years, but it's not like there were private jets and yachts seized. Two of the guys arrested had less than a dollar on them. Anyway Alan is applying for some kind of legal aid to assist financially, but I have to get him as much money as possible. The prison system where you go after sentencing is full of people doing 10 years who had shitty attorneys, and so I really am fighting for my life (and sanity) right now.

Love you all loads. Sorry for any disappointment or hurt this may have caused. Keep in touch, but follow the mailing rules.

Shaun

In the letters to my parents, I hide the dangers of the jail so as not to terrify them. I also have to be careful about mentioning my crimes in letters and phone calls because the jail has access to both. Any admission of guilt can be used as evidence against me. The letter to my parents contains a snapshot of my involvement in drugs at the time of my arrest. The only person I can safely tell about my entire drug history is my attorney. Although I deserve punishment for my crimes, I'm resenting being held when no drugs were found in my apartment because I had already quit dealing. I desperately want to be free of this life-threatening environment. And if that means beating the system due to the lack of evidence against me, then so be it. The visit from Alan Simpson reinforces my hope that I won't have to pay for my old lifestyle. Taking responsibility for my older crimes is far from my mind. Although confinement is slowly crushing my emotional immaturity and altering my destiny for the better, I'm clueless to this.

After sending the letter, I pray my parents find $50,000 to retain Alan Simpson. I feel as sick as when they first found out about my crimes because they are not rich people.

My parents came from working-class families. With hard work, they improved their circumstances. My grandmother did not want my mother to continue with her education after age fifteen. She wanted her to work in a shop or factory like her siblings as she felt women progressing was a waste of time because they marry and have children and that's the end of their careers. My mother won the argument, went to secretarial college and became a personal assistant.

My parents met in their late teens, when my mother took a second job as a waitress in a social club near where my dad lived. He'd just returned from hitchhiking around the country when he saw her at the club, dark-haired and with pretty brown eyes. His face was tanned and his hair bleached with the sun, but at first she wasn't interested. He won her over by persistence, charm and with his kind blue eyes. They fell in love listening to rock and blues and folk music in the local clubs. They married at age twenty – the year of my birth – and have been in love ever since. After becoming a secretary, my mum went on – with my dad's encouragement – to get a teaching certificate and later on to attend university to get a degree in English and Psychology. Wanting to make a difference where it mattered the most, she first taught students with special needs and language difficulties and, later on, college students.

My dad started out going door to door selling insurance and built himself a loyal customer base. As a child I sometimes accompanied him. His customers loved him. Everywhere we went, he was offered tea and biscuits and always took time for small talk. I'd return home with my pockets full of gifts of chocolates and money.

When I learn my father has to cash in his retirement account to pay the $50,000, I'm relieved but my guilt is compounded. Over the years, I'd spent a multiple of that on drugs and partying – one New Year's Eve rave party alone had cost over $50,000. It hurts that my parents are paying for my wrongdoing. Fifty thousand is their life savings. *I'll do my utmost when I get out to pay them back.* Many of my neighbours have been disowned by their families, so I feel blessed to have such support.

CHAPTER 12

"C'mon, Shaun, white-boy meeting in my cell right now," Billy the Hippy says after the morning headcount.

"About what?" I drop off my bunk.

"The guards rolled Outlaw up to a pod for sentenced prisoners, so we've got no head of the whites. The woods are voting on a new head."

"OK." *Does Outlaw's departure mean the whites will stop trying to intimidate me into asking Claudia to bring drugs in?*

We arrive at a cell packed with topless sweaty men swathed in tattoos. Swastikas. War eagles. Norse runes. Skulls. Swords. SS lightning bolts. Castles. Celtic crosses. Confederate flags. Tear drops. On one skinhead's chest: Hitler admiring Jews dying in a gas chamber.

"Look, woods," says George, a mountain of a hillbilly who shocks us by never wearing sandals in the shower. "Carter's been down the longest. He's affiliated with the Aryan Brotherhood. He's the most qualified to represent our race. I say Carter should be the head of the whites."

Oh no. Anyone but Carter. I don't want to vote for him, but the mood is such that I suspect if I don't I'll end up drowned in the toilet. We elect Carter unanimously. *As he's the one who suggested Claudia bring drugs in, things are probably going to get worse for me.*

"Thanks, woods," Carter says. "I've got an announcement to make."

The mood turns deadly. All eyes shine with attention. *He's going to tell us to charge down the stairs and attack the blacks.*

"I'm about to get married, and you're all invited to my wedding party," Carter says.

Our laughter echoes in the day room.

Scared of sounding naïve, but curious, I ask, "How can you get married in jail?"

"Over the phone," Carter says.

While Carter recites marriage vows on a three-way call to his wife and minister, I fetch cookies from my cell to contribute to the wedding buffet. From the balcony, we watch Carter give the thumbs-up, signalling he is married. Cheering erupts in the day room. Smirking and puffing his chest, Carter raises the phone so his wife can hear. The prisoner on the phone next to Carter extracts his hand from his crotch and pats Carter on the back.

The whites are helping themselves to the food by the time Carter returns to D14. He leads the men in drinking hooch and snorting lines of crystal meth and crushed-up psychotropic medication. The food disappears. Fights almost break out over the crumbs.

Billy jumps onto the tiny steel table in the middle of the cell, undoes his ponytail and lets his hair down. Gyrating like a stripper, he undresses while we sing. Down to his pink boxers, he grooves his hips and lashes us with his hair. "Congratulations!" he shrieks. With his back arched, he sticks his tongue in Carter's ear and pinches Carter's nipples. "Take a Pac-Man." He places seizure medication on Carter's tongue.

The maximum occupancy of a Towers' pod is forty-five men. Turnover is high and the racial balance keeps changing. What never changes is that the race with the most members picks on the race with the least. In our pod the whites are presently the majority, the blacks the minority. Something is brewing between them.

The day after Carter's wedding, the guards move Gravedigger – a six-foot-four cage fighter – into our pod. He isn't massive, but he has muscular thickness and definition in all of the right places. He has a narrow ill-tempered face and beady brown eyes that shine with a primeval lust for violence. His ink includes skulls, demons and racist slogans. The tattoo that stands out the most is on his chest: the devil as a puppet-master. He is in jail for kidnapping and torturing a rapist. His presence increases Carter's smugness and the threatening behaviour of the whites towards the blacks.

Gravedigger strides into D10. "Who's the English guy in here?"

He sounds so angry, I brace for trouble. "I am." I rise on my bunk fast.

"Here you go." He throws a small piece of carefully folded paper at me. "It's a kite from the crazy English dude in Tower 2. I gave him my word I'd hand it to you personally."

"Thanks, bro." Excited, I open it hastily.

Shaun,
Sign up for Catholic mass. I'll meet you there.
Love you loads,
Wild Man

Gravedigger projects his gaze onto Troll. "Hey, Troll, front me some cookies till store day." His tone leaves Troll no option.

"Sure, dog." Troll slides a commissary bag from under the bunk. "Heard you just got out of the hole." He extracts a rack of cookies.

Gravedigger snatches the cookies. "Yeah, dog. I had to smash some toads in Tower 2."

"How come?" Troll asks.

"Two toads owed a white boy, my Russian buddy, Max. Max went in their cell to collect on store day and they smashed him. You know the blacks ain't getting away with disrespecting our race like that. Not when I'm head of the fucking whites. So I just bombed in there myself. I don't need torpedoes to fight my battles. I knocked the first one out with one punch. Motherfucker had a glass jaw. The other shit bricks, ran into the day room like a little bitch."

"No shit," Troll says.

"So I'm chasing him round and round the fucking stairs with everyone watching. I caught him, put him on the floor with a kung-fu takedown and pinned him in a wrestling lock. I'm slamming his face with my elbows like this." Gravedigger sets his elbows in motion like two giant chisels. "Blood is coming out everywhere. The guy's all fucked up. The blood around us was getting bigger and bigger. And Officer Noble's just watching it from the fishbowl, enjoying it, waiting for backup. It took a long time for the guards to respond, so I just kept pounding him. Blood splashing all over me. Everyone watching."

"You're no joke, dog," Troll says. "You ain't nothing nice."

Gravedigger glares at Troll and leaves.

Yet another maniac for us to contend with.

Before breakfast the next morning, Billy takes me to his cell. "I'm just giving you a heads-up. You're in danger. Shit's about to pop off in your cell."

"What do you mean?" I ask, panicking.

"Some fucked-up shit's going down with Troll. I don't agree with it, but there's nothing I can do. I suggest you stay out of it, too."

"What's going on?"

"Look, Shaun, Carter and Digger's gonna smash Troll."

"Why?"

"For playing cards with the blacks and dealing too much with the other races."

"That's crazy."

"That's just their front so they can jack Troll. Carter and Digger owe Troll for store. So when Troll rolls up after they smash him, the debt will be squashed and they'll just take all the store Troll has left."

"Maybe I should try talking to Carter and Digger?"

"It's no use. They've made their minds up. If you try get in the mix, they'll just smash you, too. Look, I'm gonna tell you more, but don't tell anyone this."

"What?"

"Carter told Digger you and Troll are the two white boys least representing the white race."

"No shit. Do you think they'll smash me?"

"No. At least not yet. Carter thinks you might be able to bring drugs in."

The drug thing has been nagging away at me. "Look, there's no way I'm bringing drugs in. What should I do?"

"I really don't know. Carter's instigating all this shit. Digger just loves to fight."

"When's this supposed to happen to Troll?"

"After breakfast."

Expecting chaos in my cell, I dash back to D10. *The threat to Troll is imminent. I can't just look the other way and let Troll get smashed. During our time together, we've bonded. If I was in danger, I reckon Troll would at least forewarn me. But what can I do? I can't go up against Carter, Gravedigger and their torpedoes. I'll be annihilated. OG loves to fight, but the rules of racial division prohibit him from interfering in a dispute among the whites. Wild Man is in Tower 2, at the opposite end of the jail, where he can't help on such short notice. I'll tell Troll over breakfast. I'll advise him to roll up to Tower 2 where he'll be safe with Wild Man.* Having solved Troll's problem in my mind, I worry about Carter getting Gravedigger to put pressure on me to bring drugs in.

"Chow's in the house! Line up at the door with your IDs!"

In the day room, the friction between the blacks and whites is palpable. When Mordhorst exits to serve the next pod, Carter yells at SmackDown, a beefy young boxer and the head of the blacks, "You need to stop sweating the woods, dog!" SmackDown has been bullying members of every race out of commissary. Carter is telling SmackDown to stop bullying the whites or else. The day room hushes.

From the blacks' table, SmackDown yells, "Who've I been sweating?" He speaks like an East Coast rapper.

"I can't name names," Carter says, "but as the head, people have been complaining about you bulldogging them."

"I ain't bulldogged nobody!"

"That's not what people are saying."

"Well if fools have got a problem with me, they need to come and tell me to my face."

"That's what I'm talking about. The people you've been sweating are afraid of you."

"Fuck 'em then!"

"You need to keep yourself in check! People are sick of your bulldogging!"

"I ain't putting myself in check. You can go fuck yourself, too!"

"You calling me out?"

"Hell, yeah, I'm calling you out! Ain't no punk-ass white boy telling me how I'm supposed to behave around here."

One of the worst things you can call someone in jail is a punk. A punk is a sex slave who can be traded or rented out. Being called a punk leaves a head of a race no choice but to fight. If a head doesn't fight, his own race will smash him. I don't envy Carter's position – SmackDown has never lost a fight in the jail. Troll previously told me that the guards had moved SmackDown from our pod for fighting, but he'd smashed so many people in so many other pods, he's right back where he started.

Everyone stops what they are doing and joins their races. Whites. Blacks. Mexicans. Mexican Americans. Four armies posted around their heads, poised for war.

"You'll see who's a punk!" Carter yells, tilting his head back. "Let's take this to cell 3!" Cell 3 is under the stairs, making it less visible to the guards and the most popular spot for fights.

The residents of cell 3 rush inside and stash all of their property under the bottom bunk, so it doesn't get damaged or bloodied.

"What're we waiting for?" SmackDown swaggers into cell 3 and assumes a boxer's stance, displaying SMACKDOWN tattooed on his right forearm.

Carter charges in and spins SmackDown around. Smack-Down almost loses his balance but steadies himself and delivers a hook to Carter's head. Cockiness disappears from Carter's face. A flurry of desperate kicks from Carter gets nowhere. SmackDown simply shifts slightly, frowning, remaining focussed, biding his time. A jab strikes Carter's head and sets him bouncing all over the place, dodging punches in a wild dance. He loses his footing and stumbles forward, taking a blow to the head. He crouches and lashes out with a kick aimed at SmackDown's groin. As if anticipating the kick, SmackDown shifts into the perfect position to launch an uppercut at Carter's chin. *Bam!* The audience gasps. Carter's knees buckle, but he doesn't fall. SmackDown moves in closer and throws more blows. Carter leaps away, dashes out of the cell and totters to the whites' table, his expression stuck on disbelief as he sits down.

Stood in the cell doorway, SmackDown yells, "What the fuck was that? Get back in here! We ain't through!" He pants and flares his nostrils.

Voices rise from all tables:

"Handle your business, Carter!"

"Finish the fight!"

"You can't just run away from a fight like that!"

"Yeah, Carter, get back in the cell!"

Carter blushes. "I went in already." He can barely speak. It's all coming out in spurts. "We fought. He won. I handled my business."

Yelling rises:

"What the fuck?"

"You're supposed to be the head of the whites!"

"You have to fight, dog!"

Even his torpedoes turn against him:

"You're our head!"

"You're making us look bad to the other races!"

"You have to go back in!"

"Go back in, Carter!"

"I already fought," Carter says, his face crimson. "He fucking beat me!"

"Fucking punk-ass bitch!" SmackDown yells. "Get back in

here, motherfucker. I'm calling your punk-ass out, you fucking bitch!"

Gravedigger rises from his stool and puts his hands on his hips. Glowering down at Carter from his great height, he shakes his head. The jeering stops. As much as I dislike violence, I'm rooting for Gravedigger to smash Carter. It might end the threat against Troll and me. Gravedigger shakes his head and says in a low voice, "Man up, wood." The evil glow in his hyena eyes intensifies.

Obediently, Carter stands. "Fuck it. I'll fight him again." He returns to cell 3.

SmackDown has regained his breath. He retreats into the cell and raises his fists. Carter raises his. SmackDown feigns a few jabs. Lacking energy, Carter skips like a man whose heart isn't in the fight. He receives a cross to his left eye. Dropping his guard, he sways. He gets kicked in the leg and blows pulverise him, but he isn't knocked out. Unable to withstand the blows, he dashes from the cell so fast that he collides with the stairs. The prisoners jeer. Panting, disorientated, he leans forward and rests his hands above his knees.

Gravedigger marches to Carter. "Roll your shit up! I'm the new head of the whites! Does any of you woods have a problem with that?" His eyes pan from white to white prisoner. No one objects.

Carter limps from the pod with a battered face, a rolled-up mattress and his property. Billy tells me that Carter's property includes photos of his wife that he didn't show to the whites because if he had, they never would have crowned him their head. She is Mexican American.

CHAPTER 13

The prisoners respect Lev Egorov because of his tough aura and association with the Russian Mafia. He is short, has a solid physique and cropped brown hair with flecks of grey. Right down to the wrinkles on his forehead, he looks like a KGB agent. Introduced to chess as a child, he is an enthusiast I play daily. As immigrants, we bond quickly. The topics of our lively discussions range from geopolitics to the corruption in the legal system. When an East European limps into our pod – a Muslim from the Balkan Peninsula who doesn't fit into any of the four major racial categories and has been smashed everywhere he's been housed – Lev rounds up some of the saner whites, including me, and we agree to protect him. Unfortunately, the guards move the Muslim a few weeks later, and he is beaten and hospitalised. We never see him again. Lev is the only person I see criticising the drug users to their faces. In a deep angry voice and strong Russian accent, he yells, "You fucking Yankees have sucked your brains out by doing dope! If the Yankee didn't do the dope, maybe the Yankee would have more intelligence. The dope is destroying this country. It is the greatest weapon against the Yankee."

It's generally not a good idea to ask prisoners what their charges are until you get to know them. Questions along those lines from newcomers can make the more established feel disrespected. Burning with curiosity about Lev, I wait until I've known him for a few weeks before I ask, "How did you end up in jail?"

"Ha! First, let me tell you the story of how I came to America."

"OK," I say, sitting on my bunk.

"I deserted the Russian army and ended up in a German jail. I contacted the American embassy and offered to trade them knowledge of the Russian military for US citizenship. They agreed. I signed a two-year contract to work for the CIA. I did this to save my sister's life."

"Save your sister's life?" I ask, confused.

"She was stuck in Russia dying from the effects of the Chernobyl nuclear accident. I came here, introduced her to a Yankee, who married her so she could come here legally and get the correct medical treatment. The Yankee doctors cured her, and now she is living here and has remarried and has her own family."

"Good for you, man!" Tired of hearing farfetched crime tales, I'm nourished by Lev's story. "So how did you end up here?"

"Almost ten years ago, I was involved in cocaine in Arizona. Someone murdered my business partner. I went looking for the murderer. I entered the house of the murderer's brother with a gun. The murderer was not there. The brother was. He called the cops. They charged me with assault with a deadly weapon and attempted kidnapping."

"Assault and kidnapping?"

"Yes, because he said I pointed the gun at him, which I didn't. But I did shoot the floor when I was yelling at him. I was arrested and released. They didn't do anything for years, so I thought it was dropped. Then they recently extradited me from Washington, where my family lives and I was working as a mechanic."

Why are some people arrested, released and then rearrested on the same charges years later? I imagine bureaucrats in police departments reopening certain cases to fill their quotas. "It sucks that they had Washington ship you back years later." His case is so old, I sympathise. His actions, such as risking his personal safety to stand up for the Muslim, suggest he's matured into a well-meaning person.

Lev is my next workout partner after Sniper. Using a towel, we tie the broomstick in the day room to the handle of a mop bucket full of water. Holding the stick horizontal, we do weight-lifting exercises. We wrap our pink socks around sections of the metal-grid stairs to make handgrips for pull-ups. In his youth, Lev had won prizes for gymnastics. His ability still shows. He breezes through sets of pull-ups, starting with fifty reps, working his way down to thirty – with many onlookers awestruck – and he dismounts gracefully. I grow tired around five pull-ups. He supports my back, so I can do more. At first, my lats remain sore for days, but that soon wears off. The increased strength I feel in that region takes me by surprise.

The heads of all of the races arrange a chess tournament. Each contender contributes a commissary item of food to the jackpot. Inmates bet heavily on the two favourites: Lev and me.

To put my mind in overdrive prior to the tournament, I eat several brownies. I hang a bag made from toilet rolls in a sock from the top bunk and punch it until my knuckles bleed. Psyched up, I bounce down the day-room stairs, shadow boxing, singing "Eye of the Tiger" by Survivor, my eyes mad-dogging Lev the whole time. I take a stool at one of the steel tables and commence my first game, radiating chess expertise. Surrounded by onlookers – half of them yelling advice that would cause anyone who takes it certain ruination, the rest telling them to shut up or else – I beat all eight contestants, including Lev. I expect to receive the jackpot, but Gravedigger, who has bet heavily on his cellmate, Lev, says that the top four contestants now have to play three games each against each other. In the zone and feeling invincible, I agree.

Lev and I crush the competition and play each other. Concentrating on the available moves, the opportunities each move presents, Lev's possible responses to each move and my responses to his responses, I can almost feel my neurons firing. About ten minutes in, I have to stand to stop trembling. The atmosphere intensifies as we each win a game. Due to the large amount of side bets, the audience remains riveted as the third game begins. Mid-game, my energy level slumps. The audience's cockfight wisecracks start to irritate me. *I'm in trouble.* Lev is also taking longer to move and making silly mistakes. *Maybe his brain is more frazzled than mine.* I make a series of moves I regret and lose key pieces. My morale sinks. Sensing my downfall, Lev's supporters, egged on by Gravedigger, heckle me more. Lev can checkmate me in three moves, so I position my king for a stalemate, staring blankly at the board so as not to betray my sneakiness. But Lev knows me well enough to see through that strategy. Biding his time, he checkmates me. As the crowd mock me for losing, I almost collapse from exhaustion. Lev congratulates me on being a worthy opponent and secures the jackpot: mostly melted Snickers and Kit Kats. "You played well and deserved to win," I say. Vowing never to let that happen again, I order a chess book.

A Space Hopper of a youngster moves into an upper-tier cell. Eighteen-year-old Alejandro, a 400-pound half-Mexican half-Native American, shot an AK-47 at a car full of rival gang members, all teenagers, who'd ventured into his westside neighbourhood. Some of his victims are in critical condition, and if any die, he will be facing a sentence of death by lethal injection.

Every night, just before the news is about to begin, Alejandro emerges from his cell with an expression of dread and positions himself at the back of the noisy prisoners clustered in front of the TV on the day-room wall. When the news starts, he moves forward as if yanked by its familiar jingle. Sweating, he urges everyone to hush. Out of deference for his situation, the gang leaders order the youngsters to shut up. By the time the condition of his victims is reported, the unusual quiet – which implies something bad is happening to somebody somewhere – draws the attention of the card and domino players and even extracts the hermits from their cells, doubling the size of the audience. I'm sure that the men watching from the balcony and every corner and table of the day room are thinking the same as me: *Will a victim die? What's it like to face the death penalty?* Alejandro stands there, arms folded, his bulk swaying slightly, with a fear in his eyes as if he's not watching a TV that barely tunes in, but a gun pointed at him. The prisoners usually remain quiet, except for the night a reporter reveals that one of Alejandro's bullets had exited through a girl's nipple. The prisoners groan and shake their heads. The reports invariably end with his victims in critical but stable condition. None dead. After digesting this, Alejandro sets off relieved. He trudges up the metal-grid stairs. The hermits disappear into the cells in front of him and the noise in the day room picks up behind him.

The heat makes him sweat and stink so much his race holds a meeting about whether to get rid of him. Bad hygiene can get you smashed. In Alejandro's case, a compromise is reached. Under threats of violence, Alejandro has to shower every few hours and afterwards members of his race coat him in baby powder.

Sensing a frightened child inside the gunman, I try to befriend him. "How much is your bond for shooting those people?" I ask.

"Only ten gees, homey," Alejandro says.

"Ten grand!" I say, envious. "I've got drug charges. Mine's three-quarters of a mill."

"That's way too much for drugs, homey. They got me on attempted murder. Hey, I'm gonna get bonded out real soon." In a soft tone, he asks, "Think I should go on the run?"

"I can't recommend that. It could open me up to new charges. But even if none of your victims dies, they're going to put you away for a long time. I'm not recommending you do anything illegal, but if it were me, and my bond was only ten gees, I'd disappear into Mexico and *never ever* come back to Arizona."

"I've been told I'm dead as soon as I touch down on a prison yard."

"How come?"

"That neighbourhood's got a hit out on me for blasting their homies, and my victims have family members in the prison system."

I don't know what to say to comfort him. Hearing he is facing life sentences and possibly the death penalty puts my situation in perspective. I steer the conversation around to parties. He reminisces about his rave experiences.

To see a doctor you have to beg a guard for a form called a medical tank order. If the guard is in a good mood he might give you one on his next security walk. You then have to return the form to the guard, who has to sign it, and hope it survives its journey through various departments to the medical staff. The medical staff decide who gets seen. Depending upon how serious they classify your complaint, they might call you to Medical in a few days' time at the earliest, or call you weeks or months later, or not call you at all. The staff assume that most of the sick inmates are fakers. They often turn away genuine cases, resulting in a few deaths every year, including diabetics.

Someone decides Lev is the closest thing we have to a doctor. Inmates from all races inundate him with demands for treatment due to a menace from the insect world: spiders that crawl on us during the night and bite while we sleep. The culprit is rarely seen. Some think it's the brown recluse, others the Arizona brown. Whatever the spider, the result is always the same: during the first few days, the bite slowly expands from a small white blister to a pus-oozing sore; over the next few, tissue sloughs away from the abscess leaving a sunken ulcerated crater, exposing underlying tissue and sometimes even bone. These holes can be as broad as the palm of a hand. Other side effects include fever, chills, vomiting and shock.

Alejandro is so big, his flab creeps up the wall as he breathes during sleep. With no room for spiders to manoeuvre around him, he is bitten. His written requests for treatment are ignored. When the pus begins to leak out and Officer Mordhorst rebuffs his pleas for help, inmates sympathise.

"Give him treatment!" Gravedigger yells at Mordhorst in the day room.

"He must go to Medical. Look at his damn back! He must see a Yankee doctor," Lev says.

"It's getting worse and worse," Alejandro says, squinting.

"It's growing. Look! There's pus coming," OG says.

"I already told you guys: the Medical Unit does not treat insect bites. That's the jail's policy," Officer Mordhorst snarls.

"That's fucked up," Troll says, playing spades.

"You're shit out of luck, Alejandro," Billy the Hippy says.

"You're burnt," Gravedigger says.

Later that day, Lev enters my cell. "These damn Yankees think I am a doctor." He seems strained yet proud. "Now they want me to take care of Alejandro's spider bite. Will you help me?"

"How?" I ask, honoured.

"Gravedigger and the others are going to hold Alejandro, so the big bastard doesn't move, while I squeeze the pus out, and I need from you some salt and perhaps you will help me put salt on the wound?"

"Count me in." Plagued by mouth ulcers due to stress and malnourishment, I've been collecting the tiny salt packets served with the red death because gargling salt water temporarily relieves the burning sensation the ulcers cause. I retrieve the salt packets from under my mattress and follow Lev into the day room.

The bullet-wound scars on Alejandro's back pale in comparison to what looks like a baseball of yellow plasma attempting to exit his body. *How can a spider cause that?* When Lev fingers the wound, thick yellow pus runs down Alejandro's back, triggering my gag reflex.

"That's fucking gross!" Billy says.

Gravedigger smiles.

"It hurts like fuck! Are you sure you know what you're doing?" Alejandro asks.

"Trust me. I was in the Russian military. This wound is easy."

"He ain't no doctor!" yells the big hillbilly, George, sitting with the TV-watching crowd. "The commie bastard'll make you worse!"

"The irritation will be less when I am finished. Someone bring me toilet paper!" Lev catches a toilet roll launched from the balcony, unspools some and swabs up the pus. "Men, I need you to hold him steady," he says like a commander prepping troops for battle.

Gravedigger yanks Alejandro's right arm and locks it between his forearms and biceps. Two men secure Alejandro's left side.

Lev presses his thumbs against the wound.

Alejandro moans. The wound gushes. "It hurts," he whines.

"It hurts! Ah good! It will hurt less when I am finished." Lev presses harder, freeing more pus.

Does he really know what he's doing?

"It fucking hurts!" Alejandro says, scrunching his face.

"More toilet paper!" Lev's eyes track the pus streaking down Alejandro's back like egg yolk.

Sweat is streaming from Alejandro's short black hair, converging on his neck, branching out into tributaries on his body and coagulating with the baby powder coating his skin.

I pass Lev toilet paper. *I hope that's the last of the pus.*

"We done yet?" Alejandro asks, swaying, destabilising the men holding him.

"Keep him steady! We are not done! The poison is still coming out! More toilet paper, please!" Lev booms.

I quickly unspool more toilet paper. "Here you go."

Lev cleans up the fresh pus and applies pressure to the rim of the lesion.

Groaning like a dying elephant, Alejandro shifts, dragging along the men holding him.

"We need more guys to hold him," Gravedigger says.

Everyone in the day room ceases their activities to watch the volunteers steady the big man.

"I think that is it. One moment! Let me see. No! No! We are not done." Gazing fanatically, Lev discovers a new region of pus to finger.

On the verge of fainting, Alejandro groans and shifts again.

"More toilet paper!" Lev yells.

"That must be it," Alejandro says, sweat dripping from his ears and chin.

The prisoners ease their hold on Alejandro.

"Wait, men! Let me see." Lev thrusts his fingers into the sore. The ejaculation of pus, the biggest so far, surprises Lev, delights Gravedigger and shocks the rest of us.

Alejandro stumbles forward, tugging everyone holding him.

They steady him again. A pint of pus must have come out by now.

"More toilet paper!" Lev massages the area, liberating the last of the pus. "Now I will apply the salt."

I open the tiny packets, tip salt onto Lev's palm and cringe. Lev sprinkles salt onto the wound and rubs it in. Alejandro wails so loud the hermits rush from their cells.

"There. Thanks to my Russian military training and the solidarity of my Yankee and Limey assistants, you are all fixed up now." Lev smiles.

With their bee stripes stained by a combination of pus, sweat and baby powder, the men release Alejandro to applause. Alejandro sways but doesn't collapse.

Alejandro's back improves. He is released on bond, but I have a feeling I'll see him again.

CHAPTER 14

In July, Officer Alston stops by my cell with a smug smile and a copy of the *Phoenix New Times*. "Have you seen this?"

"No," I say, expecting him to drone on.

"You're the cover story! English Shaun's Evil Empire. Don't tell anyone I gave you this. Read it. I've got some questions for you later on." He hands me the paper and continues his security walk.

Ba-dum-ba-dum-ba-dum goes my heart when I see the cover: a portrait of me resembling the vampire Nosferatu, with four of my co-defendants, including the Wild Ones and Cody (my head of security), in the foreground, my arms encircling them like an evil puppeteer; in the background, a horde of tiny ravers in a strobe-lit inferno, dancing with their arms in the air. *Unbelievable!* Frantically turning the first page, I tear the paper. I scan the contents page. There is a ten-page article. Stunned, I climb onto my bunk and comb through it as fast as I can. *Surely this will damage my case.*

Evil Empire

Investigators say he is bigger than Sammy the Bull. His minions say he ruled the drug trade in the Valley's rave scene. Now, authorities have "English Shaun," the man they claim reigned over a night-time empire of ecstasy, meth, violence and excess.

By Susy Buchanan and Brendan Joel Kelley Thursday, Jul 18 2002

Ethan, Will and others who were there still talk about the scene that night. Two girls — a stripper and her friend — walked arm in arm through the living room of a villa at an East Valley resort hotel. Braless in matching bright halter tops, the girls wove their way through the crowd, sharing balance among their four feet. They wore naive, synthetic grins, eyes lolling about the room. Near the kitchen, their gazes landed on a six-foot-tall bald man. He was, Ethan recalls, crushing and chopping pills, spilling the granules into a pile of powder on the smooth glass of a picture frame that had been taken off the wall.

The tall guy, 30 years old but younger-looking than that, was the host of the party: English Shaun.

It was the fall of 1998, days after Halloween. Afternoon sun poured into the villa, which was rife with the smell of cigarette smoke and chemical sweat. Hunched over the picture frame, English Shaun and Ethan — who ran drugs for Shaun back then — combined powdered ecstasy, Xanax and ketamine into a large pile. "Zek lines," Ethan calls them. After enough mixing, the two aimed rolled-up hundred-dollar bills into the middle of the pile and snorted. Moments later they both slumped on the couch, eyes slightly open but quite literally unconscious.

"I thought we OD'd," Ethan recalls. "We blacked out for 20 or 30 minutes. I thought we were dead."

When consciousness returned, they went back to the drugs. Throughout the villa stood piles of cocaine, methamphetamine and ketamine. Outside in the fall sunshine, picture frames lay flat with liquid ketamine drying into crisp disks of crystals on the glass. Pills were strewn throughout countertops and pockets — painkillers like Darvocet and Vicodan, along with a large quantity of ecstasy, English Shaun's trademark product.

Then there was concern at the locked door to the bathroom. An internationally famous DJ — the guest of honor for the party, in town for a rave — had disappeared into the bathroom more than an hour ago and turned on the shower, but now he wasn't answering to knocks and shouts at the door.

Will, a drug trafficker and distributor for English Shaun, kicked the door in. He found the star lying in the bathtub with the water still on, breathing but unconscious. He lifted him from the shower and took him out to a couch. And as soon as the celeb came to, the party started up again.

It was a full two days later that the fete finally trickled to a close. The villa sustained considerable damage. Picture frames were destroyed, and glass was strewn throughout the villa. A lampshade caught fire. There were craters in the walls where English Shaun had smashed his head while high on GHB, a liquid anesthetic. Dried wax covered the carpeting and bed, a souvenir of Shaun and Will having hot candle wax dripped on their naked bodies by strippers.

Looking back, the people who were there that day couldn't have realized that this would be the pinnacle of their decadence, the crest of a wave that now threatens to drown them.

Arizonans are by now familiar with Sammy "the Bull" Gravano's exploits as leader of an ecstasy ring, which he ran with the help of his son Gerard and a group of thugs called the Devil Dogs, until his arrest in 2000. Few, however, are familiar with Gravano's contemporary — and, some would say, competitor — English Shaun, and the organization he reportedly referred to as "the Evil Empire." Investigators from city and federal agencies who have been tracking English Shaun since January 2000 now charge that for years he piloted a syndicate of drug importers and distributors that supplied the bulk of ecstasy in the early days of the Valley's rave scene, and eventually branched out to include meth, pharmaceuticals, designer drugs and marijuana. In the process, it made English Shaun an urban legend in the rave underground. In May, "English" Shaun Attwood and 12 of his alleged associates were arrested and indicted for a sum of 155 felony violations, including conspiracy, participating in a criminal syndicate, and illegal enterprise. Attwood denies all the charges against him and has pleaded not guilty.

Since the arrests, the legend of English Shaun has flourished in clubs and private parties, and the stories told on the streets these days are elaborate rehashings of antics that crescendo with each retelling, tipping the scales of freak. Rumors of guns, strippers, threats, superstar DJs and enough drugs to kill a herd of elephants. They peak with tales of outrageous parties and heavenly bills, and end with the bald-headed Englishman chained at the legs and wrists in court, staring at nothing, as attorneys discuss what remains of his supposed empire.

Sammy the Bull had the name, and his ride on the ecstasy merry-go-round made headlines around the nation when the former hit man was arrested. The drug, and the rave scene that favored it, had sprung up seemingly out of nowhere. The quantities of pills he brought into the Valley at the time were unheard of. But law enforcement sources now agree that while Gravano had muscle and flash, he was no English Shaun. Gravano lacked Shaun's intelligence, organization, and diverse array of products, they say. They also claim that Attwood easily moved millions of dollars' worth of meth, ecstasy, pharmaceuticals and marijuana through parties and raves in the Valley over the past few years, and they are careful to qualify that estimate as conservative. English Shaun was bigger, in other words, than Sammy the Bull.

And in more ways than one. Attwood is tall, lanky and bald, with pale white skin and pinched features. His accent is where the "English" comes from, a Mad Hatter tea-time lilt. He has braces on his teeth, his lips are thin and pursed, and his blue eyes glimmer mischievously, even in a mug shot. Friends and former roommates describe him as a sort of vampire — largely nocturnal, with a thirst for the GHB they say he drank like blood, and a more than passing resemblance to Nosferatu. He could be proper, charming, polite, with an intelligence that matched his magnetism...

On and on it goes, mostly the accounts of ravers, some who know me, some who don't and are fabricating. When I read that the prosecutor has classified me as a serious drug offender likely to receive a life sentence, I go into shock. Serious-drug-offender classification carries 25 years. *I thought I was getting out. My attorney's filed for a bond hearing.* I add 25 to my age, 33. *I'll be 58, near retirement when I get out! My life's over. I'm fucked.* Propelled by the urge to take action – even though I don't know what – I drop down from my bunk. Unsteady on my feet, I feel as if everything is spinning around me. Dizzy, I fall onto my knees as if I'm overdosing on drugs. My throat spasms. Afraid of retching, I approach the toilet on all fours like a dog. Due to my empty stomach all I puke is bile. Sitting on the floor in a daze, I finish the article. *They've made me sound like a villain from the Marvel Comics I collected as a child.* Frustrated, I want to punch the wall. *Oh, fuck, my parents might see this.* My fury rises when I read the prosecutor's contribution:

"You know, as I was driving to work today I was listening to that Aerosmith song, 'Livin' on the Edge,'" she says after the court hearing. "When you live on the edge, you can't keep yourself from falling. That's what this case reminds me of. Once upon a time you thought you were so powerful, and now you're invisible, in chains in a courtroom."

How is that legal? Surely this has prejudiced my case.

The criminal behaviour I hid from my parents has burst into the open, and even worse, the article portrays me as a cross between Tony Soprano and a vampire, not a hedonistic stockbroker gone wild on drugs. *I must stop my parents from reading it.* I dash downstairs and call my aunt Ann.

"Please don't let my mum and dad see it!"

"It's too late, Shaun. There's an Internet version."

Holy shit! An Internet version! I want to rip the phone off the wall.

While I fume, she explains there is no way to prevent my parents from reading it. It would be best to forewarn them before they find out from a less friendly source. She points out that no one will believe such an over-the-top article. She rings my father and emails him the online version.

My mother reads it. Her mental deterioration begins after giving a college lecture. In the staff room, she approaches a group of foreign students who are waiting to see their tutor, imagining they've read and are talking about the article. "They all know what's going on!" she screams, darting at the students. Busy at their computers, the teachers pause to watch her shouting abuse and pointing at students until someone calms her down. My father rushes to the college to take her home. She ends up on medical leave from work.

Her initial anger at my lack of concern for my family turns into a deep depression. She can't understand how I could do this to them. Her anger turns to shame and guilt. She is ashamed of what the son she's been so proud of has done. She doesn't want anyone to know I'm in prison. She keeps it all a secret for months, not even telling her only sister. She lives in fear of her house being vandalised by people who've read the article. She imagines the words "DRUG DEALERS" daubed on the front of the house. Every time she goes near a newsagent, she is afraid to glance at notice boards or stacks of papers, thinking my story has made headline news in the UK. She thinks her friends will turn against her and she'll lose her job.

Her doctor prescribes anti-anxiety medication, which helps her sleep and blocks out to some degree the constant unease she feels about my safety. Overriding the guilt and shame is her concern for me.

With numerous counselling sessions and cognitive-behaviour therapy my mother learns to deal with the situation. When she does finally break down in tears at work, she tells her manager, who can't believe she held it in for so long. From that moment, she receives nothing but support from her co-workers, friends and family.

My father, who always appears strong, suffers panic attacks, and my sister has counselling. During one of the sessions, her counsellor suggests she write me a letter expressing the anger she feels about what I've done to my family. The letter is ten pages long. Karen waits a week to find the courage to mail it.

In the letter, Karen is furious about my uncaring and selfish behaviour towards our parents before my arrest. She reminds me how I hardly ever called them, how I constantly lied to them and how they never knew what I was doing. She accuses me of behaving as though I don't care about them.

She asks why I married Amy – who I was with before Claudia – without telling our parents and why I think it's acceptable to be so secretive even though I expect them to bail me out if something goes wrong.

She lambasts me for not paying off Mum and Dad's mortgage when I was rich, for not trying to make their lives easier and for blowing a fortune on my raver friends. She reminds me that this is a time when our parents should be slowing down, taking it easy, enjoying a holiday home with grandchildren, but instead they are spending a large part of their lives frantic with worry about me, their entire life savings sucked up by my lawyer's fees.

She says that I've been a constant disappointment to her. That she felt rejected during our childhood – due to all of the teasing I did – and years later, whenever she came to the States for a visit. That she is hurt by my lack of interest in her life. She admits she'd visited me and Amy in Tucson because she thought it would be good for Mum and Dad for the whole family to be reunited. Yet I had still almost ruined that trip with my "fucked up life" by being out of control on drugs.

She says that the person I was before my arrest doesn't deserve the deep love and devotion of someone like Claudia. I've wrecked Claudia's life with my selfish behaviour, so how can I talk about loving her?

She questions my present behaviour, my pronouncements about living a good life, and she asks whether I've really learnt what a massive impact my behaviour has had on everyone. She reminds me that Mum and Dad are ill with stress, all their plans for the future have been shelved, and that she too is ill from the stress of seeing how badly Mum and Dad are doing. She says they are all furious for being dragged into my mess.

Finally, she says she's never bothered telling me how much

I've upset her in the past because she doesn't think I'm worth it or capable of understanding. She hopes I've changed and not just somehow intellectualised a change by reading about how a good person should behave. She will only be able to tell when I get out.

Her letter throws my mind into turmoil. I feel more physically sick than when I read the *New Times* article because these words are from someone I love and most of what she says is true. My family's suffering is a result of my choices and my arrogance in imagining I'd never get caught. Guilt and shame consume me. I spend all day worrying about my family, the possibility of getting a life sentence and the effect getting a life sentence might have on them.

The guards circulate the *New Times* article in the jail. They cut out pictures and post them to the Medical Unit's notice board for all to see. When Claudia visits, some guards harass her about the article. Officer Alston extracts me from the pod to ask what I've really done. He says I don't fit the newspaper's portrayal of me as the Antichrist. He says I should have committed my crimes in his hometown of Chicago where they only arrest black people. I appreciate his sympathy but not his racism. My infamy spreads throughout the jail. Inmates ask for my autograph and put me on the phone to say hello to their wives and girlfriends. At breakfast, I receive extra milk and cheese from trusties eager to serve "English Shaun" – a persona I regret ever creating now that I realise how badly it's going to affect my case. Even Gravedigger stops by – drunk on hooch and in an expansive mood after knocking out a Mexican who crapped in the shower – and offers to silence any of my co-defendants I think might cooperate with the prosecutor.

Alan Simpson says the article has damaged my right to a fair trial in Phoenix. He files some motions. The judge issues a gag order on the prosecutor and Detective Reid because of their contributions to the article, but refuses to move my case out of Phoenix. The damage is done. I'm dissatisfied with the outcome of the motions.

Making matters worse, a second group is arrested – thirty-nine more co-defendants – increasing the size and complexity of my case. The prosecutor states that there is too much legal discovery on the case to be printed out. The tens of thousands of pages of police reports on the "Attwood Organization" will have to be downloaded onto computer discs. The motion filed to reduce my bond, which had raised my hopes of getting out, is denied. The growing complexity of the case, my attorney says, means that I'll probably be in jail for at least a year.

The deterioration in my attorney's optimism crushes my hopes of probation or a short sentence. According to Simpson, even though the prosecutor didn't have much of a case in the beginning, so many people are being arrested some will inevitably agree to testify against me. When I try to imagine what serving years in prison is going to be like my brain shuts down. It won't accept it. It wants me to fight. I convince myself I can deal with and deserve five years or less but the thought of ten or more overwhelms me. *It would break me.* With uncertainty gnawing away, I pray for a speedy resolution, so I can be transferred to the prison system where conditions are better than in Arpaio's jail (according to the prisoners who've been there). Coming to terms with spending a year in here is hard. I fear for my health, safety and sanity.

July 2002

Dear love,

Just finished chow. The rice was water-logged and crunchy. Luckily I saved half of a breakfast brownie but I feel bad after eating that crap. We have no air conditioning and showers still. I am writing stuck to my clothing and all of my chocolate bars have melted.

Besides that everything else is going good today. I'm 2-2 with the Russian chess champ and I just got back from church where I saw Wild Man and had a good sing-a-long.

The whole pod was buzzing when I walked upstairs with boxes of my case paperwork. Thanks to that and the New Times article I'm getting more status. At classes and church I'm getting more hellos and fist bumps. People were bowing down in church whispering Evil Empire. People love talking about raves and the scene.

If I can sue the New Times and get some funds then I wouldn't feel as financially helpless as I do now. I feel sick to my stomach that my parents are paying my legal bill and I will do anything to take that burden away from them.

In one of your letters you said the weeks are going faster. Well that's certainly the case. The August court date will be here in no time, and we'll have a better idea of what's going on. One of the guys in the pod used Alan Simpson for his previous case. He shot at people in a Circle K and was looking at 15 years. Simpson got it down to 3.

In one of my classes we talked about freeing ourselves from our bad apples. That we are trees. Bad apples include drugs, violence, etc. even fear of flying. She says we must get rid of all our turkeys as well. Those are people encouraging us into negative environments, and people making us feel guilty or bad so that we will help them. Well I guess I have been growing bad apples and been surrounded by turkeys for quite some time. This experience should free me of all that so I can be with you 100%.

Love,
Shaun XXX

Dearest Fiancée,

Today is a very strange day in jail. No sooner had I called you than they declared headcount and no sooner had I got back on the phone than they declared lockdown. Whilst sitting bewildered in my cell, a guard came by. He said hello and explained that something had happened. I asked him if someone had been murdered and he said he wasn't allowed to answer that question.

So here I sit. Troll is passed out on the bottom bunk. OG is on the top bunk contemplating whether he'll be struck down by God if he uses pages from the Bible to roll cigarettes with. Both lie in their pink undies. The pod is unusually quiet. People are miffed. First they took our food, and now we are trapped in our cells. The noise of the constantly leaking water from the shower pierces the silence. Every now and then an inmate listening to the radio joins in with a partial song. There's no mail today. No visits are allowed on lockdown. The spirit of the pod is in dismay.

Troll just rolled out of the foetal position and blurted, "Where am I? What day is it?" He giggled and coiled himself back up.

Chow should be here soon. The first and only opening of the cell door for the evening, aside from the continuous headcounts. Yesterday's chow was cowboy beans, 2 meat tostadas, and watermelon, carrots and onions mixed together in a greasy sauce. I used the bread provided with my breakfast to make bean sandwiches of which I ate 5. I traded my 2 tostadas for 2 juices with other white inmates. The juices are half ice and are gone in a few swigs but in the unairconditioned environment provide excellent thirst quenching. Even after the juice is quickly drunk, I utilize the ice in the cups by dropping it into used plastic bottles, which are filled with lukewarm tap water to hide its tepid taste. Nothing is wasted except when the food is so bad the returned trays pile up with the uneaten garbage.

I love you dearly and deeply,
Shaun

CHAPTER 15

Church on the Street starts as usual. We are sitting in rows of plastic chairs in a large bare room without any windows, singing along with the chaplain, Pastor Walt, who insists, in the face of numerous obstacles put up by the jail, on holding a weekly Christian service. Pastor Walt is an ex-Vietnam vet, Satanist and alcoholic whom God restored to His flock in 1976. In drainpipe jeans and a lumberjack shirt, tiny Hillbilly Ed is strumming a vintage guitar and tapping pointy snakeskin cowboy boots against the concrete. There are no guards present, affording more privacy for the devout to commune with God and the faithless to misbehave.

There is power, power, wonder working power
In the blood of the Lamb;
There is power, power, wonder working power
In the precious blood of the Lamb.

Would you be free from your passion and pride?
There's power in the blood, power in the blood;
Come for a cleansing to Calvary's tide;
There's wonderful power in the blood.

Clutching the Bible, Pastor Walt takes a few steps forward. His keen eyes, bulging and bloodshot, appraise the audience. "Tonight this is God's room. This is our church. This is the time and place to worship Him, and I expect you all to behave yourselves, especially the scoffers and mockers in the back row." Pastor Walt's eyes scan the back row and halt on a known disrupter of religious ceremonies: Wild Man, who stops whispering loudly to me and smiles dementedly at Pastor Walt. The expression on Pastor

Walt's sun-leathered face sours, his gaze intensifies. When Pastor Walt finishes shaking his head at Wild Man, his eyes settle on the inmates clustered in the front rows, clutching soft-bound Bibles and rosary beads, some with tattoos of crucifixes, Jesus and the Virgin Mary. The communing of eyes between them restores a calmer look to Pastor Walt's face. "You see, scoffing and mocking was predicted in the Bible. The scoffers and mockers were expected during the End Times. How many of you are familiar with Revelations?"

All hands shoot up in the front rows, not so many in the middle, at the back, none.

"If you've read Revelations—"

Two men burst through the door right behind Pastor Walt, startling him. One, a Rolling Stones type in tight-fitting black clothes and a headband, unsheathes a guitar with a gay-pride rainbow sticker and doesn't speak or alter his facial expression. Wearing sandals worthy of an apostle and well-faded jeans, the other is bald and beaming a smile not of this earth. Through John Lennon specs, his eyes radiate happiness. His cheap white T-shirt proclaims: I LOVE JESUS.

Regaining his composure, Pastor Walt says, "Some of you may already be familiar with Jumping Bill."

The bald man raises a hand. His smile intensifies. The inmates who recognise Jumping Bill clap as if we're in for a treat.

Pastor Walt gazes for a few seconds at the new arrivals tuning their strings. "I'm just gonna step out of the way and let Jumping Bill take over."

Jumping Bill centres himself in front of the congregation. His partner remains near the wall. "How many of you love Jesus?" Jumping Bill whispers.

Only the front rows respond.

"How many of you love Jesus?" he says a little louder, nodding at us.

More rows respond.

"How many of you love Jesus?" he says even louder. He strums his guitar and lunges forward.

Most of us respond.

He smiles over his shoulder at his expressionless partner who nods. Rotating his head from side to side like a mannequin, Jumping Bill engages us with eyes that proclaim, *I am about to open the gates of Heaven for you.* Still lunging, he rocks back and forth and sings in a soothing whisper:

Worthy is the Lamb
Worthy is the Lamb
You are Holy, Holy
Are you Lord God Almighty
Worthy is the Lamb
Worthy is the Lamb

Jumping Bill leaps into the air, surprising us, his guitar flying out to one side. He dashes down the aisle, casting the net of his smile over the rapt audience. Strumming faster, he homes in on the back row. He stops in front of men, nodding and smiling, not saying a word, melting the meanest looks from faces. When my turn comes, he looks so happy, I think, *My God, I took drugs to feel like that.* The force of his smile is so strong, I cannot resist smiling back. His aura raises the hair on my arms. He runs to the front, back to rocking in a lunge.

He shouts, "Repeat after me, everyone!" and sings, "Worthy is the lamb."

"Worthy is the lamb," we chime in.

"You are Holy, Holy," he sings.

"You are Holy, Holy," we repeat.

We cheer when the song is over.

"Excellent! Excellent!" He plays more songs, whispers to God, sings loudly, weeps, sings in Spanish and dances and dashes around the room. "OK, everybody, at the end of this song I want you all to jump up and down with me as high in the air as you can."

When he shouts, "Jump, everybody!" he jumps. Some men begin to pogo dance. Others scan the room as if wondering what to do. I jump alone in my area, embarrassed at first, but quickly joined by a few others whose jumping eases my self-consciousness. Smiling at Bill and the other men jumping, I'm free from the stress of my case and the environment. I'm free to push down hard on my feet and spring as high in the air as possible and land in a way that jolts my body and sends my anxiety out in shockwaves through my feet. I feel the force of the irrational joy sparkling in the eyes of the men jumping. I'm finally at one with the insanity of the place.

"You are going to be free-free-free-free…" Jumping Bill yells. "C'mon, everybody, jump with me!"

Around the men jumping, more join in. The mass of jumping men expands across the room with late jumpers enthusiastically matching the intensity of early ones. Even Wild Man is jumping and yelling, "The devil is in me!" The men jumping nearest to Wild Man are eyeing him cautiously and maintaining a safe distance. IDs shoot from the top pockets of some of the jumpers. Men push and shove each other and play fights break out. When shower sandals and chairs are launched across the room, Pastor Walt calls order. Much to my disappointment, Jumping Bill and everyone stop jumping. I'm back in the jail.

When Pastor Walt steps back, Jumping Bill yells, "One more time! You are going to be free-free-free-free…"

The cheering men jump, converting the room into a punk-rock concert. To a boisterous ovation, Pastor Walt announces the end of the service. Most of us have stopped jumping by the time the guards rush in to investigate the commotion. They command us to return to our pods, but we are so many and they are so few we ignore them. Relishing our defiance of the guards and the afterglow of jumping, we linger to hug Jumping Bill.

CHAPTER 16

Returning from court, OG breezes into our cell singing "Another One Bites the Dust" by Queen, grinning in a self-satisfied way that looks peculiar on a man lacking front teeth. His case was dropped. At the back of the cell, he ties a towel around his arm, clenches his hand several times and shoots up a celebratory hit of heroin. He sings until 2 a.m. and tickles my feet every time I fall asleep.

Troll and I pray not to get another maniac cellmate. Our prayers are answered in the form of Doug, a mellow fifty-year old who's spent half of his life locked up. He is short, thin, with gentle blue eyes and a large nose reshaped by ancient prison fights. Caught with a tiny amount of black-tar heroin, he is facing five years for violating the terms of his parole. As Doug has served more time than all of us, the inmates respect him. Even Gravedigger stops by to congratulate us for having an all-white cell with a well-respected wood.

Around the time Doug arrives, our pod receives the biggest man in Towers jail, Houston, an ex-pro footballer. Six foot eight, he towers over everyone and is crowned the head of his race by virtue of size. His presence puts an end to the day-room affronts on the blacks – even Gravedigger modifies his behaviour. When there is a black-on-black dispute in a neighbouring pod, the guards take Houston there to settle it. He tells me about travelling the world with his football team and the partying he did at Stringfellows nightclub in London. Along with sports success came a cocaine addiction. Drugs destroyed his career. He was arrested selling cocaine to finance his addiction. I tell him I threw my stockbroking career away to party. After chatting with Houston, I return to my filthy cell, dwelling on what I lost.

At the peak of my Ecstasy business, a typical day involved rising around noon in a million-dollar mountainside home in Tucson. Sometimes when I went outside, deer would be gathered around. When it rained, a beautiful waterfall would form behind the house and a stream would gargle past our little wooden gate. With the sun high in a usually cloudless sky above the Sonoran Desert, I would wake myself up by jumping in the pool with my ex, Amy, an undergraduate who became a strip-tease dancer in order to seduce a female co-worker. After swimming, we'd head to our favourite Indian restaurant. Later on, my right-hand man, Cody, would arrive to discuss my illegal business, including who needed more Ecstasy, who was having problems paying for drugs, and how much cash he'd collected and secured in an apartment I rented for that purpose. Hoping to avoid police detection, we only discussed business in person. If everything was running smoothly, I'd splurge at a fancy restaurant with Amy, take drugs and make love all night. If problems arose or key business associates such as the New Mexican Mafia wanted a face-to-face meeting, I'd head to Phoenix, pick up my two toughest friends, Wild Man and G Dog, and try to fix things. *How powerful I felt strutting around with those two. And just look at me now. Reduced to nothing…*

Houston isn't with us for long. Trouble brews after he's moved to another tower to promote racial harmony. Lev warns me about Gravedigger's plan to have SmackDown – who is now the head of the blacks again – smashed. After smashing Carter, SmackDown behaved himself for a few weeks but he's now bullying commissary from members of every race again. There are only a few men left that SmackDown hasn't tried it on with. As smashing the head of a race is a declaration of war on every member of that race, I expect chaos.

SmackDown corners me in D10 when I'm on the stool writing a letter to Claudia. "Hey, England, I see you get store. Give me a Snickers till store day, dog, and I'll pay you back two-for-one." In shower sandals and bee-striped pants, he steps towards me, reducing the distance between us as if to pressure me into saying yes. He inhales loudly, expanding a broad and powerful chest rising from his narrow waist like a triangle.

Troll has previously warned me that if the prisoners know I'll give them store, there'll be a line at the door to take my commissary. "I've only got enough to last till store day," I say, hoping he leaves it at that.

SmackDown steps closer, breathing the force of his presence upon me. "You don't trust me 'cause I'm black. You don't think I'll pay you back," he says, anger rising in his voice.

My body tenses. "That's not it at all. I'll starve in here if I give my store away," I say, which is true. It's also true that I don't trust him. He knows it and is trying to milk that truth. The reason I don't trust him isn't racial. It's because I can count on the fingers of one hand the amount of people I trust in here.

"Y'all motherfucking racists up in this cell."

Aware he's trying to exploit any emotional reaction and wary of triggering his violent nature, I strain to remain pleasant. "Look, I can't eat red death or green baloney. I'll starve if I give my store away," I say, determined to hold my ground.

"Fuck, man, all I'm asking for is one lousy Snickers."

"If I give my food away, I'll run out before store day and end up hungry."

Troll walks in. "What's up, dogs!"

"I'm motherfucking hungry," SmackDown says. "Got any honey buns?"

"Best I can do is a few soups, bro." Troll reaches under his bunk for a commissary bag.

The soups send SmackDown on his way, but I know he'll be back. A part of me appreciates what Gravedigger is about to do – the same part that rejoiced when SmackDown smashed Carter and Gravedigger sent Carter packing. SmackDown has threatened my food, which I value highly. Hassled, I understand why so many are against him.

Gravedigger uses the numerous incidences of SmackDown bulldogging inmates to convene a meeting for the heads of all the races except the blacks. He says that if a torpedo gives Smack-Down the usual ultimatum, "The fellas have decided you need to roll your shit up or else we'll roll it up for you. What's it gonna be?" SmackDown will smash the torpedo and claim he's earned the right to stay. To get the job done properly requires three torpedoes to corner SmackDown and more to wait outside his cell just in case. Eager to get rid of SmackDown, each head volunteers a torpedo to smash him and more as backup.

While on the phone in the day room, I notice men gathering suspiciously on the balcony. Most of the blacks are playing cards downstairs, as three torpedoes – a white, a Mexican and a Mexican American – enter SmackDown's upstairs cell. More torpedoes guard the stairs.

"Each of the races has decided you've got to go, SmackDown," yells the white torpedo, a tough forty-year-old ranch hand from Nebraska. "Now roll your fucking shit up!"

"For doing fucking what? Who wants me to fucking roll up?" SmackDown yells, shifting away from them.

"Come on, SmackDown, let's do this the easy way, dog."

"I ain't fucking rolling up!"

The white torpedo dashes behind SmackDown, while the other two approach from the front. He puts SmackDown in an upright headlock while they punch SmackDown's head and stomach. SmackDown lurches backwards, sandwiching the white torpedo between the wall. He flicks his head forwards and backwards, breaking the white torpedo's nose. Noisy crosses, jabs and uppercuts ferment into a bloody mess. The yelling and pounding of knuckles against flesh catches the attention of the blacks, who charge half way up the stairs before the torpedoes push them down. One of the blacks weighs about 400 pounds. He falls down the stairs, knocking men out of the way like a bowling ball mowing down pins, dragging more men into the fight. Two of the blacks fight their way to the balcony. Inmates of all races emerge from the upper-tier cells and fight those two. The battle for the stairs is raging below them. The fight at the bottom of the stairs is spreading throughout the day room. Several blacks are trying to gain ground on the stairs until a hefty Mexican American attacks them from behind with a mop stick. Everywhere I look a black man is bravely fending off multiple assailants. From his cell downstairs, Gravedigger is admiring the spectacle as if he has unleashed the satanic puppet-master on his chest.

Mordhorst turns the phones off. "Lockdown! Lockdown, now!" he yells over the intercom. "This is a direct order. Lockdown right now!" Ignored by everyone, he puts on a space suit and grabs a fire-extinguisher-sized canister of chemical spray.

With Mordhorst about to decimate the riot, I redouble my attempts to get up the stairs behind Troll and Doug who are struggling to elbow through the fighting men. Struck by flailing arms, I raise my forearms to shield my face. Progress is impossible. We advance a few steps and get pushed down. The torpedoes at the top of the stairs are pushing the blacks down onto us. I've never been in the thick of a room full of people fighting. Caught up in the atmosphere, I'm soon elbowing and pushing men of all races away with increased force. Gripped by the rush of the battle, I'm doing what is necessary to get up the stairs. Mordhorst is descending the control-tower stairs, wielding the canister, seconds away from entering the day-room door directly behind me.

I need to get the hell out of Mordhorst's way!

Sane guards wait for backup before entering a riot situation, but not Mordhorst. Watching over him in the control tower, Officer Alston activates the sliding door to our pod. As Alston yells, "Lockdown!" over and over, Mordhorst turns sideways to get through the half-open door and charges into the day room. A Mexican pulling ninja moves with a mop stick is sprayed first. An awful smell assaults us, as if a thousand bird's-eye chillies are being deseeded simultaneously. The spray scatters the men from the stairs. Falling over each other, eyes smarting, my cellmates and I rush into D10 and slam the door. From the safety of the cell, I watch Mordhorst dash around fumigating prisoners as if exterminating vermin. Coughing and wheezing prisoners rush into cells.

Many lock down in the nearest cells they can find just to escape from Mordhorst. The Mexican and Mexican American torpedoes slip out of SmackDown's cell just before Mordhorst gets there. Mordhorst locks the door and sprays the cell for several minutes.

"I'm fucking blind!" SmackDown keeps yelling.

By the time backup charges into Tower 6, Mordhorst has put out half of the riot. Guards drag away anyone still fighting.

"My eyes are killing," I say, panting by the cell door.

"Wet your towel and wrap it around your head," Doug says. "It'll stop the spray. Blink as much as you can, so your tears wash the chemicals out."

I put a wet towel around my head but leave a gap to monitor the day room. Guards are charging up the stairs, racing towards the fighting noises still coming from SmackDown's cell. The guards open SmackDown's door and rush in, yelling orders to stop fighting. They emerge with SmackDown.

"You'll all be fucking sorry for pulling that three-on-one bullshit when I get back out of the hole!" he yells. Barely able to open his eyes, he otherwise looks unscathed as they escort him to lockdown.

They extract the white torpedo whose bleeding nose is pointing in a new direction.

"Your nose is crooked," mocks a guard.

"Can I fix it before you handcuff me?" the white torpedo asks with a polite cowboy twang.

The guard looks perplexed. The white torpedo places the palm of one hand against the side of his nose and strikes his nose with his other hand. *Crunch.* Holding his hands out in readiness for the cuffs, he smiles with satisfaction.

Due to the riot, we are confined to our cells. I read and play chess. Deliveries of mail and chow break up the monotony. On the third day of the lockdown, the noise of inmates yelling obscenities and banging on their doors and walls draws me and my cellmates to the door. Seeing a larger than usual goon squad in the corridor, I brace for another raid. Dwarfed by the guards, a small pot-bellied man with thin greying hair slicked to one side emerges from the goon squad, wearing square-framed spectacles and a beige sheriff's office shirt with a brown tie. The yelling and banging spread throughout our tower.

"Fuck you, Arpaio!"

"Rot in hell, Joe!"

"Stop feeding us red death, motherfucker! You try eating that shit!"

"Turn the fucking air on! We're dying up here."

Having only seen Sheriff Joe Arpaio on TV, sometimes surrounded by adoring inmates – obviously staged – other times organising the collection of fruit from rat-infested neighbourhoods, I'm surprised by this powerful man's small stature. I'm unsurprised by the inmates' reaction, which heightens as Arpaio talks to the guards at the foot of the control tower, circled by bodyguards, unexposed to danger. In solidarity with my neighbours, I yell and bang the steel table with both fists – aware that the architect of our suffering is unmoved – but enjoying a release of tension after being cooped up in the cell for days. The energy of animosity saturating the building is so strong that if the inmates had access to Arpaio they would probably tear his limbs off. After Arpaio's brief appearance, the atmosphere remains charged with antagonism for the rest of the day.

CHAPTER 17

Before my arrest, my parents booked a hiking holiday in Switzerland. Reluctant to waste money that might be needed by my attorney, they cancel, losing their deposit. They want to fly to Phoenix, but I tell them not to incur the expense. Ashamed, I don't want them to see me in here, but Mum insists on coming. Putting aside my dread of her being in the jail, I write home, excited about her visits. I appreciate her travelling 5000 miles.

When the first visit is called, I'm happy but afraid. I'm concerned that when she sees me – malnourished and in bee stripes – she might have another nervous breakdown. My situation is far removed from when she visited my mountainside home.

I first glimpse my mother from the visitation holding tank. She looks smaller and more fragile than usual. Struck by guilt, I try to reassure her by putting on my widest grin. She's sitting at a table, pale and tired, glancing around expectantly until she spots me waving. Momentarily, her eyes light up and the sadness lifts.

After Officer Green gives his speech to the visitors, I'm allowed in. I rush to Mum's table. "Thanks so much for coming all that way."

Tears well. She's obviously shocked by my appearance. "You look as though you've lost weight," she says, appraising my sunken cheeks and skinny frame. "Are you getting enough to eat?"

"Thanks to Claudia, I'm getting Snickers, peanuts and peanut butter from the commissary," I say, smiling but shook up by the toll my situation has taken on her health. "How was your journey?"

"Long and tiring, but it was worth it to see you."

"I really appreciate it."

"I had to come. I had to see you in the flesh. I needed to know you're all right."

"I'm all right. I was in shock at first, but I've adjusted. The longer I've been here, the more allies I've made. That's what keeps you out of trouble. The *New Times* article – as exaggerated as it was – gave me some street cred with my neighbours."

"So in jail, everything's turned on its head. What's bad is good and vice versa?"

"Kind of. Well, actually, only in some cases. Sex offences and crimes against kids can get you killed. But if you're a murderer – and you've not murdered a woman or a kid – then you're at the top of the pecking order."

"What's Alan Simpson saying?"

I don't want to burden her with the stress of my legal situation. "He says my case is going to take longer to resolve than we originally thought because it's a complex case."

Mum frowns.

"Alan's one of the top attorneys in Phoenix. I'm sure he'll eventually get the best possible plea bargain." *I'd better change the subject.* "So how's your stay gone so far?"

"Everyone's been so helpful. Claudia's been an angel."

"I know. I don't know how I'd cope without her visits and constant letters."

"She picked me up and drove me here and is waiting to take me back. She said she'd do that every visit and drive me anywhere I want to go."

"Good. She'll enjoy spending time with you. She told me she'd look after you."

"How she copes with getting in here I don't know. It's horrendous. It's so distressing seeing the people in the waiting room, mothers with toddlers and small babies, crying and restless, all crowded together in a hot stuffy room. It's dirty and littered. The toilets are a disgrace. I was sat there for hours, waiting to be called."

"Claudia's told me about some of that stuff. I'm so lucky to have found someone so caring."

"And when I was finally called after going through security, feeling the heavy door close behind me, shutting out the world, I felt an inkling of what it must be like to be a prisoner."

"At least you can go back out through that door," I say, glad to see her smile. "There's people been in here for over a year."

"Held un-sentenced for over a year?"

"Yes, over a year. Can you believe it?"

"The system here stinks! The guards treat the visitors like dirt. They're abrupt. They look down on everyone. It's so unfair. A lot of the women waiting are Mexican and obviously poor. They've committed no crime, but they're treated like criminals. Outside, we drove past a woman pushing a pram down the dusty road. Too poor to afford a taxi, I suppose. The officers in charge of Visitation are rude and ignorant. Which, having a boss like Arpaio, doesn't surprise me. The nastiness comes down from the top. I don't want any special treatment, but they just don't seem to care."

"When the visit's over, Officer Green locks us in the strip-search room for hours. It's a bloody nightmare. But some of the guards are OK. Some hate working for Arpaio and aren't afraid to tell us."

"I suppose it takes all sorts. They're probably not paid very much. The dress code gets me. They complained this shirt reveals my collarbone and were about to refuse me entry. I had to plead ignorance about the dress code. They allowed me in – only because it's my first visit – but warned me to cover my collarbone next time. I can understand them banning miniskirts and cleavage but not collarbones. Who's going to get excited by my collarbone? I hate to think of it!" she says, her face brightening. "We drove past Tent City. I couldn't believe what I was seeing."

"Arpaio's real proud of Tent City. If you think we've got it bad, imagine those poor souls out in the desert in old army tents from the Korean War. The news reported temperatures in the tents of over 130 °F. And because it's outdoors, the gangs get weapons and drugs thrown over the fence."

"If this were a developing country, I'd understand it. But not in America. No one would believe it."

"Arpaio does what he wants. The old people in Sun City

keep voting him back in 'cause he's out doing tough-on-crime PR stunts every week. But in reality, he's all spin. He's created an environment that just breeds more crime. There's no hope for youngsters coming here. They get recruited by the gangs, and are soon shooting up drugs like everyone else, and contracting diseases like hepatitis C."

"You've been writing a lot about the food. Are you getting enough to eat?"

"Yes. Enough to get by because Claudia's put money on my books. The guys with no money are constantly begging everyone else for food."

"Starving people in the land of plenty. It's shameful." My mum says how my dad and Karen are coping. "They're both still shell-shocked and just taking it a day at a time. Karen's working hard. She'll be a top journalist someday. But she gets upset and anxious for your safety. You hear so many tales about violence in prison. I try not to think about it."

"It's like a video game in here: you're surrounded by danger, but you have to just get through it. So far – it's like I have a guardian angel or something – I've managed to get through unscathed."

"It's a relief to know you're safe. That someone's looking out for you."

"I'll be OK. Try not to worry. The longer I've been here, the more friends in low places I've made."

We laugh.

"Your dad is just getting on with it. What else can he do? He's strong, and although he's worried sick about you, he keeps positive, which helps me survive each day. We are a strong family, and we won't let this pull us apart. You know we love you very much, and we'll do anything to get you out of this mess."

"Thanks," I say, overwhelmed.

Officer Green announces visits are over.

"I'll phone you at Ann's tonight," I say.

"I look forward to it. I love you. Take care."

"Love you, too."

During her two-week stay, my mother visits at every opportunity, sometimes with Claudia, sometimes with my aunt Ann. She gets used to the ordeal of getting in and out. She even befriends people she meets in the waiting room. Although I'm traumatized by my legal situation, her visits begin to restore hope. Her constant expressions of support are reassuring. During the last visit, we are both sad because we know it will be a while before we see each other.

August 2002

Dear Claudia,

We are on 24 hour lockdown because a fight broke out this morning. I'm not sure what happened but a bloodied little Mexican emerged from the shower area after some thumping noises were heard. For once the guards were on it right away and locked the whole pod down.

Despite lockdown, we've been in good cheer. Rather than give us our chow room-service style, each cell was called down the stairs. This led to a kind of frenzied atmosphere. As each 3 cellmates went on their walk down the stairs to get their chow the rest of the pod hollered and screamed obscenities. Troll walked down the stairs with his bum hanging out to massive applause. When a guy who's always asking me to spoon with him on his bunk went down, we all screamed slut, slut, slut! Ah, the small joys of mocking the system. After chow another guard came in and threatened a 72 hour lockdown if we didn't shut up.

The chow was gross, love. I ate 2 cabbage sandwiches and had to eat an extra Snickers to fill up. I eat a Snickers for lunch because we get no lunch. I order 7 a week, so I'll run out early now, but I still have plenty of nuts left, so I won't starve.

Gravedigger didn't get a bond reduction so he's depressed. My Russian friend Lev is having to take his case to trial so he's also pretty depressed. Troll got granted mental health status, so he is in good spirits today.

August is here now and my court date. I wonder if I'll ever get to listen to the wiretap evidence. It would be nice to hear the full extent of the calls so that I can find out what was really said as opposed to the police's hang-the-bastard interpretations. I'm not expecting much from court. The lets-scare-the-new-inmates-to-death procedures are likely to continue. If the prosecutor could she would up the 25 years I'm facing to the death penalty. I expect some offer of many many years designed to scare me and make me feel like I'm getting a deal later on when they reduce it.

I L U forever,
Shaun XXX

Dearest loveliness,

So court was just a continuance yet again. Surprise, surprise. I've slept about 2 hours in the last 24 with the up-all-night court routine. At least Alan said I've been doing good work in these legal visits listening to the wiretaps. I feel more confident after listening to the calls because I'm not really on many of them or saying much. It puts things in perspective.

The guards played a prank on Wild Man this morning. Out of 50 inmates they chose him and Gerard Gravano, Sammy the Bull's son, to be chained together. Gerard seemed nice though and we got to ask him more questions about his Ecstasy ring case, which is similar to ours. Apparently, most of his co-defendants have agreed to work with the prosecutor. I hope that doesn't happen in my case. Alan said we'll find out when the prosecutor starts offering them sweetened deals to testify against me.

It's so hot in here tonight, it's insane. Sweat is just dripping down my face as I write this. It keeps dripping on the paper and fucking my writing up. I pray that they will fix the fans soon. I drink tonnes of water all day long. I'm so sick of the swamp environment and the new mosquito invasion. I'm going downstairs in a minute to do a few hundred push-ups with the boys. I'm trying to do more exercise each week despite the hot conditions. It just requires 3 showers a day. The exercise helps me stay sane.

After two nights of cabbage sandwiches I couldn't eat, tonight's meal was emu burger, soggy rice and corn on the cob. I took one bite of the emu burger and gave it away. I am out of Snickers, so I ate 2 rice sandwiches, so I would not starve.

The guys 2 cells down from us got searched today. They had to strip to their pinks and were then handcuffed and taken downstairs. As the guard searched, we heckled him. An hour later we were handcuffed and taken downstairs, and our cell was searched. They took our spare towels and sheets and stuff. We had to sit at the dining table in our pinks while the inmates tormented us for 10 minutes, yelling stuff like, "Look at his ass. Nice ass. Search his ass. It's in his ass!"

We are so bored at nights we name a letter then have to think of movies beginning with that letter. Each letter can last up to an hour, so we only do 1 or 2 letters a night.

Ta-ta!

Shaun

XXXXXXXXX

CHAPTER 18

To promote racial harmony following the riot, the guards move half of our pod to other towers, including Troll, Doug and Lev to Tower 2. Losing my cellmates and chess partner on the same day hurts. I've defined myself through friendships with relative strangers – primarily those three – and without their companionship buoying my spirit I'm lonely.

Into D10 the guards moved Busta Beatz, a young Mexican American who thinks he is a rap star and arrives with a pet cricket in a box. With a round face, slanted chestnut eyes and short spiky black hair, he looks like an Eskimo. His skin is an Etch A Sketch of mismatched tattoos, including smiley faces on his fingertips, BUSTA in rickety writing on one forearm and BEATZ on the other. After taking psychotropic medication, Busta Beatz circles the day room with a vacant stare and raps. His attorney has filed a Rule 11, so he is undergoing tests for severe mental impairment. Something the psychiatrist should take into consideration for Busta Beatz's Rule 11 is his love of red death. He can't get enough of it. It is common courtesy for anyone leaving red death to give it to Busta Beatz. He receives up to ten trays daily. By tray pickup, he is usually still eating, so he bags the red death, puts all the mustard he can scrounge into the bags, bites the corners off the bags and squeezes the red death into his mouth. This food lasts until the next day and makes our cell stink of rotting meat.

Curious about this bizarre character who delights in catching me off guard and pulling my trousers down, I ask him about his life.

"I'm state-raised. Foster homes," Busta Beatz says. "When I was eleven, I was kidnapped off the streets by a guy and a chick. They took me to a house and made me take crystal meth. They kept me there while the guy raped me and his friends raped me.

They'd suck me off and give me crystal and tell me everything was gonna be all right."

Repulsed, shocked, I say, "Hey, look, you don't have to tell me this stuff if you don't want. I was just–"

"It's all right. I can deal with it. They raped me for three days, then just dropped me off where they found me, so I went back to my foster parents. After that, I started to run away a lot. Did drugs. Sniffed a lot of paint. To buy paint and drugs, I shoplifted and robbed houses. I ran away to Phoenix where I didn't know anyone, ended up living on the streets, mostly West Van Buren. The Mexicans recruited me for their gang, Doble. They gave me a gun, so I'd go to 35th and Van Buren and stickup shoppers. Doble took half. I kept half for paint, drugs and fast food."

"So you were busted for sticking someone up?"

"No, for breaking into an empty house I was gonna sleep in."

I encourage Busta Beatz to get some books to improve his reading. He reads erotica to a mosquito he keeps on a small island of soggy toilet paper under an empty peanut-butter container. Worried the mosquito might escape, he rips a wing off. Feeling sorry for it, he attempts to feed it a morsel of Snickers, but the mosquito backs away.

"Bad mosquito! Don't walk that way! I'll have to punish you again."

He rolls six inches of toilet paper to the diameter of pencil lead and hovers it over the mosquito's rear. "You are not being a good slave! I'm going to have to spank your ass again! Here I come!" He taps the mosquito's rear with the toilet paper. "Good slave! No! Bad-bad-bad-bad slave! I'm gonna have to spank you again." He does this for two days until the mosquito dies – then he eats it.

During the night, lying stomach-down on the cell floor, he writes rap songs in the company of his cricket, which is unable to jump away as he's removed its legs. Practising raps in a loud whisper, he often wakes me up.

His most popular rap with the inmates is "Dead Body Hoes"

– about him defiling the corpses of famous women including Christina Aguilera and Britney Spears. The inmates demand that song every day.

When Claudia's next visit isn't announced at the prearranged time, I wait a few hours and call her.

"What're you doing home?" I ask, worried.

"They wouldn't let me in," she says.

"What?" I ask, furious.

"It's really hard to visit. The staff are always giving me a hard time, and today one in particular had a problem with the way I dressed," she says, on the verge of tears.

Has she been insulted or sexually harassed by a male guard? "Who is it? Which guard?"

"Some fat lady at the front with attitude from hell."

"What did she say?"

"She said don't try to come here no more unless I follow the rules for outfits and dress properly, so I started crying and asking her how I broke the rules, and she told me something along the lines of my shirt being too tight, you can't show the shape of your boobs. I want to show her the shape of my middle finger." We laugh. "I was dressed like a schoolteacher, and she's telling me my clothes are too formfitting."

"Take no notice. She's probably just jealous of your looks."

"Do you know if that counted as a visit?"

"I don't know. I'll file a grievance if it did."

"I want to come back down as soon as I can. What makes me mad is half the other people were wearing shorter or less clothes and tighter than me, and getting in no problem."

"I'm sure they'll let you in next time, love. I really appreciate what you go through."

Claudia is allowed to visit, but no matter what she wears that particular guard keeps harassing her.

CHAPTER 19

Young Marco is a new arrival to our pod. Within days of him moving into cell D15, he has the guards fetch two of his friends, Paulie and Hugo, from other towers to join him. No one knows how he's arranged this – I'm flabbergasted – but rumours soon spread that he is the son of a Mafioso and bribery is involved. Supposedly he's won trophies for kickboxing, but he doesn't look the fighting type. He is short, with an innocent expression and usually smiling. He has large affectionate eyes and eyelashes long enough for women to envy. With thick brown tresses and an olive complexion, he looks unique. From a distance, he seems unimpressive, but up close, his self-confidence sweeps you away. He's in for punching someone. We share the same attorney, Alan Simpson.

Lanky and with stately slicked-back salt-and-pepper hair, Argentinian Hugo idolises Marco and acts as his butler. The son of Italian immigrants, he speaks Italian, Spanish and English. Although in his forties, he's prone to emotional outbursts, which he puts down to his South American upbringing. He writes love letters to his wife signed in his own blood. He often weeps during church services and while listening to inmates tell sad stories. Facing deportation to Argentina, he claims he is blacklisted as a political dissident and the government will execute him on arrival. I pay him cookies to teach me Spanish, which I'm determined to master.

The stocky Italian New Yorker, Paulie, is Marco's goon. He has beady brown eyes, a boxer's flat nose and hairy fingers that generate a nutcracker of a handshake. Every few days, he vents his anger on Hugo much to our amusement. But, like Hugo, he is prone to crying, especially when talking about how much he misses his wife and kids.

Much to the astonishment of the guards and inmates, a drawing of the Italian flag and a sign goes up on the door of D15: LITTLE ITALY. Laughing aloud every time I see it, I can't believe my eyes.

Following the race riot, Gravedigger was moved to Tower 2, so we have no head of the whites. A white-boy meeting is convened, to which I'm uninvited. I know the whites are voting on two candidates: Marco and the skinhead with a tattoo of Hitler admiring Jews dying in a gas chamber on his chest. As most of the Aryans were moved from our pod following the race riot, Marco wins the vote by a narrow margin, a result that amazes and gladdens the other races and me. The skinhead is peeved. I fear jail movements are such that it's only a matter of time before the Aryans regroup and launch a coup d'état on Little Italy.

"Hey, England," Paulie says, entering D10 with a scowl that makes me squirm on my bunk. "I've come to you 'cause I know you're the only one in here that'll give me a straight-up fucking answer."

"What is it, Paulie? You know I'll help you if I can," I say, sitting up fast.

"You promise me you'll tell me the truth no matter what I fucking ask?"

"Of course I will."

"Well then. Tell me this then: do I have a fucking anger problem?" he asks, gazing sternly.

I push thoughts of *Why me?* away and search for something safe to say. "Here's what I think, Paulie. You're a really nice fella, but you do get a little excited every now and then. You're an emotional person and everyone likes you."

"So you're saying I do have a fucking anger problem then?" he snarls.

Stunned, I pause to find a better answer. "I try and stay as calm as possible during stressful situations, but I can see how you handle things a little differently and like to speak what's on your mind."

He gazes up as if in deep thought. "So are you saying I *do or do not* have a fucking anger problem?"

Cornered, I risk being more specific: "I'd say you don't have an anger problem, but you do get angrier than most of us." I study his face.

He scratches his chin. "So you're saying I do have *a little bit* of an anger problem?"

The jokey high-pitched way he said *a little bit* encourages me to mimic him. "Maybe *a little bit* of an anger problem, but nothing to lose any sleep over."

He leans towards me. I flinch. His hand appears to be coming for my face, but it finds my shoulder. Rocking my shoulder, he says, "Thanks, England. I really appreciate your honesty." Much to my relief, he marches away. He stomps down the day-room stairs towards Hugo, who's stood watching TV. He stops when his face is inches away from Hugo's and yells, "England said I don't have no fucking anger problem!" He thrusts his palms at Hugo's chest, knocking Hugo over a table. I feel partially responsible. "You don't know what you're fucking talking about!" Jabbing his index finger into Hugo's face, he yells, "Don't ever talk shit to me again about no fucking anger problem!"

Into D14, Marco moves another friend, Nick, a Golden Gloves boxer, who's won many fights in Tower 5. Slightly bigger than Paulie, his handsome friendly face makes him seem less fierce. He puzzles everyone by obsessively shaving his arms and the back of his hands with a stolen razor he keeps hidden in his trash bag. When not knocking people out, he's a mild-mannered erudite conversationalist. I discover he traded the stock market. We share finance books. Our fiancées befriend each other at Visitation.

When Nick invites me to his cell to drink the juice of stolen oranges freshly squeezed by Hugo, I figure we must be close enough for me to ask about his charges. "You seem out of place here, Nick. How'd you get busted?"

"I was set up by my fiancée's ex," Nick says, perched on the bottom bunk.

"How?"

"He's a rich guy, a martial-arts expert. He was hassling Susan, so I pulled out a knife, and he tried to kick it out of my hand and it got stuck in his foot. Not only did he call the cops and say I assaulted him, he filed a police report saying I stole $500,000 from him and filed an insurance claim to get the money."

"How come the cops aren't busting him for that?"

"The cops are in on it. He paid them off. So I've got armed robbery and kidnapping and all these charges for defending Susan."

Before my arrest I thought dirty cops were a product of moviemakers' imaginations, but now I believe otherwise.

"Did I ever tell you about my first day at Towers?" Nick asks.

"No. What happened?"

"You're gonna love this. After suffering two sleepless nights at The Horseshoe, they finally ship me to a cell at Towers. It's a nightmare. I'm exhausted, but it's still before lockdown. Anyway, I'm trying to sleep and I hear two black guys next door arguing over a pair of slippers. One says, 'Whose are these shoes?' The other says, 'Them's my motherfucking shoes.' Then the other one shouts, 'Well, they're my motherfucking shoes now!' I hear, 'Oh no, they isn't,' and 'Oh yes, they is.' I'm thinking, *What is this madness?* and then it gets worse. One says, 'You touch my motherfucking shoes and I'm gonna stab your ass.' The other says, 'You ain't gonna fucking stab nobody – no sirree!' 'Don't make me do it,' shouts the other. I hear, 'Don't lay one finger on my shoes!' and then I hear a scream, '*Aaggghhhhhh!*' and one of them comes rushing out of the cell with a golf pencil stuck in his chest. I'm thinking, *What am I doing here?*

"Anyway, it quietens down. I'm lying there, tired, but still too nervous to sleep, and then they call, 'Lockdown!' This homeless-looking guy enters my cell and gets on the bunk below me. I'm finally trying to get some shut-eye and I hear this weird noise. I did my best to ignore it, but on it went. I still can't sleep. I'm really curious, so I peep down over the end of my bunk and see this guy jerking off."

"Wow! I haven't had a celly like that yet," I say. "It's probably just a matter of time."

"Fortunately, Marco knew where I was. He got me moved to Tower 5 the next day. There was a lot of crazy violence in Tower 5, but nothing's as bad as the shock of your first few days in jail."

Due to Nick's association with Marco, the guards allow his visits with Susan to exceed the maximum time allowed. If Claudia were to arrive at Visitation with Susan, Nick says, he can have the guards extend my visits. Visitation time is golden, and I'm honoured to be included with Marco's perks. I desperately want to break the news to Claudia, but I can't on the recorded phone lines or in a letter the mail officer might intercept. I wait until her next visit. She is delighted. Showing up at the jail with Susan even puts an end to the harassment from the female guard.

During the extended visits, Nick and I monitor the guards. Whenever they are distracted, we lean forward and kiss our fiancées above newly-installed table divides. Those kisses are the highlight of our week.

"I got five kisses in," Nick says, walking back to Tower 6 after the strip searches.

"Only three," I say, grinning.

"Marco gets legal visits," Nick says.

"What do you mean?"

"Look, you can't tell anyone."

"You can trust me, Nick."

"He had a guard put his girlfriend into the computer as a legal visitor."

"You're kidding!"

"She came dressed in a business suit and they both got put in a private room."

"Lucky bastard! I can only imagine what he got up to."

"The guard told him not to go all out and get caught having sex, but they fiddled with each other and she gave him head."

Every week I hear an incredible story about Marco, but this

tops them all. "I've never seen an inmate run the guards like him."

"They won't do it for me. Marco has more pull. Don't mention this to anybody. We don't want to get that guard fired."

November 2002

Dear Mum and Dad,

I hope all is well over the pond. I'm sitting on the arse-aching steel stool with my tiny golf pencil.

Someone in cell 15 is singing "Rudolph, the Red Nose Reindeer" to the whole pod. The sense of humour in the American prison system is far more acute than in the average American sit-com. There are some hilarious inmates, a lot of cynics and much black humour. Something that breaks the ice on an otherwise bleak pond. There is hope for America after all. Some of them are bloody funny.

The stress of not knowing what is going to happen to me is psychological torture. It's the worst part of being an un-sentenced inmate. I dream every night of personal disasters. I dream of being chased, confined, killed. I dream of nothing else.

I really appreciate your kind acts, your love and support, and I am deeply sorry for the emotional trauma this has put you through. I am lucky though to have been brought to focus on what really matters most to me. You have saved my life or a good portion of it and have flown half way round the world to support me. You have given me inspiration when there was only despair. I have extra love for Karen for coming to see me. She has truly touched my heart. This situation has completely changed my outlook on life. Gone is my complacency. I now realise how precious every moment is in the outside world. To suffer this pain, to bring me closer to my family and make me enjoy my future time with them is but a small price to pay. Maybe all of this is necessary for this purpose.

Hopefully things will be resolved soon and I will be getting on with my new life, with Claudia as my wife, happily trading stocks. That is all I ask for.

Thank you so much for everything,
Love Shaun

CHAPTER 20

I wouldn't wish jail on any of my friends, but it's always a pleasure to run into one in here. I'm delighted to see Joey Crack, whom I know from Tempe, in Tower 6's punishment pod. As a favour to me, Marco uses his influence with the guards to move Joey Crack into my cell. Emaciated by drug abuse, Joey Crack arrives with a face as gaunt as an Afghan hound's. He is taller than me, high-spirited and full of strange quirks. He shocks the inmates and guards by inserting the circular bottoms of black chess pieces into his ear lobes as if he's following the customs of voodoo tribesmen.

Joey Crack likes to alter the jail-issued postcards that show Sheriff Joe Arpaio in publicity poses. On the bottom bunk, I watch Joey Crack on the concrete, surrounded by tiny body parts he's cut from magazines with a stolen razor, sticking a pair of breasts to Sheriff Joe's jowls. His glue is soap shavings mixed with the high-fructose corn-syrup jelly that comes in the Ladmo bags. His cards are in high demand. Most of them make it out of the jail – the guards usually laugh at them – but some are intercepted, deemed illegal due to the alterations and Joey Crack receives numerous verbal reprimands for promoting contraband.

After the evening chow, Joey Crack is pacing, warming up to describe a fight he saw when Little Italy file into the cell. The Italians appear dapper in new bee stripes they've bribed from the laundry officer.

"What's up, fellas!" Marco says.

"What's up, dogs!" I say, offering my fist from the bottom bunk.

"What's up, Joey Crack and England!" Paulie says, grinning and winking at me.

"What's up, dogs!" Joey Crack says.

After fist bumping, we urge Joey Crack to tell the story.

"Yeah, Crack, how many guys has Kyle made shit themselves?" Paulie asks.

"I wasn't present when Kyle knocked the shit out of those guys. I missed those gems," Joey Crack says. "I was, however, front and centre for many good smashings he inflicted. My personal favourite is the one I call The Naked Cage Match, which I must admit, I somewhat helped instigate."

"How did you manage that?" Paulie asks.

Marco takes the stool. Settling in, the rest lean against the wall.

"It was gonna happen regardless, but I had to put my own two cents in to make things more entertaining. I don't remember what the original beef was about, but then again what does it really matter – Kyle just loves to scrap!"

"Hold on a minute," I say. "What's Kyle look like?"

"That's the thing," Joey Crack says. "He's just a skinny youngster. He doesn't look like much of anything, so these big dudes pick on him, and he always smashes the shit out them. So anyway, there's this guy who's having some kind of problem with Kyle. Kyle takes this guy into a cell and touches him up. Seconds later they both emerge and this guy has some bumps and bruises, so we make him get into the shower to clean himself up. When he gets out, wrapped in only a little pink towel, he proceeds to tell us that he's OK and that Kyle hits like a girl!"

"Oh no!" I say.

"We know exactly where this is going," Marco says, grinning.

"Saying that was hilarious enough considering he's standing before us with his face swelling black and blue. But he also tells us that if he had been ready for it, Kyle wouldn't have stood a chance. We laughed our assess off and informed Kyle that he had been incompetent in not properly smashing his opponent. The guy's walking around protected only by his little pink towel, talking all kinds of shit about Kyle. We warn the guy that he might want to get dressed ready for the next round, but of course he fails to listen. Kyle comes rolling in full of piss and vinegar ready to do battle and make up for not doing things right the first time. Then suddenly – *bang!* Kyle knocks the fool for a loop and we all spill out of the cell in order to make room for this little rumble. As expected the towel falls to the floor, and now we've got ourselves a naked cage match!" Joey Crack's voice intensifies. "Kyle throws the guy into a headlock and proceeds to beat his face into disfigurement. You've never seen anything so funny as this little naked man grunting like a baboon in distress trying to escape from Kyle's fists of fury. Lucky for the little bastard, Kyle didn't go too far. He simply needed to show him that not only could he beat him down once but he could do it twice, and with the challenger being naked, he put icing on the cake by keeping a straight face the entire time."

We laugh and bond over stories, filling the cell with camaraderie. In this lonely place, I'm delighted to feel part of something and grateful for their friendship. Joey Crack tells stories about the Wild Ones. Intrigued, Paulie adds that he's heard about Wild Man and asks to arrange a meeting with him. I send a note smuggled through the jail by inmates to Wild Man, requesting his presence at the next Catholic mass to meet Little Italy.

CHAPTER 21

The high demand for Catholic mass is not from prisoners seeking absolution from their sins, but from those eager to exchange gossip and drugs with their friends from other towers. Problem is only ten are allowed to attend from each forty-five man pod. When the guards announce, "Catholic mass! First ten at the sliding door only!" dozens charge for the exit, leading to squabbling, pushing, shoving and occasional bloodshed. Fortunately, when it comes to the battle for the ten spaces, my friendship with Marco gives me an advantage. Thanks to inside information, Marco often knows the actions of the guards in advance. Ten minutes before the guards are due to announce Catholic mass, Marco tells Joey Crack and me to line up at the door with Little Italy. With the Italians eager to meet Wild Man, we set off.

In a black cassock and white alb, tall bespectacled Father O'Donnell greets us at the door of the windowless religious-services room, but he's not his usual chirpy self. We rush past him and secure the back row of plastic chairs. When Tower 2 arrives, Wild Man gives me a bear hug and sits in-between Joey Crack and me. The seats fill quickly. The latecomers stand.

"This is Wild Man," I say to the Italians.

"Ah! So this is Wild Man! We've heard so much about you," Paulie says in his gruffest voice. He leans across me to shake Wild Man's hand, pressing my stomach so forcefully that my seat tilts back.

"In the name of the Father, the Son and the Holy Spirit…" The gossipers hush as the introductory rites begin. As the mass progresses, Father O'Donnell's serious demeanour becomes more apparent. Before the distribution of Communion, he explains why. His mother is on her deathbed in hospital. He asks us to pray for the restoration of her health. Her illness arose unexpect-edly. Describing her condition, Father O'Donnell weeps. Tears stream from Hugo. His sobbing attracts attention. He buries his face in his hands and bows his head. Marco and Nick turn teary eyed. Marco makes the sign of the cross and closes his eyes. Paulie weeps openly, rubs his eyes, dries them off, calms down, looks at Hugo and weeps again. Marco pats Hugo on the back. The more Father O'Donnell sobs, the more the audience reacts. Some weep. Others offer sympathy. I feel moved, but not enough to cry. The crying peaks when Father O'Donnell starts sputtering. He pauses to ground himself and travels the rows, feeding the men Commu-nion wafers, which, due to our perpetual starvation, are devoured rapidly. My stomach growls. When Father O'Donnell reaches the back row, Hugo declares that we'll pray for his mother and she will recover. Revisiting the subject of Father O'Donnel's mother provokes another round of tears from Little Italy.

My saliva is gushing by the time I receive my wafer, the only fresh food in the jail. It tastes like cardboard with a wheaty over-tone. To appease my stomach, I gulp it down. As Father O'Don-nell returns to the front, I fantasise about snatching the rest of the wafers from him and cramming them into my mouth.

"What's everyone crying for?" Wild Man says. "Look how old he is. His mum must have one foot in the grave by now. She's probably 100-years old." The congregation tsk-tsking only en-courages Wild Man. He spits an intact wafer into his hand and puts it over an eye like a pirate's patch. "Look at me! Ha-ha-ha-ha-ha!" Vibrations from Wild Man's maniacal laughter penetrate my chest.

Prisoners stop praying and crane their necks to watch Wild Man.

"You're all fucking sinners! You don't fool me! You're all going straight to hell!" His laughter draws more attention.

Inmates elbow each other until most have turned around to watch Wild Man. Reactions from Little Italy range from an ap-palled Hugo to an amused Paulie.

Wild Man removes the wafer from his eye and launches it at Father O'Donnell, who is approaching the front of the room with his back facing us. The onlookers' heads follow the trajectory of the Body of Christ as it ascends steadily. When it skims the ceiling, a few men say, "Wow!" The skim should have knocked it off course, but it continues, undaunted, descending at a steady rate, arcing relentlessly towards the priest as if under the guidance of an invisible evil hand. When Father O'Donnell places down the ciborium, a few arms from the front row shoot up but fail to stop the wafer from hitting the priest square in the back like a perfectly aimed Frisbee. The congregation gasps. Wild Man says, "Bull's eye!" The worshippers shake their heads or snicker but none challenge Wild Man. Nick and Marco are speechless. In a show of disapproval, Hugo moves his chair to the front row.

"He's a fucking lunatic," Paulie says, grinning. He whispers in my ear, "He's worse in real life than in Joey Crack's stories."

Fortunately, Father O'Donnell doesn't see the wafer roll across the floor and settle under the table he's set up with holy water and pamphlets. When mass ends, Hugo discreetly pockets it.

Wild Man continues his antics in the corridor. "Fucking church, eh? That priest can kiss my arse!" He drops his pink boxers and moons the prisoners, failing to notice the arrival of a female guard.

"You're on report! Give me your ID!" she yells, furrowing her brow. She calls backup, who handcuff Wild Man and take him away.

The following week, Wild Man is still in lockdown, unable to join the rowdy cheering in Catholic mass when a joyous Father O'Donnell announces his mother is out of hospital and on the mend.

CHAPTER 22

By the end of 2002, Marco and his Praetorian Guards seem to have more control over Tower 6 than the jail administration. Every day, the guards choose Little Italy to serve chow and turn a blind eye when they steal the leftover Ladmo bags and trays and divvy the food out to the heads of all of the races. They are applying Troll's law – *he who controls the food controls the prisoners* – on a mass scale. Business is booming for the "two-for-one store" Marco runs out of D15, which enables inmates to buy commissary provided they repay double on "store day" – the day of the week our commissary orders are delivered. Whenever the goon squad is due to raid our pod, Marco knows in advance. During such searches, the guards confiscate our extra clothing, towels and sheets, but Marco simply gets the next shift to walk Little Italy to the property room. They return with mountains of fresh laundry, grinning triumphantly.

Marco deals with disgruntled inmates sympathetically. He presides over the kangaroo court of white-inmate conflicts, and when he banishes inmates from our pod or decrees they must settle things by fighting, most of the prisoners comment on how fairly he's adjudicated. His power is such he can have the guards move any inmate in or out. He is inundated with requests from inmates wanting to move into our pod because it's humming with the vibrancy of Little Italy.

CHAPTER 23

Settling into a disciplined study and exercise regimen helps time pass. Lying on my bunk at angles that minimise the discomfort of my bedsores, I read for hours. At first, the abundance of time to read rekindles my teenage obsession with stock-market books. But a prisoner urges me to read two novels: George Orwell's *1984* and Aldous Huxley's *Brave New World*. Before my arrest, I thought reading fiction was frivolous. *To Kill a Mockingbird* was the last novel I read – required reading in high school. But in the dystopian jail environment, I relate to Orwell's Big Brother and Room 101. Reading Huxley, I see parallels in my life with the characters taking grams of the hallucinogenic drug soma and orgying. These books dramatize two things I constantly dwell on: the excesses of my lifestyle and the justice system.

My sister is worried about me losing my sanity in the jail. A practitioner of yoga, she mails me *Yoga Made Easy* by Howard Kent. Although grateful, I hide the book under my mattress out of fear the prisoners will see it and brand me a sissy. Over several weeks, the book gathers dust. In her letters, my sister keeps asking if I've tried yoga. My guilt grows. *If I try the exercises one time and don't like them I can at least tell her I gave yoga a go.* I wait until my cellmates are downstairs and retrieve the book. On the floor beyond the doorway and the toilet is just enough space to do yoga. I try several basic postures to the best of my ability, bending this way and that and rotating my spine, worried that I'm going to pull a muscle in my stiff body. Holding the positions for up to one minute is harder than it looks in the book. Sweating in forward bend, I strain to touch my toes, but my fingers refuse to go any further than my shins.

At the end, thankful the routine is over and no one saw me

doing it, I lie on my back in corpse pose and close my eyes. For the first time in jail, I feel all of the anxiety over my safety, the conditions and the uncertainty surrounding my case melt away. In particular, my shoulders are so relaxed that all of the tension concentrated in that area and the back of my neck feels as if it's oozing out. I'm breathing slower and the constant worries have emptied from my mind. It feels so good, I stay there longer than the few minutes the book recommends, tuned into my heartbeat and out of the mayhem in the day room just a few feet away. *How's it possible to feel this good without drugs?* After yoga, I remain relaxed for a few hours until the worries and anxieties resume.

Craving more of the yoga fix, I abandon my inhibitions and start doing it daily. Fortunately, my cellmates spend most of their time in the day room watching TV or playing cards. I'm soon proficient in postures such as cobra, forward bend, cat, dog, side bend and seated spinal twist. I yearn to master the harder ones such as headstand.

At the end of each routine, I try to spend a few minutes meditating, but meditation doesn't make any sense. The book instructs me to sit cross-legged and to try and halt the flow of my thoughts, but every time the discussion in my head slows down, a thought intrudes and my brain speeds back up. I'm clueless about meditation, but the physical side of yoga is working so well, I resolve to persist with the mental. Over the weeks, I make little progress with meditation. Having lived such a fast-paced life, one of the hardest parts is having the patience to sit for longer than a few minutes. Just when I'm managing to still my brain, a thought pops up about something pressing – I need to tell my lawyer this, I need to write to that person… – and before I know it my body is springing off the floor to handle what's on my mind. To keep such thoughts at bay, I pay attention to my breath by saying to myself, *in, out, in, out…* After a few minutes of using this technique, I stop monitoring my breath, and my mind goes quiet for a little bit at first, increasing over time.

When Marco invites me to work out with little Italy, I feel

honoured. For weights, we use the mop bucket. By attaching a towel to the mop handle we perform rowing, curling and shoulder exercises. Other than Mordhorst, most of the guards don't mind us working out with the bucket in the corner of the day room. Every now and then one yells through the speakers, "No working out with the cleaning supplies!" which usually means his superior officer has entered the tower. Chatting while exercising, I get to know Marco and his friends better. With people in the dayroom noticing that I'm working out with them, I feel somewhat safer as no one messes with Marco's inner circle.

CHAPTER 24

The glut of drugs and cigarettes in Tower 6 is thanks in part to the keystering skills of the car thief Magoo, a tall bespectacled hippy with greasy straggly hair and a spattering of crystal-meth sores on his face. He prides himself on his ability to stuff long packages into his anal cavity. Magoo sets himself up as a mule for hire. His fee: a percentage of what he smuggles in. At Visitation, I watch Magoo observing the guards through thick-lensed glasses. When a querying visitor distracts Officer Green, Magoo receives cellophane-wrapped packages under the table, which disappear into his trousers. He doesn't even flinch as he deposits them deep enough in his behind so as not to peek out during the strip search. He receives numerous visits each week from strangers bearing such packages and never gets caught or sent to a dry cell to crap, even though after each visit he walks in a bandy-legged leaning-back way as if he's been speared in the behind.

Our sense of community spirit rises when we adopt a needy youngster named Slopester as our son. Eighteen-year-old Slopester was living on the streets of Sunnyslope, a crack and crystal meth hub of Phoenix, with his younger sister. With his mouth closed, he's handsome. But he smiles constantly, displaying a graveyard of brown teeth. Caught shoplifting clothes from Dillard's in Paradise Valley Mall, he'd pulled a butterfly knife on an employee. Arrested in the parking lot, he was charged with assault with a dangerous weapon. In minimum-security, the gangs had preyed upon him. After receiving numerous tickets for fighting, he was reclassified to Towers jail. Marco puts him to work offering a hand-laundry service. The jail replaces our laundry once a week, but in the meantime our underwear and towels collect filth and sweat. For one item of candy, Slopester hand-washes two items of clothing. "Bleach is free," he titters as he closes his sales. Prior to visits from Claudia, I take advantage of his laundry service. I also pay him to barter for state cheese. He brings me so many oily processed slices that they repeat on me for hours. Even though I'm ravenous, I have to tell him to stop because the cheese is making me ill. Needed and cared for, Slopester blossoms. We rejoice to see him happy. Other youngsters notice his growing importance and he becomes the king of the waifs.

The atmosphere grows increasingly circuslike. Newcomers add to the furore. Kyle arrives from lockdown. His last fight had yet again resulted in his opponent crapping. Upon regaining consciousness, his opponent had been ordered by the head of the whites to clean the crap off the floor. Kyle and a skinny black inmate do daily back-flip shows off the chow tables. The competition between them delights us.

On Christmas Eve, we parade around singing "Felice Navidad" and our favourite Jumping Bill songs. A few days later, seeking adventure outside of the pod, Marco takes most of the whites to Muslim services. We outnumber the Muslim congregation. Anticipating a race riot, the frightened imam radios the guards, but Marco settles the imam down, sends the guards packing and encourages the imam to teach us the Arabic alphabet. At the end of the service, we kneel with the Muslims in prayer to Allah. The imam invites us back.

With exuberance running rampant, Joey Crack takes things to another level. Desirous of a Prince Albert piercing, he sharpens the end of a paperclip, spends a few seconds studying his penis and sticks the paperclip into his frenulum and out of the urethra. Undeterred by the blood trickling into the toilet, he shoves a tiny silver bar through the hole he's made. I never imagined I'd see the day when I'd stop what I was doing to stare at a man's penis, but it's hard to concentrate on writing when such things are going on. Sitting on the stool, I'm amazed he has the nerve and/or insanity to gore his precious organ. Some inmates are astonished, others sickened as he walks onto the balcony waving red hands, blood dripping from his penis, with an intoxicated look in his eyes. "Look, fellas, I've put a bar in my cock, and 'cause the bar's straight it feels like it's ripping me apart. So what we've got to do, fellas, is, I'm gonna put my cock between the cell door and the wall, and I want someone to put their fingers in the same spot, 'cause we need to close the door on my cock, and hopefully the door will bend the jewellery, but I don't want to completely close the door and crush my cock, so if one of you guys has your fingers in the same spot then we can judge how far we can close the door without anyone's fingers or cock getting hurt. Got it? Who'll put their fingers in the door and who'll slowly shut it?"

I'm too queasy to volunteer. Slopester puts his fingers between the door and the wall. Joey Crack inserts his penis and positions the silver bar, so that the force from the closing door will bend it. Magoo slowly closes the door. The jewellery slips twice. Joey Crack's penis appears to be crushed between the door and the wall. It's hard to watch. I press my legs together as if it's happening to me. The audience in the day room gasps. The jewellery holds steady during the third attempt and the bar bends.

"That's fucking great! My cock doesn't feel like it's being ripped apart any more, but it's gonna hurt like hell when I take a piss! Thanks, fellas!"

December 2002

Dear Mum and Dad,

Thanks for the Xmas card. Very groovy. I hope that everyone had a merry Xmas and a Happy New Year. It was good to talk to you both last Wednesday.

So the madness in the courts continues. It amazes me how things are developing. It is obvious I was arrested without a case prepared in the hope that they would find evidence and hence be able to form a case.

The prosecutor is now trying to stop Alan from playing the wiretaps. Isn't that the evidence against me? Isn't it a good thing for the prosecution to hear the evidence against me? In normal circumstances one would think so. This action confirms that they created a case by selecting a misleading choice of wiretaps and are now worried about being exposed.

Apart from court, everything plods along as usual. I've now been in Towers the longest in my pod out of the whites.

I talked to Claudia about St Bede's for our wedding and she sounded very excited with that idea. She said she has seen a picture of St Bede's already. I'm so glad Karen and mum really liked Claudia when they met her. I feel like I'm doing the right thing this time.

The pod is freakier than ever in its composition of inmates right now. There's John the Baptist, a skinny 6ft 4 inch hippy/Jesus-looking type who stores a diamond in his arse. Three Sopranos live in cell 15 and there's a guy here who runs the Aryan Church. Yes it makes for an interesting Xmas.

Sometimes I think I've gone completely mad and that I'm actually in a mental hospital but don't really know it. The vibe here is mighty amusing. John the Baptist runs around screaming "Repent!" and another inmate makes a realistic voice of a baby crying all day long. It fooled the guards. Good character building stuff.

Love you loads,
Shaun x

CHAPTER 25

Under Little Italy's rule some prisoners are acting as if jail isn't all that bad. I fear what's going to happen when the good times run out. In the New Year, the mood shifts.

Shortly before lockdown, the Mexicans are tossing a grapefruit. A poor lob results in a missed catch. The grapefruit flies over the head of its intended recipient and hits Magoo in the leg. In accordance with the convict code of not backing down from any act of aggression, Magoo retaliates by lobbing the grapefruit at the Mexicans. Four of them stretch but fail to catch it. It travels over them and hits their leader, Carlo, in the head as he is playing spades. After the shock wears off Carlo's face, he casts Magoo a stare of death. The Mexicans advance towards Magoo.

Watching what's unfolding, Marco dashes between the Mexicans and Magoo. "Look, he never meant to hit you with the grapefruit like that. And I apologise for it being a wood that threw it." Turning to face Magoo, he yells, "You need to apologise!"

"Nobody is telling me what to fucking do!" Magoo stomps up the stairs to his cell.

The Mexicans look at Marco, who says, "Please don't get involved. This is white-boy business now."

The next morning, I'm under the stairs doing pull-ups when I notice Marco's crew gathering at either side of Magoo's door. Officer Mordhorst is just finishing walking our pod. As soon as he exits, Paulie enters Magoo's cell and the familiar thumping noises commence. A few minutes later, Paulie emerges, panting like an exhausted pit bull. Everyone in the day room looks up at Magoo's door. Magoo appears, dishevelled, battered, minus his glasses, swaying like a drunkard. "What the fuck was that all about?" he yells. He turns, but not in time to see a right hook hit his chin.

The fist belongs to a muscular Mexican American covered in Aztec tattoos who took a dislike to Magoo prior to the grapefruit incident. The Mexican American slams Magoo's head against the iron railing running along the top tier with such a clunk that many prisoners gasp. He knees Magoo in the groin. Magoo collapses on the balcony. Having seen so much violence in the jail, I'm becoming desensitised. Instead of fear and apprehension, I'm watching out of curiosity. As Magoo is conscious and alive, I mark the violence low on the scale of things that happen in here.

"You need to roll your shit up!" Paulie yells at Magoo.

Magoo grabs the iron railing, pulls himself up, staggers into his cell, gathers his property and re-emerges with his face starting to swell. From the stairs, he yells for the guards in the control tower to open the sliding door. The guards let him out, but don't lock us down – the normal procedure when someone is smashed. The look of complicity on Officer Alston's face implies he knows what's going on and is accommodating Marco.

Magoo is in the corridor waiting to be rehoused when Slopester struts up to the Mexican American who walloped Magoo and says, "That was white-boy business. You Chicanos shouldn't be getting in the mix. That was for us woods to handle."

"So fucking what? Are you gonna fucking do something about it?" the Mexican American snarls.

Inmates usually go into the cell under the stairs to fight, but the Mexican American and Slopester trade blows in the day room. Marco's Praetorian Guards charge over and stop the fight. Minutes later, the Mexican American and Slopester share a reconciliatory cigarette in a cell.

A few days later, Paulie returns from Visitation boasting he just smashed a sex offender in a holding cell. Later on, he swears at a female guard who is reprimanding him. For disrespecting staff, he is transferred to the maximum-security Madison Street jail to go on the loaf program – two meals a day of leftover food cooked into burnt bread that smells like shoe polish.

"Now Magoo's gone, I've been asked to take some visits," Joey Crack says.

"You really want to risk getting busted bringing drugs in, getting another five years added to your sentence?" I ask, concerned about my friend.

"It's just tobacco."

"That's what they tell you! Think this through, man. It's not worth the risk."

"I already gave them my word."

"Who?"

"I've been asked not to tell you. I've said too much already."

"I don't know, Joey Crack. I'd pull out if I were you."

Joey Crack fails to return from Visitation. Rumours start. I'm devastated. Listening to prisoners in the day room bemoan the fate of their drugs while expressing no concern for Joey Crack, I guess who hired him. Angry with them, I pace the cell expecting the goon squad to raid my home at any moment because Joey Crack is busted. A few hours later, Joey Crack shows up grinning, erasing my bad mood.

"Everyone's saying you got busted," I say.

"Listen to this. I go to the visit and the guards are suspicious from the get-go 'cause I don't know who my visitor is, and she usually visits someone else. Anyway, I find her. She's some sketched-out twitchy tweaker. She tells me the package can't be delivered 'cause it's too big, and she doesn't have it with her."

"Good."

"I was relieved 'cause after speaking to you, I wasn't wanting it to happen. It seemed out of sorts, and my gut feeling was not to do it. So we're at the table for all of three minutes when a guard comes over and says, 'I think there's something going on that shouldn't be.' They know her face 'cause she usually visits some guy who has non-contact visits. They tell her I'm gonna be searched, and if anything is found on me she'll be charged with promoting prison contraband and our personal favourite: conspiracy. I'm laughing 'cause we have nothing on us. I'm stripped naked and nothing is found. Then a female is brought to search my visitor. I'll never forget the look on her face! She was truly scared beyond all control. Her jaw was twitching, her lips doing something I can't put into words and her hands were everywhere. I realised then that she might have told me a fib. They search her. I'm told to get against the wall, interlace my fingers on top of my head and slowly move to my knees. Later, I found out she got busted with meth, tobacco and weed."

"Your new friends in here were more concerned about the package getting seized than your welfare."

"I know. The main guy's more concerned about losing his dope than his girlfriend getting busted and going to jail. It would have been ugly if she'd passed the package. Never again. No way."

Officer Mendoza appears at the cell door. "Roll y...y...your shit up! You're g...g...going back to the hole."

"For what?" Joey Crack asks.

"Conspiracy and susp...sp...icion...o...o...on of attempting to smuggle drugs int...int...into the jail system."

My bad mood returns. I fear the consequences for Joey Crack and dread playing the cellmate lottery. Making matters worse, Busta Beatz is moved out with no explanation given. I brace to receive two new cellmates.

CHAPTER 26

Receiving new cellmates involves adjusting your routine to accommodate theirs. I prefer cellmates who spend a lot of time in the day room, so I can concentrate on reading, writing and doing yoga in the cell. By luck, I receive two such cellmates.

Tiny Honduras has short black hair, friendly brown eyes and speaks little English. He is a coyote: paid to escort illegal aliens into Arizona from Mexico, part of a Mexican Mafia operation that uses cell phones to communicate with lookouts stationed on mountaintops in order to avoid Border Patrol agents. He was arrested for allegedly holding at gunpoint a freshly-smuggled Mexican who'd refused to pay the transportation fee. Charged with armed robbery, kidnapping and extortion, Honduras is facing fifteen years, yet is calm about his case. "*Tengo suerte!*" – I am lucky! – he often remarks. His Mafia boss hired him an attorney, who advised him not to sign a plea bargain or to cooperate. He spends most of the day out of the cell with the Mexicans. To improve my Spanish, I often join them in the mornings watching soap operas called telenovelas. The racists ask, "Why're you celling with a wetback?" I ignore them. Some gripe when I watch TV with the Mexicans, which is odd because the most watched TV show by all of the races is *Caliente* – a dance-music show on every Saturday morning, so esteemed that prisoners fiddle with the wonky TV set five minutes before the show begins to tune it in as best as possible. Even the neo-Nazis can't resist the lure of señoritas in skimpy bikinis shaking their hips to house music. Having increasingly noticed that the rules of racial division are dropped whenever it's convenient for the gangs, I'm starting to play around the gang rules, just like I've learned to work my way around the guards' rules.

My second cellmate, Stalker, is in his mid-thirties and slightly bigger than Honduras, but made of much frailer stuff. After the breakdown of his twelve-year marriage, he went on a crystal-meth and alcohol binge. He started following his wife around and leaving threatening messages, which she played to the police who charged him with stalking. Unlike Honduras, Stalker never ceases fretting about his case. Sometimes, he breaks down and sobs. Repeatedly, I reassure him that a prison sentence isn't the end of his life. Even Honduras pitches in with, "*No problema. Poco tiempo.*" No problem. You won't get much time.

Stalker delights in plaguing us with his farts. He claims to intentionally withhold his farts all day so he can unleash them on us after lockdown at night. He signals their arrival with fits of giggling. He lets one round off and there'll be silence until the stink is almost gone. Then he lets loose again. Time-released farts. They are especially bad after he's eaten red death. The best Honduras and I can do to protect ourselves is to hide our heads under our sheets, but the potency of his farts is such that defensive manoeuvres only minimise our suffering. With his average run of farts lasting close to an hour, we have to surface at some point. Through this torment I learn some less polite Spanish phrases:

"*Pedoro.*" – Fart man.

"*Culo mugroso.*" – Filthy ass.

"*Culo sucio.*" – Dirty ass.

Stalker's rapid-cycling bipolar disorder is such that one minute he's spitting out farts and giggling himself purple, and the next he's telling us through trembling lips how he needs to slash his wrists so he doesn't have to go to the big house. I read his paperwork. Sexually abused as a child, he'd used alcohol and drugs to self-medicate multiple mental disorders. I encourage him to sign up for the few classes available. Worried about him, I repeatedly try to coach him into thinking positively. I tell him that a prison sentence will put the brakes on his cycle of self-destruction and enable him to sort his thoughts out. "I know that everything's gonna be all right. I'm lucky to have you two buddies as cellmates," Stalker says, raising my hopes for him, only to threaten suicide ten minutes later.

January 2003

My Darling,

I'm riding the rack because my bum is so sore. Today I woke up with massive swollen tonsils, and screamed, "Get me out of this bloody place!" The day started with "Chow's in the house!" Tuesday is peanut butter. I was hungry because last night I gave my whole macaroni tray away for a pack of chocolate chip cookies. After grabbing my Ladmo bag, I put it on my bunk, and jumped in the shower (which is finally fixed). I was first in the shower and went back to the cell to eat the chow. My cellies had already eaten theirs and were back asleep. No sooner had I finished chow and lay down to read, they shouted "CAB class! Roster only!" Returning from Confronting Addictive Behaviour, they stripped us of our boxers and we pleaded for recreation but to no avail. I then hopped on my rack, and did a Spanish crossword and conjugated some Spanish verbs. I ate an orange and some peanut butter. So I was studying and they locked us down for the plumber. He worked and we had a headcount. When they took us off lockdown, there was an immediate scramble for the phones, so I'm sorry I wasn't able to call you. Shift change came and we commenced working out. We have to wait for shift change because the morning guards will not let us work out with our tops off. After working out, came, "Chow's in the house! Diets first!" Burnt veggie burgers. I soaked them in the sink, and they were so burnt I had to swill water in my mouth as I ate them. I hope my burnt veggie burger breath has gone for your visit tomorrow.

See you soon,
Shaun XXX

Ps) Last night I discussed Stalker's revolting farts (*los pedos*) with Honduras. We cracked up and couldn't stop laughing.

CHAPTER 27

"Everyone, roll up! All medium-security inmates in Tower 6 are moving to Towers 2 and 5!" Officer Mordhorst announces.

"Moving all of us! I don't believe it!" I scramble off the bottom bunk.

"They're gonna split us up and we're gonna have fucked-up cellies," Stalker says. "I really like you guys."

"It's as good as it gets." I join the worried prisoners gathering on the balcony.

The guards assign my downstairs neighbours to various pods and cells in Towers 2 and 5. Everyone is upset with the move except for Little Italy. *Are they up to something?* The prospect of being rehoused and having to adjust to new cellmates has me on edge.

Officer Alston announces, "Everyone on the top tier, grab your shit, you're moving to the top tier in Tower 2, A pod."

The tension on the faces of the men on the balcony melts into incredulous smiles. Marco winks at me. *He must have arranged for the top tier to be moved as one, so Little Italy will remain intact.*

The upper tier in 2A is empty due to a race riot ignited by the Aryans. As we move in, the Aryans from the lower tier announce a mandatory white-boy meeting. We fall under the rule of their existing head of the whites: Iron Eagle. Dreading the new rules the Aryans will enforce, I join the white-boy meeting in a crowded cell downstairs. Marco is present, meekly sizing up the Aryans, no doubt running the calculations for his next power play.

"Any woods kicking it with the other races are gonna get smashed," says Iron Eagle, a musclebound thirty-something with a shaved head and an angry expression stamped on his square face. There is a big swastika on his chest, surrounded by a pattern of white-supremacy tattoos. "That means no playing cards with them, no going in cells smoking with them, no selling commissary to them. If you've got money on your books, you need to break bread with your own race, help the indigent white boys out. Also, we heard some fucked-up rumour about a bunch of woods in Tower 6 going to Muslim services. If you woods know who the race traitors are, we wanna know about it."

The eyes of Iron Eagle and his torpedoes roam over us. My face heats up. No one volunteers that all of us new arrivals had gone to Muslim services with Marco that day.

The next day, Iron Eagle corners me in my cell. "Hey, dog, how about kicking in some store for the indigent woods?"

"Sure, dog," I say, resting my golf pencil on the table. "What do you want me to order?" I have no problem helping out penniless inmates. I remember how strangers offered me stamps, writing supplies and hygiene products when I arrived at Tower 6.

"Some toothpaste, so they don't have to use that state shit."

"I'll put it on my commissary list."

"How about hooking me up with something to eat, wood?" The violently hungry look in his eyes is common in the jail.

Feeding him will be seen as weakness. He'll be back for more every day. If I don't comply, he might take it personally. "I'm low on store. How about I order you a rack of cookies for store day?" I've agreed but on my terms. He'll have to wait a week for the cookies to be delivered, and with the friction between the Aryans and Little Italy, a lot could happen in a week.

As the week progresses, I'm dismayed to see the hostility of the Aryans towards Little Italy increase. The Aryans have slightly greater numbers, so Marco goes on a recruitment drive. He receives a note from the head of his Praetorian Guard, Paulie, who's finished the loaf program at the Madison Street jail and wants to be moved from Tower 5. When Marco moves Paulie in the next day, I'm delighted. Paulie weeps in Marco's arms and goes cell to cell on the upper tier bear-hugging everyone. Crushing me with his body, he says Marco needs to speak to me. Eager to find out what Marco wants, I follow Paulie to Marco's cell.

"How many people have been arrested in your case?" Marco asks.

"I stopped counting. They arrested them in groups. The last group was thirty-something and they're still arresting people."

"You've got co-defendants all over Towers?"

"Yes."

"And you're their ringleader?"

"Alleged ringleader."

"Yes, alleged ringleader. After the Aryan Brotherhood and Mexican Mafia, you've probably got one of the biggest crews in the jail."

"I know, but I'm not trying to run anything as it could be used as evidence against me."

"I've got a proposition for you."

"What?"

"Shit's about to go off between my people and the Aryans. Look, Shaun, we work out together, and I know if something goes off, you've got my back. But I was thinking it would be safer for all of us if I moved some of your co-defendants into this pod."

Excited by the prospect of joining forces with Little Italy, I'm apprehensive about where it might lead. *The more friends I have in this pod, the less chance of anyone smashing me.* "Good idea."

"Cool."

Doubts creep in. "Isn't going up against a prison gang way out of our league?"

"Yeah, but we're not in prison. This is jail. It's far more every man for himself here. The Aryan Brotherhood are far stronger in the prison system than in the jail. Most of their shot-callers are locked down in the super-maximum-security prison. A lot of the guys in here are just wannabes. I don't see the Aryans here attacking us if we have greater numbers. If I move your people in, I need to know will they have my back?"

"Of course, Marco."

"Then draw up a list of who you want moved in."

"I'll get right on it. Wild Man's at the top." *Wild Man will intimidate most of the prisoners, but he might instigate trouble with the Aryans just for the hell of it.*

Marco moves three of my co-defendants into one cell. The jail's computer system prohibits Wild Man from being housed in the same pod as me, so he ends up in the adjacent pod, 2D. Joey Crack also has Marco move Kyle the kickboxer over. At Durango jail, a gang of youngsters smashed my oldest co-defendant, Little Ben. He'd been moved to Tower 1, so we move him to Tower 2. Little Ben – yet another co-defendant I've never met – is an old-timer who supplied crystal meth to Wild Woman. He arrives with a cut and bruised face. My crew is now six strong in Tower 2. Although Wild Man is in the next pod, Marco has the guards let Wild Man visit our pod for hours on end, and people take notice. The inmates nickname us The Evil Empire, after the title of the *New Times* article.

The five Aryans and torpedoes are not enough to move against ten of us. When Wild Man isn't in our pod, he comes to the window to chat with me in sign language, surrounded by a band of thugs. He shaved his eyebrows off to pay a gambling debt and looks like a monster. Another regular at the window with Wild Man is Troll, who's recently signed a plea bargain for almost ten years and is sporting a bruised face after getting smashed over a drug debt.

Unable to take us on, the Aryans pick on the smallest of us, Little Ben. They send an overgrown hick with a husky voice and scaly facial skin, to extort tobacco from him. The hick corners Little Ben in his cell. The first I know about it is from the familiar sound of a body getting thrown around. Used to that sound, I dismiss it as just another fight, until Slopester runs into my cell, yelling that the hick is smashing Little Ben. I spring off my bunk.

The rest of the Aryans are trooping up the stairs as I rush from the cell with adrenaline pumping my body up. Little Italy, my co-defendants and Kyle are stampeding across the balcony to Little Ben's. I arrive just in time to see Marco threatening the hick who is about six inches taller and broader than him. I've never seen Marco erupt. He is roaring in a deep voice, fists balled, expanding his chest with every heavy inhale.

The Aryans try to push their way through us to get into the cell, but we stop them. Surprised by our resistance, Iron Eagle assures us we are all dead as soon as we step foot into the prison system. I shudder at the prospect of running into Iron Eagle in prison, where I'll be after sentencing. My bravery dwindles as I imagine the Aryan Brotherhood shanking me to death in a shower.

Inside the cell, the argument between Marco and the hick turns physical. Outside, Kyle is feinting jabs at the Aryan torpedoes. The *thud-thud-thud* of Marco converting the hick into a punching bag prompts the Aryans to plough into us, restoring my courage. It's more of a pushing match than a fight. Surrounded by large friends, I shove back, equal parts animated and terrified. The fists I've heard so much about go to work. Kyle lets loose a flurry of blows. Blood splatters from an Aryan torpedo's nose. More blows knock the torpedo back, his eyes fading in and out as if his brain is crashing.

The control guard's voice crackles from the speakers, "Lockdown right now!" The older Aryans yank Iron Eagle back and retreat. The guard keeps yelling lockdown. Paulie pulls Marco off the hick and they return to their cell just as the backup guards file into the day room. Afraid of getting caught and punished for being a part of it, I'm worried about Iron Eagle retaliating against us. I envision the Aryans picking us off one by one. The guards cuff and extract Kyle and the torpedo he smashed. We remain locked down for the rest of the day.

Wild Man offers to smash the hick at Catholic mass, but Marco says no. A few days later, the guards move Iron Eagle to Tower 5, further incensing the Aryans who accuse Marco of working with the guards. The hick continues to menace Little Ben. Wild Man comes over to our pod and blatantly cheats at cards while playing the hick. "You cheating-ass punk!" is all Wild Man needs to hear from the hick. Wild Man picks the hick up and twists and pile-drives him head first into the chow table. Wild Man breaks his own thumb. Wriggling around on the floor, the hick is out of action. The Aryans don't attack Wild Man because it looks like a one-on-one fight over a card game and such fights are routine. A guard escorts Wild Man and the hick to lockdown. I speak to Marco, Marco to the guard, and the guard brings Wild Man back with no disciplinary action. The hick never returns.

There is nothing the few Aryans left can do now. We vastly outnumber them. They don't object to our decision to crown Marco the head of the whites. Their behaviour towards us slowly becomes more respectful. They know we'll fight back, and the gangs respect that when it suits them. I still feel unsafe. *If I'm moved to another tower without my co-defendants or Little Italy, the Aryans will easily get revenge.*

In the back rows at the next Catholic mass are my co-defendants, Little Italy and Aryans from various towers who know what has happened, including one with colourful flames tattooed on his skull. Now they outnumber us. Bracing for a war to break out, I fear we will suffer. With them is Carter, who still hasn't regained his swagger since being smashed by SmackDown. Father O'Donnell keeps stopping the mass to hush Wild Man who is incapable of whispering quietly. But instead of attacking us, the Aryans laugh at Wild Man throwing his communion around and disrupting the service. I'm relieved. They even praise Wild Man for smashing a baby shaker – the baby had been blinded in one eye and suffered a broken arm according to the culprit's legal paperwork.

"The doctors took me off the Thorazine and told me I'm normal. I'm normal!" Wild Man boasts loudly. "Everyone who says I'm a Rule 11, you don't know what you're fucking talking about! I'm not a Rule 11!" Demonic laughter. "I'm fucking normal!" More laughter. "If the doctors say I'm normal, then I must be fucking normal!"

"That Wild Man's fucking crazy," says a portly redneck, the oldest Aryan from our pod. "But I fucking like him. He reminds me of me at his age."

Later on, the redneck visits my cell and describes how he'd nailed a man to a wall and hit golf balls at him. He is especially proud of how well-dressed he'd been that day and what fine clubs he'd used. He asks if he can move into my cell. Alarmed, I say that I'd be glad to live with him but I'm trying to keep it a non-smoking cell. Afterwards, I ask Marco to obstruct any attempts by the redneck to move in.

CHAPTER 28

Alejandro, whose pus-filled spider bite I'd helped salt with Lev, is rearrested for threatening witnesses and housed in pod 2D next door to Wild Man. Facing a sentence in excess of a century for shooting multiple teenage gang rivals with an AK-47, he says he regrets not going on the run in Mexico when free on bond. Glad to see my friend, I'm saddened that someone so young and with a childlike mind is probably going to spend the rest of his life in prison.

The guard who selects him and Wild Man – with a combined weight of 700 pounds – to serve red death must be a prankster. In the corridor, besides steel feeding carts stacked with 180 trays, the ravenous twosome put on hairnets and proceed to steal everyone's dessert – a stale but beloved chocolate-chip cookie. Watching them shove cookies into their mouths until their cheeks are at capacity and hide plastic bags full of cookies inside their trousers, the inmates bang on the Plexiglas, shake their fists and mouth threats, but the twosome just laugh them off. The angry prisoners blame the guards for the disappearance of their cookies. The two big men are banned from serving chow.

Young Officer Hernandez – who's recently purchased a video game heavy on British slang – starts yelling on his walks, "Oh no, it's the filth!" in a mock English accent. "The filth" is UK slang for the police. The prisoners make a sport of parroting him. Mesmerised by this, Slopester consults the man he assumes is the resident expert on UK slang: me.

"When Officer Baptist does his walks, I call him the filth and he goes bright red. I need more shit to throw at him. What do they call prison guards in England?"

"Screws."

"What other bad words you got?"

"You can call someone a plonker, a pillock or a daft git," I say without giving a second thought to the consequences.

Slopester leaves giggling and bombards Officer Baptist, an averagely built, effeminate forty-something wearing big square glasses. Baptist scurries from the pod. Worried he might call the goon squad, Nick and I ask Slopester to behave himself, which he does for a few hours, but when Baptist is supervising the inmates serving red death, Slopester opens up on him again in an English accent:

"Look who it is! It's the filthy screw! He's a pillock and a plonker, too!"

The laughter in the day room ascends to the lead paint peeling off the ceiling.

"Yeah, that filth…I mean filthy screw. What a daft git he is!"

Officer Baptist's face turns purple, a show of weakness the inmates pounce on with more fake English accents:

"Who's the filth?"

"That pillock Baptist is!"

"He's a filthy fucking screw!"

"Who's a screw?"

"Who's filthy?"

"Baptist!"

"He's a filthy screw and a plonker."

Startled by everyone joining in, Officer Baptist panics. "You, lockdown," he says to Slopester in a wimpy way as if close to tears. He steps out of the sliding door, fumbles with his radio and urges Officer Hernandez to close the door from the control tower.

Slopester refuses to lockdown.

"Everyone lockdown!" Officer Hernandez announces.

As a dozen men haven't been served, the prisoners threaten to riot.

"Lockdown now!"

Backup guards run into Tower 2 and try to force us back to

our cells by yelling and waving pepper spray at us. As more arrive, I retreat, regretting arming Slopester with the ammunition to cause havoc. The last men in their cells are left unfed.

The next day, the unfed complain to the shift commander who rewards them with double rations of red death. Marco reprimands Slopester. The jail enrols Officer Baptist in assertiveness classes. The classes apparently work: he surprises us by getting promoted to Sergeant Baptist.

March 2003

Dear Claudia,

It was nice to see you in court today, albeit briefly. I am shattered. I hate the post-court jetlag effect. It makes you feel so shitty and miserable. The judge denied the evidentiary hearing/remand motion. That made me feel a little despondent as well. So I guess we file motions attacking the wiretaps next. We also must argue against us being tried in groups, which is not a good or a fair idea. All this bad news from court is terrible. I just want to know what's going to happen to me, so I can make plans for when I'll be in your loving arms. I'm so weary. I know I sound down today. I'm sure I'll be back to normal tomorrow for when you and Aunty Ann visit.

All the guys are downstairs watching *Goodfellas*. They're all wannabe gangstas. The whole pod is out. Standing room only.

I love you,

Shaun XXX

CHAPTER 29

The commander of the jail discovers that Paulie was moved from Tower 5 to Tower 2. He moves Paulie back and Slopester with him. A few days later, Marco has different guards bring Paulie and Slopester back. This incenses the commander. A tug of war begins whereby every few days Paulie and Slopester are moved from one tower to the other. In the end, Slopester is allowed to stay, but not Paulie.

Hugo finds out he is going to be released, and Marco is sentenced. The news purges a depression from Hugo who fears being met by a death squad if he's ever returned to Argentina.

All of the sentenced inmates in Tower 2 are moved to Tower 5 – except for Marco. He's arranged to stay in our pod until his penultimate day at Towers. Hugo ropes a banner across the upper tier to prevent access to Marco's cell. It reads: "V.I.P. Visits by appointment only!" The banner flabbergasts inmates and guards, especially when they watch Hugo attach and reattach it to let people in and out. But the newly-assertive Sergeant Baptist is having none of it. He arrives with the afternoon shift change, pounces on the unprotected banner and tears it up. When the Italians emerge from their cell and surround Baptist, his bravery vanishes. He turns red, trembles and slinks away with the Italians mocking his timidity and yelling that he needs to retake the assertiveness classes.

As the day of Marco's departure nears, the inmates and even some guards sadden. I'm worried that the close community and minimisation of violence he's engineered is about to end and it won't be long before the Aryans regain control. Dreading the return to chaos, I work out with him during his final days, enjoying his company and wondering in a sad way if I'll ever see him again.

The Arizona Department of Corrections is scheduled to collect Marco from Tower 5. He decides to leave our pod on the eve of his departure. It's a lengthy process involving devastated expressions on the faces of his inner circle and unprecedented levels of bawling by Hugo. Hugging Marco, I know I'll miss him deeply. I tell him he exceeded my wildest expectations of what I imagined anyone could achieve in the jail. When the guards escort him away, the day room cheers and whistles and tables are banged drum-like. As he disappears down the corridor, our anxiety heightens. Our discontent lifts an hour later when Marco reappears to a chorus of cheers fit for a war hero.

"I told the guards I'd forgot some personal property items, so they brought me back," Marco says.

The guards collect him an hour later. He leaves to rounds of applause and even louder cheering and banging than earlier. Thirty minutes later, different guards bring him back to collect more forgotten property. This time Hugo bawls and the fanfare and drama escalate to the highest levels of the day. With their eyes full of wonderment, the men mob around Marco, slapping him on the back and praising him for outwitting the guards. When he leaves again, the inmates place bets as to whether or not he will return. Some press themselves to the Plexiglas in the hope of being the first to spot him and announce his return. Sadly, we never see him again. A week after his departure, the guards free Hugo. Little Italy is over.

CHAPTER 30

Capitalising on a run of undefeated fights, Nick becomes the new head of the whites. He moves Slopester into his cell as a gofer. When problems with individual whites arise, Nick settles them with his fists rather than sending torpedoes in. Every few days he fights and wins. A Mexican American annoys us all by standing under the stairs crooning like a Backstreet Boy. One afternoon, he refuses to pipe down even though Nick is on the phone. Nick hangs up and corners him in a cell. A punch to the face propels the singer into the day room. Nick chases him around the stairs. When Sergeant Baptist steps into the pod, the singer dashes out of the door, never to return.

Nick's next three fights last slightly longer. They end in submissions from his opponents who emerge battered and dazed. The whites, intimidated by Nick's prowess, behave themselves for a few weeks, during which Nick doesn't have to fight.

Three Mexican Americans move into our pod: two older Chicano gang members who hate Mexican nationals, and Busta Beatz, stuck in the system pending mental-health reports. Nick and I have our fiancées try to locate Busta Beatz's foster parents, who we hope might offer him support and help with his legal situation.

During one of Stalker's nightly fart storms, Honduras warns me that the two Chicano gang members plan to stir up a race riot between the Mexicans and the Mexican Americans by using Busta Beatz as a torpedo to smash a Mexican. Racial tension escalates.

I'm returning from court when Nick diverts me to his cell. "Shit's getting out of control with the Chicanos and Mexicans," he says. "I stopped a fight in your cell today. One of the new Chicanos tried to smash Honduras."

"Over what?" I ask, dismayed.

"The TV channels. They took it to your cell, so I went in before your property got bloodied and destroyed."

"I appreciate that, man," I say, shocked the violence entered my home and someone picked on my harmless little cellmate.

Later on, Busta Beatz barges into a mellow Jehovah's Witness who's been my neighbour since my arrival in Tower 6, who is eating red death with the Mexicans. The Mexicans rise fast as if to attack Busta Beatz.

Nick springs up and orders Busta Beatz to apologise to the Jehovah's Witness.

"I ain't apologising! Are you gonna fucking make me?" I'm disappointed in Busta Beatz as Nick is helping him find his foster parents. Even worse, he's "called out" Nick in a way that leaves no choice but to fight.

Nick tells Busta Beatz to see him in A7, the cell at the end of the bottom run he prefers to fight in because it's the furthest away from the control tower. As they enter A7, the day room hushes to tune into the violence. When the fight lasts much longer than usual for Nick, the whites express concern and the hermits emerge from their cells. The fight drags on. More prisoners cluster in the day-room's vantage points. Rooting for Nick, I see him pin Busta Beatz against a wall, yelling, "Give up! Give up!" Busta Beatz surrenders, but as soon as he is released, he leaps on Nick, who subdues him again. Ten minutes later, both are still fighting and exhausted. Nick puts Busta Beatz in a headlock and urges him to give up.

"I give up. You win," Busta Beatz says. Nick turns to leave the cell, panting as if he's just sprinted several hundred yards. Busta Beatz springs onto the small table and jumps on Nick's back. Nick throws him off, his face contorting with fury. He unleashes punch after punch on Busta Beatz's face, punches that would knock out an average man. Blood gushes and streams all over Busta Beatz's face. Blood splatters on the walls. A volley of punches forces Busta Beatz backwards, cracking his head against the wall. I worry Nick might kill him. As Busta Beatz loses his balance, Nick pounds his head relentlessly, until he falls unconscious.

"Fuck, I think I broke two knuckles," Nick says, emerging from the cell half-covered in blood. He spits bloody saliva and pieces of teeth onto the floor.

The Mexican Americans file into A7 and rouse Busta Beatz, who is barely able to stand. "Go back to your cell and clean yourself up." He staggers out, painting the concrete red with a trail of blood.

The Mexicans, including the Jehovah's Witness, thank Nick for standing up for their race.

Over the following days, Nick's hand swells up to the size of a grapefruit, and Busta Beatz's face turns purple and blue. Nick declares he will never fight another Rule 11 inmate.

A week later, the Jehovah's Witness goes to court. The Mexicans see his story broadcast on the news. The report claims that he and his wife molested their own daughter. Carlo, the head of the Mexicans who's shared a cell with the Jehovah's Witness for a year, ordains the usual justice for a sex offender. As the Mexicans await the Jehovah's Witness, the atmosphere in the day room turns hostile. Inmates are vigilant and unfriendly. Watched by cautious eyes, the Jehovah's Witness is welcomed back by the Mexicans. They lure him into his cell. They time the attack for right after a guard has walked through the pod, so they'll have at least half an hour before the next security walk. When the thudding and stomping begins it sounds like a normal smashing. Questions are yelled harshly in Spanish, followed by the Jehovah's Witness pleading for mercy and eerie wails of pain as they torture him. I'm in the cell next door, listening to the sickening sounds, occasionally shuddering. Eventually, he stumbles and sways down the stairs and to the sliding door soaked in blood from his hair to his feet, unrecognisable, disorientated, as if searching for somewhere to die. When the door opens, he takes a few steps and drops into a heap. Showing no signs of life, he is extracted on a stretcher. The pod isn't even locked down, probably because the guards approve of sex offenders getting attacked. Sometimes they even tip the prisoners off.

CHAPTER 31

Attempting to reduce the misbehaviour in Tower 2, the guards round up suspected troublemakers and move them to Tower 5. Wild Man, Alejandro and Joey Crack end up as cellmates in Tower 5, where a guard with a reputation for being tougher than Mordhorst wakes them up every day at 6.30 a.m. by blasting the national anthem over the speakers.

At church, I ask Joey Crack for an update on Wild Man and Alejandro.

"Wild Man's back in the hole," Joey Crack whispers on the back row.

"What for this time?"

"Me, Alejandro and Wild Man were all in the cell when the guards decided to do a cell search. Wild Man was told a number of times to shut up, but he continued to be his insane obnoxious self. He kept running his mouth till the guard had had enough. The guard asked him to face the wall, place his arms behind his back, and he refused. So the guard pressed his panic button and within seconds twenty guards came running in ready for the worst. They surrounded Wild Man with their pepper sprays out, but he just stood there laughing at them. A guard said, 'Do you want to do this the easy way or the hard way?' Wild Man looked them up and down, waited till they were just about to spray him, and said, 'Let's try the easy way.'"

"What a nutter!"

"He loves the attention. He just laughed in their faces."

"How's Alejandro?" I ask.

"He got 46 years."

"Holy shit! How's he handling it?"

"They've moved him to a suicide-watch cell at the Madison

Street jail. He didn't handle it well at all. Wild Man made it worse by tormenting him the whole time."

"What do you mean?"

"During the trial, Wild Man woke Alejandro up at all hours of the night for absolutely no reason and pelted him with rotten grapefruits. Alejandro was too preoccupied to react much."

"That's way out of order."

"Alejandro had to get up after midnight, and go to court all day long, so he was only getting a couple of hours' sleep. He ignored Wild Man, which sent Wild Man crazy 'cause he wasn't getting a reaction."

"Good for Alejandro."

"Wild Man ended up smashing grapefruits all over the cell floor, so Alejandro would slip around as he got ready for court."

"I'm sure he works for the devil."

"The insanity never stopped. The citric acid stained the floor, and Wild Man started hallucinating, saying he was seeing faces of every sort on the floor."

"I told you he's a Rule 11."

"Another thing I noticed about Wild Man is a strange 6-6-6 system that he keeps. He had a picture of Wild Woman taped above his rack, and all day long he tapped it in sets of 6-6-6. What he was trying to achieve, I haven't the slightest, but it's what he does."

In Visitation, I'm sitting at a table alone, listening to wiretaps playing on my attorney's laptop, when Wild Man arrives to meet his attorney. He has no eyebrows, a goatee and a shaved head. His attorney – a tall thirty-something Mexican American – is sitting at a table close to me. I don't acknowledge Wild Man, so she won't know I'm there. Her face puckers when she sees him. To eavesdrop, I turn down my headset volume.

"Hello!" Wild Man says in a deep giddy voice. He sits down opposite her and shakes her hand.

"How're you doing, Peter? How's the broken thumb?" She

frowns at a thumb that has turned blue and shed its nail.

"OK. Everything's OK," Wild Man says.

"As you know, the prosecutor's offering eight years. Considerably less than the 25 you're facing," she says in a slick salesperson's tone.

Wild Man nods. "I never got busted with no drugs. Don't you only get 25 if they can show twenty-five grand in drug sales?"

She sighs theatrically. "Not necessarily. Who's been telling you this?"

"Co-defendants."

"I know Attwood's telling you this," she says. "He has a paid attorney. He'll tell you anything, but in the end you'll be the one that ends up doing the time. You're best taking the plea now. It's the best you're gonna get."

According to my co-defendants, their public defenders are all saying similar things. I'm keen to hear what else she might add.

"As this is my first plea, I'd rather roll the dice and see what happens."

"It's your life you're gambling."

"It's not like I haven't heard that before."

"Quite frankly, I think your co-defendant, Attwood, is going to get a lot of time, and he's going to take you down with him."

My pulse jumps. Wondering what basis she has for her claim, I listen extra carefully.

"Save yourself while you still can! I can get a settlement conference with the judge and prosecutor. See if we can work out a deal if you like?"

"Uh, OK. But I didn't get caught with any drugs. I won't do more than five years."

"The prosecutor's a very reasonable woman. But from eight down to five, I don't know. Let's just go ahead and set the settlement conference shall we?"

"Uh, OK, if you'll ask for five. I like the food here, me."

"The food?" she asks, surprised.

"In England you just get bread and water."

"How about next month for the settlement conference?"

"They feed you bread and water all week long. People complain about the food, but I love it. I just can't get enough of the red death."

"Peter, you're completely crazy. Now let's get back to the settlement conference. With good behaviour – do you think you're capable of good behaviour, Peter?" she asks as if talking to a child.

Wild Man looks over his shoulder as if she's addressing someone else.

"If you sign for eight, with your back time and the 85 per cent kickout, you'll actually do closer to five."

"Uh, OK."

"I'll go ahead and schedule the settlement conference then."

"In England they feed you porridge." Wild Man leans towards her, his wide eyes gazing dementedly.

"Peter, you're crazy." Fear flickers on her face. "I have to go. I'll be in touch. Bye!" She stands and leaves without shaking his hand. She's received thousands from the State to represent Wild Man, yet over the course of almost a year she's only met him a few times. She has never asked what crimes he actually did or offered to prepare a defence. She just wants him to sign a plea bargain, so she can move on to her next client and fee.

CHAPTER 32

Big Wood is one of the heads of the whites from Buckeye prison. Caught with marijuana and facing new charges, he was transferred to Towers and assigned to Nick's cell. He is a massive man with a mellow disposition, likeable and reasonable. Nick and Big Wood get along. After breaking his hand on Busta Beatz's face and losing pieces of his teeth, Nick is tired of being the head of the whites. Big Wood, who commands respect due to his reputation in the prison system, takes over. He orders the whites he doesn't like to roll out of the pod, gets the rest to behave and stops the nightly felatio show in 2B, a neighbouring pod, whereby after lockdown a Native-American transsexual can be seen from our cells bobbing his head between the legs of a white inmate on the toilet at the front of the cell. Prior to Big Wood's arrival, bored prisoners had enjoyed commenting on these performances, generating lots of amusing sexual banter. Big Wood sends a note to the head of the whites in 2B saying the receiver of the oral sex is disgracing the white race and must be smashed if it continues. It stops immediately.

Honduras, whose plea bargain dropped from double-digit years down to five, notifies us that he will be leaving soon as all of the witnesses in his case have disappeared. His prosecutor offers him a final plea bargain for two years, which he laughs at. He knows they have no evidence against him, so he calls the prosecutor's bluff. A few nights later, our cell door opens. A guard shines a torch on us.

"Roll up! Roll up! Immigration are here to pick you up!"

Awakened by the guard, I shake hands with Honduras.

"*Buena suerte*, Honduras," I say. Good luck.

"Buena suerte, mi compañero de cuarto." Good luck, my room-mate. "See! I told you, *tengo mucho suerte.*" I have much luck.

"Si, que suerte tienes." Yes, what luck you have.

"Que Dios te bendiga, Inglaterra." God bless you, England.

"Que Dios te bendiga tambien." God bless you also.

"Adios."

I'm glad Honduras beat the system. Surrounded by mayhem, he kept his cool, remained sober, prayed to God and showed everyone respect.

A few days later, Stalker is sentenced to three and a half years. He will serve just over two, hopefully long enough to crush his desire to resume stalking his wife. If you must stalk someone, I tell him, try a celebrity next time and we'll get you on *Oprah*.

April 2003

Dear Claudia,

Here I lay. Riding the rack. Writing to you and listening to Spanish love songs on Amor 100.3 FM.

Last night a big young guard came in and looked at your pics. He said, "Ahhhh, these are the famous sexy pics," and was nice to me. Then 20 minutes later, after lockdown, he bombed into my cell and ripped down our clotheslines. What a U-turn! I guess he was either jealous or felt guilty for being nice to me.

I had a full day today. Razors at 7am, followed by rec at 7:30. It's nice jogging at 7:30, the weather is lovely. I got a certificate for a 3 day health course I finished today. Slopester said the teacher looked like you. She had a Chinese character tattooed on her leg. She brought a dildo in and showed us how to put a condom on. Then we watched an STD slide show. Proper horror show it was! Staring at slides of vaginas with STDs made me queasy.

An old rambling man was covered in blood as I peered through 2B's pod window on the way to class. Some guy was beating him up, and the back of his shirt was soaked in blood. I never expected an old crazy man to get beaten. He was bleeding from the back of his head. It's a shame. It is a cruel place here at times.

A lot of people got sentenced this week. A Mexican in cell 9 got 10 years for a drunk-driving incident in which someone died. The guy in cell 11 got 9 years for a $20 bag of crack that didn't even have his fingerprints on it.

The sewer got blocked somehow and is flooding the pod downstairs. In the chow tonight another dead rat was served to some poor soul in D pod. How obscene is that? The longer I am here, the more the horrors of this place become apparent. Everyone who ate the slop can now go to sleep with the knowledge that a rat (or rats) was swimming in their food.

Stalker is strung out on his new meds. He had a hissy fit at the doctor and demanded something that wouldn't make him tremble so much. Now he is on Trazodone.

Honduras is gone. What a lucky young man! I miss him already as we bonded with our little Spanish conversations. I'm guessing how the witnesses in his case disappeared, considering the coyotes work for the Mexican Mafia.

I'm reading Meditations from the Mat. The yoga way of life is starting to sink in. I'm letting go of my old ways and thought processes, and becoming a less fearful and stressed person. It is amazing how much more there is to yoga than just the exercises. It is making me stronger. For example, when there are fights, I am no longer hastening to observe them like everyone else, or getting involved in gossip. The book also mentions how we choose to punish ourselves by reacting to our environment. This particularly applies to jail. Punishment is our teacher teaching us not to punish ourselves. If punishment is my teacher then this time is a blessing.

The guard just announced that razors are now at 5am. What utter bastards. Trying to save money because they know we are sleeping. They keep finding new ways to torture us.

Love you loads,
Shaun XXX

CHAPTER 33

For months, I've been using a laptop Alan Simpson put in Visitation. Through a headset, I listen to the evidence against me: thousands of wiretapped phone calls recorded in the months after I'd quit dealing Ecstasy. Whenever I hear a drug deal between my co-defendants, I document the dollar amount. The total of all of the deals for all of my co-defendants is approximately $5700. The prosecutor never misses an opportunity to say that we are a multi-million-dollar drug ring, yet there is no evidence of it. Alan says the total trumps her claim that I'm a serious drug offender – which carries a 25-year sentence – as it requires proof beyond a reasonable doubt of more than $25,000 of drug income received in a calendar year. As no one has agreed to cooperate, and the State's own evidence seems to be in my favour, Alan says he can file for another bond hearing and for a hearing to enable him to play some of the calls in court, so the judge can hear the extent of the dealing.

Clinging to the hope offered by this development, I call Claudia. She tells my parents. Alan says it will help if people send letters of support. As my family and friends are scattered around the world, I ask a friend to set up a support webpage, including the format for writing a letter to the judge. My parents and sister contact all of their friends. Hundreds of letters arrive. Claudia's family members and my relations in Arizona pledge to attend the hearing and speak on my behalf. They even offer to use their houses as collateral for my bond. Touched by their support, I'm once again buoyed by the prospect of getting out.

I've been asleep for a couple of hours when a bright light startles me awake. I squint at the figure behind the flashlight. Mr

Big – a six-foot-four hulk of a guard whose outfit barely contains his muscles – is stood outside of my door, recognisable by his thick permed hair and old-fashioned square-framed glasses. He belongs in a 1970s magazine for bodybuilders. "Attwood, wake up! You've got court!" His voice is as deep as they come.

"What?" I ask, disorientated. I detest the monthly court appearances – a day in holding cells for a few minutes of the judge's time that always ends with a continuance – but today is different. If the judge reduces my bond, I could be out tomorrow. The possibility of freedom overrides my reluctance to rise.

"Take a shower! Be ready downstairs when you're done. Here's a razor."

I slip off my bunk and take the razor. Half asleep, I set off for the shower. The empty day room is quiet except for snoring and the flopping of my sandals. In the shower, I lather soap on my face and begin shaving by touch. No mirrors are allowed. I feel my face to detect stubble. It took months to learn to do this without cutting myself too much. The razor is so blunt, it takes a while to shave safely. The water wakes me up. My brain fills with thoughts of getting out. When I'm dried off, dressed and ready, Mr Big activates the sliding door. He orders me to wait in the corridor below the control tower. Other inmates arrive, all of them on the transportation court list.

Mr Big descends the control-tower stairs to escort us out of Tower 2. "Gentlemen, proceed down the corridor in a straight line, one after the other."

The prisoner at the front sets off. A youngster turns to Mr Big. "This is bullshit. I want to go back to sleep. You can tell the judge I'm refusing to go to court."

Mr Big walks up to the youngster and inhales loudly, expanding his massive chest into the youngster's personal space. He gazes at the youngster for a few seconds, his veins and tendons protruding from his neck like ropes. "You're going to court!"

The youngster jumps and complies.

"Proceed, gentlemen!" Mr Big follows us out of Tower 2 and

along a breezeway, where crickets are chirping cheerfully. He deposits us with a hundred or so groggy prisoners from various towers congregating at the back of the reception area. The guard at the door is shouting surnames, letting a few inmates at a time into the building and ticking names on a clipboard. He yells my name. I step forward.

"ID."

I fish it from my top pocket.

"Go in. Strip down to your boxers."

I join the back of a line of men in pink boxers, holding bee stripes, about to be strip-searched. I remove my filthy clothes.

I arrive at the front of the line. A guard says, "Throw your stripes in that basket and step into that room." I undress. "Now hand me your boxers." Stood naked, I watch him feel the lining of my boxers for contraband. "Raise your balls... Very good. Pull back your foreskin... OK. Now turn around and spread 'em... OK. Put them back on," he says, returning my boxers.

I exit the room and continue down the corridor. A trusty hands me a set of stripes, which I put on. I turn left and walk down a stretch of corridor with two holding cells full to capacity. I join the inmates collecting in the corridor.

Ten minutes later, a guard appears. "What do you stragglers think you're doing out in the walkway? Get into those cells now! Do you hear me? Now!"

We cuss and groan.

"Inmates inside move all the way to the back of the cells, so these fellas can get in!"

It's a slow process, like trying to squeeze into the mass of bodies at the front of a concert. The stench of sweat, bad breath and cheap deodorant is overwhelming.

Spotting me and still looking monstrous with his eyebrows barely grown back, Wild Man bulldozes in my direction, knocking inmates out of the way. "Hello!"

"How do!" I say, glad for his company. His bear hug and the force of the men crushing me from every direction make it difficult to breathe.

"There's way too many Englishmen in here!" someone yells. "That's what the fucking problem is!"

"Wild Man alone's more than enough," I say, raising a few laughs.

"If you have a fucking problem with the English, come and fight us right now," Wild Man says, generating laughter even though he sounds serious. Wild Man is pleased with the legal developments. The calls getting played in the courtroom should help us all.

The bored and testy inmates stare at the walls, the ceiling and the back of each other's heads. When the cell door opens an hour later, we cheer.

"When I call your name, step out of the cell with your ID in your hand!" says a guard. Eventually, he calls six names, including Wild Man's and mine.

"Stand in a line!" yells a guard stood with two others jangling leg chains in the corridor. "Now face the wall!"

A guard comes up behind me. "Raise your left foot towards me." He secures a chain around my ankle. "Now the right foot." When all six sets of leg chains are on us, a guard yells, "Turn around!" They put handcuffs on us starting with Wild Man, who is first in our line of six. They chain our handcuffs together. I'm chained to Wild Man and an old Mexican with boils on his face.

"Bet you never thought we'd end up chained together like this," Wild Man says, grinning.

"It's my worst nightmare," I say.

"Welcome to my world. You've gone from stockbroker to criminal all within three of my visits to America."

"Go and wait in that cell!" a guard yells.

Six of us penguin-shuffle towards a large holding cell at the end of the corridor. The leg chains only permit half steps, so I have to take care to step in sync so the chain gang can move as one. We join other chain gangs in the holding cell. When all of the prisoners going to court are packed into the cell, the guards lock the door and cluster around a small isolation cell opposite us in which an irate prisoner with a freckly face and red hair in a ponytail is scowling through the Plexiglas at the guards.

"Are you gonna behave yourself and go to court?"

"Fuck you!" the redhead yells, narrowing his eyes.

"Looks like he doesn't want to be a good boy."

Head-butting the window, the redhead provokes laughter from the guards. "Fuck you!" When the guards laugh harder, he spits on the window. A glob of phlegm creeps down the Plexiglas, leaving a glistening trail.

"We'll just tell the judge you refused to see him. I'm sure that'll make him happy." The guards smile mockingly and stride away.

It's another hour before a transportation van parks outside of the jail. The exterior door buzzes open. Two transportation guards enter.

"OK. Any chains with green-coloured padlocks on them get on your way!"

The lead person in each chain gang examines the colour of his padlock.

"We're green!" Wild Man pushes through the prisoners to get to the door.

We shuffle out and down a ramp to the van.

A guard opens the back doors. "Get in slowly! One at a time! Watch your heads getting in! Slide all the way down the seat! Squeeze in there!"

The six of us cramp together on a narrow ledge on one side of the van. Six more sit opposite. Two groups of four sit in the space between the driver and us. Plastic mesh separates each group. The van doors slam shut. Trapped air stifles us.

"Can you get some air blowing back here?" Wild Man yells.

A guard in the cabin adjusts a vent, but the trickle of air struggles to reach us. Every time the van turns, the six of us slide along the ledge to the back of the van, crushing the man at the end of our chain gang. Tensing my body, I take the brunt of Wild Man's weight.

When we arrive at the Madison Street jail, the first rays of the day are illuminating the sky, tingeing the sparse clouds orangey-red. The van goes through a security gate and parks in a lot below the building.

The doors click open. "Get out! Watch your heads!"

Each man steps down, almost falling over, tugging the chain gang.

"Slow down getting out!" A guard leads us through an exterior door into a holding cell, brightly lit, with many security cameras, where we wait for a few minutes.

The interior door opens. "Proceed to your left!" yells a large guard with a shaved head.

We exit the cell, turn left and shuffle down the corridor towards many voices yelling. We arrive at a space facing four cells crammed with noisy prisoners, who've been transported from various jails to wait in the Madison Street jail's dungeon before going to court.

"Stop here! Line up!"

The guards remove our chains. A sound like sandpaper scraping against a wall attracts my attention. A trusty is sliding a plastic barrel full of Ladmo bags across the concrete towards us.

A guard opens a cell door. "Get a Ladmo bag and get in there! Fellas in the cell, make room! Push back against that wall!"

I take a Ladmo bag and follow the ultimate space maker: Wild Man. Multiple layers of filth have smothered the original paintwork on the walls, rendering them a dull yellowish-brown, dappled with dark-brown raised patches. The floor belongs to the cockroaches. Any I trample, the living eat. The toilet at the back reeks like a dive-bar's urinal at closing time, a smell that pushes me away as I go further in. The area around the toilet is coated in urine from countless men who've missed their aim over the years. Wild Man kicks a few pairs of legs out of the way as if they are sticks on a forest path. He power-gazes the men he's disturbed into conceding space. We squat. Pushing a sleeping man out of the way, Wild Man stretches his legs out.

Waking up, the man yells, "What the fuck!"

"So what!" Wild Man leans his large head towards the man who flinches and wriggles away.

"It's only fucking six o'clock!" announces an inmate at the front of the cell, gazing at the clock in the guards' room.

"Court's not till ten," I say to Wild Man. We chat, shifting positions when our pins and needles are too uncomfortable, having to raise our shirts over our faces to protect ourselves from the stink of the sporadic toilet use. Spotting cockroaches venturing into our neighbours' clothes breaks up the monotony.

A chain gang arrives outside of our cell, twelve men from the maximum-security section of the Madison Street jail. They are unchained and ordered to enter our cell.

"There's no fucking room in here!"

"Then make some fucking room!" a guard yells. "Push all the way to the back!"

The weary crowd compresses further, pushing me closer to a side wall. The twelve enter, trampling on the tangle of limbs. No one speaks up because the medium-security prisoners fear the maximum-security prisoners, many of whom are murderers. Two large Mexican American new arrivals notice a smaller Mexican American leaning against the back wall. The two whisper to each other as if plotting. After the cell door locks behind them, they head towards the toilet. The larger one veers towards the man they spotted. He grabs and drags him, kicking and yelling, towards the toilet. His head cracks against the steel. *Thwack-thwack-thwack…* All of the talking, joking, heckling, snoring, laughing and complaining stop. Mesmerised by the violence, inmates shuffle out of the way. When the victim's head cracks open, gushing blood, the two Mexican Americans stomp on him, putting their full weight on his joints as if to snap them. Watching them trying to murder someone activates my adrenaline. It affects my neighbours, too. The men at the back spring up. Within seconds, everyone rises. I scramble up but have nowhere to go. The panic seizing the crowd grips me. Fighting ripples from the back of the cell. The crowd lurches towards the front, sweeping me with it. I raise my forearms to shield myself from the flailing arms. Wild Man says, "I've got this one," shoves me against a wall and stands in front of me like a totem pole with prisoners bouncing off him, some helped on their way by his hands. Guards rush to the cell. One frantically fingers his keys and works one in. They enter fast, wielding Tasers and large canisters of pepper spray. The crowd folds out of their way. The fighting stops. They grab the three Mexican Americans in blood-soaked bee stripes and drag them out. The victim appears lifeless. The guards cuff the culprits. Medical staff extract the victim on a stretcher. Trusties mop up the blood. Minutes later, the chatter resumes.

Half an hour later, guards congregate outside of the cell and start calling the surnames of the men with the earliest court times. The extracted men line up and are chained together. The cells become less crowded. Just when we have enough space to stretch our legs, a guard orders us into the cell next door, where I spot some of my co-defendants. We hug.

"Alan's trying to get the calls played in court, so the judge can hear you guys were only busted doing nickel-and-dime deals." I hand them copies of the itemised drug deals, showing the $5,700 total. "This list could change everything!"

Their eyes light up. They are tired of months of legal stagnation and their public defenders insisting they sign plea bargains.

An hour later, a guard calls us out. We are chained, led down a corridor and ordered to wait outside of a holding cell for females. Wild Woman appears, her hair streaked every colour of the rainbow.

"What happened to your hair, love? It looks like you've been to a gay festival," Wild Man says.

"How did you do that?" I ask, worried the judge will get a bad impression.

"Can't tell you my secrets now can I?" Wild Woman rasps. "Shaun, your face is all sunken in."

"I know. I can't eat red death. I dream of food, including your

Sunday dinners," I say, referring to traditional English Sunday roasts that Wild Woman generously cooked weekly for me and our friends.

Wild Woman grins. "My attorney hardly visits me or lets me know what the fuck's going on."

"You need to file for a new attorney," I say.

"How do I do that?"

"I'll see if I can get someone to mail you some info."

We travel through a tunnel and wait for an elevator. We pack ourselves in. Wild Man positions himself so he can rub up against Wild Woman. As the guard presses the elevator button, the Wild Ones kiss.

"I love you," Wild Man says.

"Love you, too," Wild Woman says.

From the elevator, we are separated into two cells: males and females. An hour later, we are escorted into the courtroom. Seeing TV crews, I panic until a guard explains a teacher who molested his students was sentenced to over a hundred years. We are ordered to sit on the rows of benches at the side of the courtroom in front of the public gallery. I'm prohibited from talking to Claudia and my local family members, so I smile and bounce my eyebrows at them.

My attorney, Alan Simpson, arrives, armed with statistics and pie charts on fancy coloured paper and a tape recorder to play calls to the judge. The co-defendants' attorneys mob him for information. He whispers in their ears. The glee spreading over their faces suggests they are expecting the great Alan Simpson to finally demolish the case after almost a year of locking horns with the young prosecutor. The prosecutor greets Alan with her usual competitive smile, but she and Detective Reid (who attends nearly all of my court hearings) seem daunted. The attorneys are whispering in the ears of my co-defendants, spreading the buzz around the room. *Something good is about to happen. I might be bonded out and back with Claudia tomorrow.*

The judge emerges, bespectacled, grim, and in a wheelchair

due to injuries from the Vietnam War. We all rise. Ignoring the judge, the Wild Ones continue laughing and talking to each other loudly. Judge Watson orders our escorting guard to remove the Wild Ones from the courtroom for horseplay. Detective Reid smirks as they are removed. *How can they misbehave on such an important day? Surely the judge is going to look at our motions less favourably now.*

Alan tells the judge that the drug deals on the wiretaps total $5,700. He says he has a tape recorder and would like to play some of the calls. The prosecutor objects to the court hearing the calls. Hearing her object to her own evidence pleases me and the co-defendants. We figure we have her. The judge says now is not the appropriate time to hear any calls. The case is continued. Disappointed, I slump. My co-defendants are cleared from the courtroom, shaking their heads.

Next is my bond hearing. Alan says $5,700 worth of drug deals doesn't justify a $750,000 bond. Members of my family – including an ex-policeman – and Claudia's familystand up, vouch for me, offer to take me into their homes and offer their homes for my bond. Their strong and emotional pleas rekindle my hope. Detective Reid's face tenses. The prosecutor speaks briefly, raising mild objections. Seemingly defeated, she sits. My supporters' eyes are sparkling. *I must be getting out!* When it's time for the judge to speak, my heart speeds up. I imagine him reducing my bond and my supporters cheering. *Claudia will probably cry with relief.* The judge says he is unable to make a decision. He is taking the matter under advisement. *The hearing seemed to go so well, surely he'll reduce my bond soon. Maybe it'll take a week or so for me to get out.* I spend the half-day journey back to Towers indulging in fantasies of freedom.

CHAPTER 34

Escorting a group of us back into Tower 2, Officer Noble says to me, "I need to talk to you."

Why's his expression so serious? "What is it?" I ask nervously.

"Wait down that corridor."

With a bad feeling tightening my stomach, I trudge away.

After directing the rest of the prisoners into their pods, he approaches me. "You've got new charges."

"New charges! How's that possible? I just had a bond hearing," I say angrily.

"If you just had a bond hearing, that's how they stop you getting out: new charges. And another thing–"

Still reeling, I brace myself.

"–you've got two new cellies."

Stunned, I pause. "How did that happen?"

"They're always moving you guys around. We wouldn't want you to get too settled now."

Walking up the stairs, I pray my new cellmates are mellow.

Big Wood stops me at the top. He tells me to step into his cell. *Oh no! Now what?* I follow him. "They've put a black dude in your cell. We're trying to get him moved to an all-black cell. He has a bottom bunk slip 'cause he has seizures. He's a bit of a loudmouth, but he's all right. We just can't have a black dude celling with two woods."

I don't mind living with a black man, but not a loudmouth. "What about my other new celly?"

"He's a youngster. Busted with drugs in prison. Here on new charges."

Determined to make the most of the situation by greeting my cellmates pleasantly, I return to my cell. I press the door open a few inches. The youngster on the toilet shoves it back in my face.

"Wait outside a minute," he says with attitude. "I'm unpacking my ass. You want to smoke?"

Having dodged living with a smoker for almost a year, I'm in no mood to deal with him on top of everything else. "No. I don't smoke. This is a smoke-free cell."

"It *was* a smoke-free cell," he says. "OK. You can come in now."

The cell reeks of his business on the toilet and the rolled cigarette he's lit. Tilting back a pale face with pockmarks, he takes another drag.

"Look, I've been here for a year and I don't appreciate you smoking in my cell," I say, scowling.

"What you gonna do about it?"

My stress erupts. "You want to handle it like that?" I ask, pointing at him.

He coolly takes a drag as if the prospect of fighting me is trivial. He rests the cigarette at the base of the window.

We are inching towards each other, fists first, when the door swings open and bangs against the wall. I whirl around.

It's not the loudmouth, but an overweight man as broad as the doorway. Wincing, he limps into the cell and says in a gruff voice, "I guess whoever's on the bottom bunk's moving out and I'm moving in." He stands, panting, grimacing impatiently.

Amusement creeps over the youngster's face. "What the fuck's wrong with you, big dog?"

Unfurling his mattress on the bottom bunk, the man says, "I was Tasered six times. Some kind of high-powered cop Taser." He collapses onto the mattress – the bunk barely containing him – and trembles like a beached whale.

The head of the blacks rushes in with two massive torpedoes. "This guy's got to go," he shouts, pointing at the Tasered man. "The guy who just moved out is moving back in," he says, referring to the loudmouth.

How did my cell get so crazy?

"Why do you think so?" the youngster yells.

"'Cause they just put him in with me. We've both got bottom-bunk slips." He's angry because the loudmouth was reassigned to his bottom bunk.

The Tasered man props himself up. "*I* just got Tasered six times. *I* need a bottom bunk."

"Do you have a bottom-bunk slip?" the head of the blacks yells.

"Not yet."

"Then you've got to move back out! The guy they moved out of here has epilepsy. He needs this bottom bunk."

"You ain't no guard! You ain't telling me what to do!"

"You calling me out?" He rests his fists on his hips.

"You need to get the fuck out of our cell," the youngster says, pointing at the blacks.

Bouncing his eyes from the blacks to the whites, the Tasered man appears to be on the verge of launching himself at the blacks.

I brace for mayhem. Not standing up for your race is punishable by your own race smashing you. I've been in jail long enough to be held accountable. Hoping to prevail with reason, I say, "Obviously he needs a bottom bunk. Look at the state of him."

"Who the fuck asked you?" the head of the blacks yells. "This is between me and him."

I'm about to say, "Hey, I live here too, dog," at the risk of irritating him more, but my name is called over the speakers. "Hold up. I think they're calling me."

"Attwood. Turn out for the Madison Street jail. You're going to court."

Hurrying to abandon my home, I scoop up my property and dash along the balcony to Nick's. "All hell's breaking loose in my cell. Will you mind my store and stuff while I go to The Horseshoe? Hopefully, I won't be gone for too many days."

"Sure, bro. What's going on?"

"My new cellies are arguing with the blacks over the bottom bunk. You or Big Wood might want to go over there to try and calm things down."

Descending the stairs, I'm glad to be away from the quarrel I can hear intensifying. Youngsters are snooping around my cell, desperate to mooch tobacco from my new cellmate. *Hopefully, things will be less chaotic when I get back.*

CHAPTER 35

Officer Noble escorts me to an empty holding cell in the reception building. My concern shifts from the situation I've left behind to the one I'm entering. *New charges will affect my case and the judge's decision on my bond hearing. It's Thursday evening. I might get stuck in The Horseshoe's filthy cells with all of the crazies who get arrested on the weekends.*

Transportation arrives hours later. Shackled by a hick transportation officer, I board an old school bus and join the minimum-security prisoners sitting two to a seat, chained to each other. Being the only medium-custody inmate, I receive some respectful nods. When I sit down, the driver revs the engine and the bus rattles off. The male prisoners heckle six females locked in Plexiglas cubicles behind the cabin, working themselves into a frenzy of lewd remarks. The women humour the men with sly smiles. I'm glad when the radio blasts, drowning out the commotion. Giving up on the women, the men sing rock oldies. The heat, noise, fuel smell, cuffs and new charges are aggravating me. Breathing deeply, I try to steel my mind for the challenges ahead. The van parks. We join the queue for the jail. The arrestees in street clothes squint warily at us convicts in bee stripes.

Police cars keep arriving, delivering fresh captures, mostly men, sullen and wide-eyed, some with scrapes and bruises and blood stains. A few are dragged from the cars. I'm reminded of my arrest and arrival. *Wait a minute.* "What's the date?" I ask our group.

"May 16th, dog."

May 16th. One-year anniversary of my arrest. Can't be coincidence. Prosecutor's playing mind games! Has it in for me. I'm doomed. Maybe not. This shows a mean but immature streak. Maybe my attorney can exploit that.

A police van parks. Three prostitutes get out – one in a mini-skirt with a dragon tattoo on her thigh – setting the males off. They taunt her, but she lashes back with the panache of a drag queen. The other two prostitutes quietly hang their heads.

Inside, I relinquish my cuffs.

An inmate yells at me, "Ain't you that guy–"

I put my finger to my lips too late.

"–that English guy on the cover of the *New Times*?"

Attracting looks of curiosity and approval, I say nothing entering the walk-through metal detector.

A large Mexican American raps on the window of a cell and waves me over. "English Shaun! I'm one of your co-defendants."

Yet another co-defendant I've never met. They're still expanding the size of my case.

A guard deposits me in a cell I remember well. Plexiglas front windows. Walls caked in brown filth. A seatless steel toilet in the corner. About forty men, many high and drunk. Everyone keeping a wary eye on everyone else. They are huddled so close on the concrete, I trip over them as I work my way in. The few in bee stripes nod at me as if to join them, but I'm in no mood for jail chat. I return to the spot against the back wall where no one wants to sit due to the toilet smell. I assume a half-lotus position and read a yoga meditation book I've smuggled in with my legal paperwork, but I'm too agitated to absorb much. Every so often a prisoner is extracted or deposited. The hot stale atmosphere wears me down.

"I need to take a fucking dump!" a plump man announces. "Who's got the fucking shit roll?" He spots a hobo using a toilet roll as a pillow, walks over and snatches it, interrupting the rhythm of the hobo's snores. He shoves past me, drops his pants and lets the toilet have it. The stench permeates the cell. I hold my breath. My neighbours gag and moan.

When a guard finally extracts me, I plod to the next cell to savour the air in the corridor.

The next cell is the same. Two young Mexican Americans

start quarrelling over who shot whom. One hits the other. We all scramble to our feet. The lightning punches of the taller one pummel his opponent's face, showering those nearest with blood. A year ago, I would have felt the fear visible in the eyes of the audience. But a one-on-one fight seems trivial compared to a pack of torpedoes cracking heads against toilets and stomping people unconscious until they look dead. A flurry of blows collapses the smaller Mexican American. The taller switches to kicks. I imagine the taller one a few days from now: recruited as a torpedo, proudly employing his skills to do the dirty work for the head of his race.

The loser crawls to the toilet, pulls himself up and washes the blood from his face in the sink. The door swings open. Everyone gazes at the guard as if expecting him to notice there's been a fight. He yells a name and extracts a man. The guard shuts the door. We all sit.

The loser rips his top off. Expanding the canvas of gang tattoos on his chest, he swaggers up to the victor. "So what the fuck you saying?" Blood is leaking from the cuts on his face.

"Why you squaring off on me?"

There is a crescendo of gang slang, two men exchanging saliva motes, but not blows. *Neither wants a rematch. The victor has nothing to gain. The loser has saved face by scraping himself off the floor and showing he is ready for round two.* Proclaiming how gladly they'll die for their neighbourhoods, they bond.

"Can I have some love?" the smaller one says, leading to hugging and gang-handshaking. With toilet paper, the taller cleans the blood from the other and massages the injuries. Knowing they would smash me to a pulp prevents me from laughing aloud. I listen, riveted by their drama.

The smaller one jumps up. "Does anyone in here look at this man any fucking differently 'cause of what just happened?"

Silence.

"All right, all right, y'all go back to your business then."

Everyone resumes talking.

I'm extracted for fingerprints and photographs. My charge

sheet shows ambiguous drug charges and a conspiracy charge with another $750,000 bond. *How can I bond out now? I'll have to wait to see my attorney to interpret the charges.* I'm ordered into another cell. I figure it's early morning. I want to sleep but fight the urge as it's too dangerous. Eventually, a guard calls us out for court.

It's the same set-up and judge as last year. The prosecutor isn't there. This time I'm more prepared. When Judge Powell asks if I have anything to say, I respond, "Your Honour, last year I asked you to reduce my bond from $750,000, and the prosecutor told you I was the head of a large drug ring. After listening to all of the thousands of wiretapped phone conversations, my attorney and I totalled the value of all of the drug deals among all of the co-defendants, and it came to less than six-thousand dollars. I ask you to reduce this bond to a reasonable level."

"Less than six-thousand dollars!" the judge barks. "I have nothing showing that! The bond stands at $750,000 cash only."

Crushed by his response, I trudge away in a daze. *I should have known better than to expect a bond reduction. Even if my regular judge reduces my first $750,000 bond, I now have a second one. The prosecutor has blocked my attempt to get out. That's why she didn't put up any resistance at my bond hearing.* I dwell on having to tell Claudia and our families.

"It's English Shaun!" someone says in the next cell. "What's Sammy the Bull like?"

"I never met him."

"We know you guys were kicking it together."

"I seriously never met the guy."

The large Mexican American who had noticed me entering the jail approaches me. "I got sentenced to a year. The prosecutor tried to get me to sign some paperwork, Exhibit A, saying I know you and was getting drugs off you, but I told the judge I didn't know you and Exhibit A wasn't true."

I thank him. Contemplating how many of my co-defendants have been asked to sign Exhibit A, I fill with outrage.

Time is imperceptible in The Horseshoe. I check with a guard on the way out to calculate that I've spent almost another day in holding cells. Going on two days with no sleep, the men on the return bus lack the energy to heckle the women in the glass cubicles. They sit quiet and despondent, their eyelids drooping, dark circles around their eyes. The bus rumbles back to the jail, vibrating me to the core.

At Towers, I want to collapse on my bunk and sleep, but my cell is full of smokers. They appraise my mood and disperse. I go to Nick's to retrieve my bags. "I'm outnumbered by the smokers now," I say.

"If you don't want them smoking in your cell, you're gonna have to settle it the old-fashioned way," Big Wood says, implying I need to fight. "It's your cell. You've been there the longest."

"Why don't you move in with us?" Nick says.

"How soon can you arrange it?" I ask.

"I'll talk to Noble today."

I return to my cell. The Tasered man on the bottom bunk appears to be in a semi-conscious state of recuperation. I chance putting my store bags down next to him. He reanimates. Rubbing his eyes with the back of his fingers, he leans up slowly. Sniffing, he drops his legs off the bunk and puts his feet on the concrete. Gazing at me like a Doberman that wants to be fed or else, he yells, "Give me a candy bar!"

Exasperated, I'm about to say something impolite, but Officer Noble announces, "Attwood, roll your shit up."

The announcement lifts some of the weight of my troubles of the past few days. I snatch my bags and rush to Nick's cell. "Thanks, man. How on earth did you get me moved in with you so fast?"

"I didn't."

"What do you mean you didn't?" I ask, shuddering.

"I haven't spoken to anyone yet."

"Better go ask Noble," Big Wood says.

Stood on the stairs, I windmill my arms at Noble in the control tower. He signals back an M sign. I shrug.

"You're being rehoused to the Madison Street jail," he says over the loudspeaker.

Holy shit! With my pulse accelerating and my body heating up, I form a Y with my arms.

"Admin's reclassed you to maximum security 'cause your total bonds are showing as one-and-a-half million on the computer."

"They're separating you from your co-defendants and putting you where the killers are housed," Slopester says. "Watch your back, England."

The weight of my troubles returns much heavier this time.

CHAPTER 36

In May 2003, I'm transferred to the cockroach-infested maximum-security Madison Street jail. I don't know anybody there and most of my neighbours have committed serious crimes such as murder. Unable to sleep with the insects tickling my limbs, feet and palms, and even trying to burrow into my ears to eat my earwax – which I discover is like honey to them – I suffer a nervous breakdown. For days, I hear imaginary voices threatening me. I see cockroaches that aren't there. Drops of water on the floor appear as cockroaches. Concerned for my mental health, I request to see a doctor. I'm prescribed medication to make me sleep.

I get a reprieve from the cockroaches and being grilled by the locals when I'm summoned for a legal visit. A giant Bosnian guard deposits me in a visitation cubicle – a bare room, two plastic seats, a small table.

"How're you doing?" Alan Simpson shakes my hand, jangling my handcuffs. He isn't smiling today.

"Not very well." I sit down.

Shocked to see my eye partially closed due to an infection, he shakes his head.

"Pink eye. Cockroaches from hell. New charges. Doubled bond. I don't know where to begin. You said the case would take a year. Well it's been a year and it's deteriorating! What the bloody hell's going on?" I've never raised my voice at him. At an all-time low, I need to vent.

Taken aback, he says, "What's going on is this." He slaps down some papers. "Take a look at your new grand jury indictment and tell me who you think the other two co-defendants are. Their names are crossed out."

I read the pages. "It says I'm charged jointly with one of the co-defendants for possessing some prescription pills on May 16 2002, so that can only mean Claudia. Holy shit! They've indicted Claudia! Does this mean they'll arrest her?" I ask, panicking at the prospect of her ending up in Arpaio's jail. On the day of the raid, the police found a few prescription pills in our medicine cabinet. I'd had them for so long, I can't remember what they were for. They hadn't resulted in any charges a year ago, so I never expected they would.

"I doubt she'll be arrested. I'll try to get her indicted by mail. What about the other person?"

"It says I used her name to deposit checks in a stockbrokerage account at E*TRADE. That can only be my ex-wife in Tucson, Amy."

"Are you sure?"

"That's my best guess. How can they suddenly indict these people after a year?"

"These charges were prepared before your bond hearing."

"So they could re-arrest me if I'd bonded out?"

"Exactly."

"Isn't it illegal to punish someone for having a bond hearing?"

"Yes."

"Anything we can do about it?"

"Not really. We can't prove these charges were brought up as a response to the bond hearing. They'll just say these things were discovered during the ongoing investigation. Besides, the judge has denied the bond reduction anyway."

"Unbelievable! But those prescription pills were found on day one. Claudia had nothing to do with them. How can they stick them on her like this?"

"They haven't found what they've been looking for in the past year, so they've resorted to tactics like this. If you're right and Claudia is indeed your co-defendant, then they're likely to stop her from visiting you. Co-defendants cannot visit co-defendants."

Flushing with rage, I want to bang the table and rip the grand jury indictment into pieces. *Has the prosecutor indicted Claudia to*

stop her visits, to sever my lifeline? It makes sense. It isn't about Clau-
dia. It's about breaking me down. How can I tell Claudia?

"When is my case ever going to be resolved?" I ask brusquely.

"I don't know. Let me call the Attorney General's Office and find out what's going on. Give me a call towards the end of the week." He zips his briefcase.

Yearning for reassurance, I resent his eagerness to leave. "I don't know how much longer I can take this for."

Sweat glistens on his forehead. "Just hang in there. Remember to call my office." We shake hands. He exits.

May 2003

Claudia love,

I am so sorry I called you this morning and I was too upset to talk. I shouldn't have called you immediately after calling my parents. I didn't want the inmates to see I was upset in here. I was beginning to cry and didn't want to break down in front of people. It was so hard to listen to my dad's upset voice and tell him the news of my move, and the loss of your visits. Karen didn't even speak. She was flabbergasted. It is torture to hear my parents get distressed about my situation. It seems unending the agony everyone is going through.

I am OK, love, but I'm suffering mentally. Don't tell anyone. I didn't want to say anything on the phone because if they find out here they strap you into the torture chair for hours "for your own protection." I probably just need a few nights of good sleep. If I didn't have you keeping me sane, I would have lost my mind by now. I have a goal that's getting me through this. It is to wake up every day safely and to open my eyes and to see you.

It's tricky here having commissary, saying no to people. I did break some bread, but I finally said enough is enough, and I got called a "Jew." I haven't even got my stereo on display except on lockdown. I tell people who ask me that I don't even have one. These people are a lot tougher than at Towers.

I called the embassy and then I got nervous and hung up. I need to calm down before I call them again. I'm losing my mind. They want to destroy me and take my life away. I'm a first time offender. This is insane. I am so confused, love. I miss your visits, and it's really upsetting me. I can't imagine how you are feeling. I think I'd better go look at your pictures again.

I just looked at your pictures. You seem so far away. It's like you are a dream and I am in hell.

This is certainly a creepy place. It's a different form of torture here. The roaches, the open shower and toilet, it's much creepier than Towers. When I went to the shower this morning, roaches were just running wild all over the day room floor. I've never seen so many. It's obscene! I can't toothpaste seal the whole pod, and they just come straight in from the day room under my door. It's tricky when you're trying to sleep and they are running across the walls inches away from your head. There's a strange scratching noise at nights in the walls as well. I suspect it's rats or mice. There is nowhere to hang my towels and undies to dry. I have no extra blanket to do yoga. At nights they turn the lights on at weird hours during the security walks. On the latest walk they came in and checked if my light or vent had been loosened. At least if the experience and suffering of Towers actually did me some good, then this will probably do the same. That's my positive outlook on the situation.

My celly is quiet. He has slept constantly. Who knows what ails him?

I told the fellas at the chow table about the rats in the red death at Towers. They responded with,

"Oh we'd just eat 'em."

"Chew 'em right up."

Not the responses I expected. They get much less bread with dinner here.

Thanks for the photos, love. You look as beautiful and radiant as ever.

Love,
Shaun
XXX

Dear Mum, Dad and Karen,

I hope everyone is doing good despite the bad news on the bond hearing. It was rather disappointing after it was presented so well in court. Alan said I may be here up to a year longer now, while they try to gather evidence against me and find witnesses. I've already done a 1 year sentence, so another shouldn't be a problem.

I've been here so long I have a better understanding of the legal system. I feel the judge was told not to drop the bond during the advisement period. Time after time I've seen him drop bonds for people with more charges than me, with higher bonds than me and from foreign countries. The whole thing is being dragged out so that witnesses can be paid off and deals struck to testify against me. I have a trial date, but I expect if they have no witnesses it will just be postponed. The Black case, a conspiracy wiretap case tried by my prosecutor's boss, was postponed continuously for 3 years until 9 witnesses were found, and then they were all successfully prosecuted, and the leaders got sentenced to decades. If Alan's motions are unable to get the case kicked out, I will ultimately have to plead guilty to whatever they want and accept the punishment. The amount of money they spent on the investigation is flabbergasting, and they must be vindicated at the end of the day. There's still hope. I don't think Alan Simpson will do much worse than getting me 5 years. If my jail time amounts to 2+ years by the time they're done, I'll be halfway through that scenario. I have one of the best legal minds in town on my side, so it is still quite possible that things will end not too bad. Maybe prison is something I need to go through to make me grow up.

Since I've been locked up, I have seen an increase in the jail population from my number, 815706, to 910000. This means that the State of Arizona alone has arrested over 100,000 people from a population of less than 2 million. They've locked so many people up that they started sending inmates to Texas. But a riot by the Arizona inmates in Texas last month put a halt on that. The people running the prisons are crying out for more money from the federal government or else "murderers will go free and the streets won't be safe." When really, from what I've seen, the prisons are being packed with mostly petty drug offenders. That's how the system stays in business, and the corrupt few like Sheriff Joe Arpaio enrich themselves. Enough said.

Love,
Shaun

Dear Karen,

My current conditions will provide good storytelling material. I get to kill cockroaches all day in between listening to one of my new murderer friends tell me whose fingers and toes he's going to chop off and exactly why. He sounds convincing and doesn't flinch as he vividly describes his future plans to me. Why me?

There are a lot of Aryan Brothers in maximum security. I've questioned them (politely) about their beliefs. Alan's New Mexican Mafia clients are a few floors above me. They are all charged with murders for hire, lots of murders, including police officers, public officials and witnesses.

Yep, it's quite a creepy place here. My visits with Ann are through plastic screens with phones. Rather like when Hannibal Lecter first met Clarise.

There's a vivid assortment of characters. Violent offenders and repeat offender drug criminals. There are a few chemists (meth) and an individual whose victim apparently lost her spleen. Most of them have done 10+ years already. I have no access to the outdoors anymore. I've spent a fortune on toothpaste sealing cracks where the cockroaches get in.

So what do you think of the new charges and the dragging of Claudia unnecessarily into the mix? Don't you think it is beyond a joke now?

Love,
Shaun

CHAPTER 37

Going through a terrible drug withdrawal, my cellmate, Joe, stays cocooned in a white sheet for almost a month, only getting up to allow food and fluids in and out. When approaching the toilet, he acknowledges me with his eyes – big, hazel and bloodshot. If I'm lucky, I get a grunt out of him. Handsome other than missing a front tooth, he is beyond the ideal quiet cellmate. It's like living with a corpse, and I'm making the most of the uninterrupted reading. Another advantage is his condition prevents mooches from staying too long in our cell. The inmate code requires not disturbing sleeping prisoners. Drug users trying to mooch commissary to buy meth and heroin are constantly doing the rounds. Whenever one pushes our door open and pops his head in, I simply point at Joe asleep above me. It works fast. The drug user acts uneasy and moves on to the next cell.

The day finally comes when Joe doesn't return to his cocoon after breakfast. He finishes his sandwiches and says, "I've got to catch up on my workouts." He gives me a parting nod and does lengthy sets of push-ups, tricep dips and squats in the day room. The prisoners don't mess with him. I'm glad they show him respect. The more people he gets along with, the less chance of violence spilling into our cell.

Resting on his bunk after working out, Joe turns to me. "Did you hear about the attempted escape?"

"Escape!" I say, sitting on the stool. Escaping from maximum security seems impossible.

"Right before you got here, they rolled the whole pod up for trying to escape."

"This pod?"

"Yup. They were digging the window-frame out. Trying to pull the window out. But they fucked up. As soon as they got so far, they started bringing in bottles of whiskey, cell phones and drugs."

"How?"

"They made a big rope with sheets, and loaded it down to the street level, so they could fish in their contraband. Trust dope fiends to fuck up their own escape attempt. Bringing in all that shit got them busted."

I tell Joe about my charges and mounting legal problems, so he knows I don't have crimes that invite trouble.

"Man, they're going after you hardcore," Joe says. "I hope for your sake, you have a good paid attorney."

"Alan Simpson."

"I've heard of him," Joe says, nodding. "When I was twenty-one, I got busted by the Organized Crime Bureau. I took it to trial and beat it."

"How much time were you facing?" I ask, amazed to hear someone actually won a trial.

"Ten years. It wasn't so much time 'cause it was so long ago."

"Hope you don't mind me asking," I say politely. "What're you in for?"

"Manufacturing methamphetamine. Possession of equipment and chemicals for manufacturing dangerous drugs. Possession of dangerous drugs. Possession of a weapon in a drug offence."

"How much time you looking at?"

"Twenty years."

Shocked, I guess why. "Because of your priors?"

"Yeah."

"How did you get busted?"

"I cooked up a batch of crystal meth in a partner of mine's house, Outcast. After we got done, me, my buddy Ed and his girlfriend were sitting around. Ed tells me, 'You know Outcast got busted in this house three days ago. The SWAT team had to extract him. He got busted for prohibited possessor of a firearm and drug paraphernalia.' I said, 'I had no idea that happened otherwise I would never have done the cook here. Call up Outcast.

He should have told me he got busted. I want to talk to him face to face.' So Ed calls up Outcast, and Outcast says he's too busy to come over. Ed hangs up, and Ed and I know something's wrong. I got a bad feeling about getting busted. So we split up the meth lab and the finished product. Ed's gonna take the finished product in one car, and I'm gonna take the lab, so we don't get busted with everything. It kind of worked. I got busted. Ed got away. The police did a felony stop on me. They found a meth lab, a gun in my trunk and a little bit – an eight ball – of finished product."

"Are you done with drugs now?"

"Look at the hell I just went through since getting arrested coming down off meth. Getting high's a sucker's game. They're building prisons all over America for people like you and me. We're the ones keeping these bastards in business. And even if the cops don't get you, the dope will get you in the long run. One way or another, it'll catch up with you. Guaranteed. See my foot." He dangles his foot off the bunk, displaying big scars. "The day I got my foot shot off, I should have been killed."

"Your foot was shot off?"

"Yup. Here's what went down. I was on a payphone, and my dope-cooking partner, Spike, was in the car. I'm decked out – Italian designer suit, gold chains, the whole nine yards – and a youngster asks me if I want to buy dope. The kid won't go away, so I figure I'll teach him a lesson. I say, 'Yeah. Get me two pounds of meth.' The kid says, 'No problem,' and asks me to meet him at some street corner later on. We pick up a .45 to rob the kid with and go to the spot. The kid shows up with his girlfriend and a car full of Mexicans. I discuss the price with the head Mexican. It's a good price, so I tell Spike it's not good robbery potential, but the guys look legit, and it may be worth actually purchasing the meth. He agrees, so I go back to the Mexicans to discuss the details. The head Mexican pulls out a duffel bag full of half pounds of meth cling-wrapped. I unwrap one of them, spilling some on their car. This irritates the head Mexican, so I open the door, so if any more spills, it spills outside. I put both of my feet out of the car onto the asphalt. Meanwhile, Spike – high on meth and paranoid after robbing some Mexican dealers for cash – figured I was being kidnapped by the Mexicans, and trying to get out of their car. I'm just calmly doing business with them. He leaps in front of the car and opens up with the .45, hitting none of them. But blasting my foot. I try to run, but fall 'cause my foot's hanging off. The Mexicans start unloading their guns on Spike, who went down. I'm trying to get away to get to the donut shop to get rid of the ephedrine I've got on me. I'm crawling away. I see the head Mexican walk up to Spike, take aim at his spine and fire point-blank. He then put the half pound of meth I'd opened into Spike's top pocket. He walks back to the car, sees the trail of blood I've left crawling away and starts to follow it. I'm thinking my number's up. There's no way I can get away from him. By now, people are gathering, and the car full of Mexicans motions to the head guy that they're leaving. He's halfway to me. He stops walking, looks at me, looks at the car, pauses like he's deciding what to do, then heads back to the car."

"Man, you're bloody lucky! I can't imagine being in a situation like that. Did the cops bust you with the ephedrine?"

"No. I booked into a hospital under an alias. They put plates and screws into my calf and foot. I escaped from the hospital and took out the screws with a power drill."

"Ouch! What about Spike?"

"He survived, but he's a quadriplegic. Lives in a wheelchair with a colostomy bag. After hospital, I went right back to doing dope. How fucked up is that? And now I'm looking at another twenty years."

I see parallels: we've both devastated our lives by choosing to do drugs and making one bad decision after another. Not only that, I've devastated the lives of my loved ones. I wonder if Joe has any family support. Joe says he booked into the jail as a Sikh to get a vegetarian diet. "In prison, they made us go to Sikh classes and chant and meditate in order to get the Sikh diet. When I see you doing your yoga and meditation, you remind me of that."

"I'm down as a Hindu."

"The things we do to avoid red death."

"I am really into yoga though. But the jail won't recognise yoga as a religion. I've been getting more into meditation lately. I'm doing it every day."

"Meditation is powerful stuff. Nelson Mandela told Winnie to do fifteen minutes a night when she was in prison. And look at the positive brainwave changes they've recorded in Buddhist monks during meditation. I just meditate lying down."

In the following weeks, Joe and I grow close. He schools me on prison etiquette. I trust him in a brotherly way. We share and discuss self-help books. I feel blessed to have him as a cellmate.

CHAPTER 38

Some of the whites resent Joe and me minding our own business. They make a sport of spilling the drama of the day room into our cell. We humour them, and when they are gone, we laugh and chant *Ommmm...* Unable to get a rise out of us, they resort to intimidation.

Larry, a torpedo for the Aryans, swaggers into our cell. I stop writing at the table. Joe rests a book on his bunk.

"Check this out, me and a couple of the guys just cleaned up the pod for you. It's your clean-up day." Waiting for our reaction, he stands tall, lean, topless and tattooed from the neck down.

I want to point out that it isn't our clean-up day, but I suspect he dislikes me. *He'll be more inclined to listen to Joe.*

Joe dangles his legs off the bunk and sits upright. "Check this out, dude. Number one: it's not our clean-up day. Number two: you can take that shit down the run to somebody who's gonna listen to you who cares."

I'm taken aback because Joe is always polite and respectful to everyone. *Maybe Joe's trying to teach Larry a lesson.*

"What?" Larry shrieks. "We'll see about that!" He rushes out.

I look at Joe for guidance.

"Get on your bunk, celly," Joe says, implying danger.

I rush to my bunk and wriggle around nervously. My pulse climbs. "What do you think's going to happen?"

"He can't fight his own battles," Joe says in a low voice. "So he's gonna–"

Larry rushes in with two Aryan Brothers: Bullet and Ace. Ace is fifty-something, an old boxer way past his sell by date with a crushed nose on a broad face, pocked and scarred. His skin is unnaturally white as if he's spent most of his life in cells deprived of sunlight. He has severe diabetes. Decades of drug use have not been kind to his health. He shuffles into our cell and tries to intimidate Joe with a voice so gravelly it makes me wince. "Hey, Joe, you need to apologise to Larry for disrespecting him."

Bullet is stood like Ace's goon, as if ready to pounce on Joe or me if one of us says the wrong thing.

"I'm not gonna apologise to anybody 'cause I didn't disrespect anybody," Joe says. "In fact, Larry disrespected me."

"Between all three of us," Ace says, taking stock of his comrades, "we've got seventy-five years in the prison system. Larry told me that you told him to take that shit down the run to someone who cares – and we're the ones down the run who care! So you need to fucking apologise to Larry!"

Out of all of my cellmates, I trust Joe the most. He has an indescribable quality – an inner peace – that I warm to. I feel safe living with him. I know he'd spring to my defence if anyone threatened me. Recent events have elevated my tension. My new indictment. My failure to get bonded out. The move from Towers jail. The meeting with my attorney. Claudia losing her visits. The last thing I need is these three venting on Joe who's done nothing wrong. The injustice of the situation makes me snap. So far, I've avoided conflict. I'm trying to use jail as a learning experience. I don't want to go to lockdown for fighting or to affect my case with bad behaviour. But the more I listen to them, the angrier I grow. The situation appears to be heading for violence anyway, so I try to calculate our chances of winning a fight. Joe has been doing 500 push-ups a day, and looks stronger than them, except for Bullet with his powerful build. Ace is all bluster and could easily be shoved to the ground. Larry lacks build, but can move fast: a reasonable match for me. If a fight breaks out, Ace will be on the floor gasping for his inhaler, leaving Joe fighting Bullet, and me Larry. Two other reasons are pushing me in this direction. I want to show Joe that I'll stand up for him, and I want to show them that they can't bulldog us. I have something to say, and I know as soon as I open my mouth I'm committed to a certain course of action. I will have to back my words up physically if it comes down to it. Taking them by surprise, I speak from the bottom bunk. "Hold on a minute. Larry came charging in here saying it's our clean-up day when it's not even our clean-up day. Whoever told Larry it's our clean-up day has caused this issue and I think that person needs to be dealt with."

Ace's face puckers as if a cockroach has crawled into his mouth. They recoil for a few seconds, as if they can't believe I dared to speak.

"You need to keep the fuck out of it," Bullet says, slanting towards me, dangling his fists at the height of my head.

There is no stopping me now. Intoxicated by my own audacity, I press on. "Whoever told Larry it's our clean-up day needs to be dealt with, not Joe. We were just in here minding our own business before all this drama came into our cell."

"You're really starting to piss me off," Ace says, shaking a fist.

"Keep your fucking mouth shut," Bullet says, thinning his lips. "You've got nothing to do with this."

"Yeah, I do! Joe's my celly. What's going on here is wrong. You guys back your cellies up when you feel the same way," I say, citing their own code.

Bullet crouches near enough to throttle me and raises his eyebrows. Staring back, I can tell from the way he is looking at me, that they are after Joe not me.

The others yell:

"Who the fuck you think you two are?"

"You fucking guys know it's your fucking clean-up day!"

"What're you fucking thinking going disrespecting Larry like that?"

"You need to fucking apologise!"

They're working themselves up to attack us. "But it's not our clean-up day!" I yell. "Whoever told Larry it's our clean-up day has caused all of this!"

"Shut the fuck up, England!" Bullet yells.

"That person needs to apologise!" I say, about to spring up.

"I won't tell you again!" Bullet yells.

Just when it seems they're going to pounce on us, Joe says, "Look, there was a misunderstanding. I apologise, Larry."

Stunned, they gawk at each other. My shoulders relax down.

The atmosphere remains combustible until Larry says, "All right, fellas. Let's go." He leads them out.

Before exiting, Bullet shoots Joe a glance that says, *I'll get you one of these days.*

When they are out of earshot, Joe rests his back against the cement-block wall and crosses his legs. "Bullet and Larry can fight, but that loudmouth, Ace, ain't shit. My crime partner shot him one time."

"Shot him! How come?" I wipe the sweat from my brow.

"Ace was in the back seat, my partner in the passenger seat. My buddy was driving. Ace says to my partner, 'Well, don't you know who the fuck I am?' My partner says, 'Man, why don't you just shut the fuck up,' grabs a .38 and points it back at Ace's leg. My buddy says, 'Don't ever point a gun at someone if you're not gonna shoot them.' So my partner shot Ace in the knee. Ace screamed like a little girl and said, 'Take me to the hospital.' My partner said, 'Fuck this dude. Take me to my stolen car.' The driver tripped out, kicked my partner out and took Ace to a hospital."

The next morning, I'm on my bunk browsing through the *Financial Times* when Bullet stops outside of the cell.

"Can you trade this stamp for an envelope?" he yells through the oblong gaps in the door.

"I don't need a stamp, Bullet, but I'll give you an envelope for a milk." A milk is considered a fair price for a stamp or an envelope.

"Keep your fucking envelope! Take my state milk from me! Motherfucker!" he punches the door and storms away, ranting. Having no opportunity to calm him down or to renegotiate, I brace for his return.

June 2003

Dear Mum, Dad and Karen,

Thanks for the books. I'm halfway through "Meditation Now" by Goenka. I like the idea of getting to the root of our problems in the mind. I have been chipping away at stuff with yoga and it has benefited me. Getting rid of the worry voice is my problem. No matter what I do it creeps in with what-ifs? What if they hold me for years? What if they send me to prison? What if I lose at trial? What if the judge has taken a dislike to me and gives me 10 years or more? Before my arrest I never really analysed my mind and compartmentalised it. I never had the need. I'm sure slight worries came in but I was relatively happy-go-lucky. My yoga meditation helps me push worrying thoughts away. But recent traumatic experiences strengthened the worry voice. It constantly creeps up through the day no matter what I am doing. When I am reading, I absorb some paragraphs and then suddenly I'll find I just read the last few sentences and I can't even remember them as I am now focused on a worry.

I am living as Godly as possible and applying all the yoga yamas (5 moral restraints) niyamas (5 observances) and I'm trying to minimise the five afflictions (spiritual ignorance, pride, desire, aversion and fear of death). I apply yoga breathing throughout the day and sometimes visualisation. I've done quite a lot to fight stress. More than most people. I can't imagine how I would be coping without yoga and spirituality.

To indict Claudia to sabotage my visits is to torture me further. What manner of justice is this? I've led a raving lifestyle and I can understand that I must suffer for my sins, but to charge Claudia who has done absolutely nothing wrong clearly illustrates that this is a far cry from any normal process of justice. Thomas Moore, the judge, said that the justice system should be tempered with mercy and not be all about punishment. Inmates keep coming and going and some even going and coming back but I just remain here, month after month.

See how easy it is to get back to negativity and worry. I switched from the wonders of meditation to my usual worry, my grim situation. If only I had a technique to address the constant surfacing of garbage in my mind. I must try to feel no anger or resentment to those torturing me. I pray for their ways to be amended. It is negative thoughts about what is going to happen to me that are drowning me. Where do these thoughts come from? Goenka says they come from very deep down.

Love,
Shaun
Xxx

Dear Mum, Dad and Karen,

Thank you very much for the book Please Understand Me II. Oddly enough it caused a chain reaction with the inmates and I'm now everybody's resident psychological test analyst. The inmates observed me on the phone asking Claudia the test and started prying into what I was up to. So now they're lining up requesting I do the test for them and help them analyse the test results for their loved ones. I already did two alleged murderers today. One came out as the performer ESFP and the other as the champion ENFP. So many people are asking me to do the test I'm exhausted and having to schedule them for later in the week. This book has caused quite a ripple in the pod.

I find psychology fascinating and I'm very grateful for the book. It has helped me interrelate with people, to understand people and to help remove some of my misconceptions, especially about the alleged murderers. It must be a criminal psychologists dream to have such candidates approaching me (a non-authority figure therefore guaranteeing honest answers) demanding I do these tests. This must remove inaccuracy as inmates boast about lying to their doctors all the time. Maybe I should keep the results.

Anyway, it's enabled me to learn a lot and have some fun. As I write this I'm watching one alleged murderer tell another inmate (of unknown criminal origin) about the test, waving his test results in his face.

Madison houses the courts so they wake you up at 5am here for court, and they immediately bring you back when you are finished. This will make all the difference in the world IF it goes to trial, from turning me into a sleep deprived nervous wreck, into actually being able to rest.

It's still "nothin' nice" here. I feel like I am being slowly cooked alive by constant unbearable heat. It's quieter though and more conducive to yoga, studies and book writing.

Thanks v much for the books, love, support etc.

Love,

Shaun

Dear Mum, Dad and Karen,

Aunt Ann came in earlier today and that visit went well. I'm glad that you got my email about the civil rights violations. I'm not asking for freedom. I'm just asking for a prompt resolution to the case.

I started month 6 in yoga today. It takes about 1½ hours. I think I'm getting very flexible because during the forward bend I previously strained to touch my toes whereas now I can touch over them to the middle of my feet, legs not bent for a few minutes. It's nice to feel the advancements. New exercises this month include the bridge and the tree. It's hard to do the tree with my eyes closed.

Recent conversations with the fellas here include how one inmate decided to remove a fellow from his house. He shot him in the arm, removing it, and proceeded to kick him out of his house while the guy was bleeding profusely from the stump. He then called his friend and said, "I shot X." The friend asked "Is he alive?" He replied "Sure he is. I just kicked him out of the house." I've got to see massive scars from various biker accidents and to hear tales pertaining to biker accidents and shootings. An Aryan Brother showed us a 12" scar covering his calf muscle and described a biker accident after which he found his leg stuck over his shoulder with his calf hanging over his face. He was completely unable to move, stuck watching the contents of his calf dribble out.

Love everyone,

Shaun xxxx

Mum, Dad and Karen,

It was nice to speak to D and K today. Sorry I missed you mum. Happy Birthday and Anniversary and stuff! I'm glad you got the card.

People from prison state that county jail time is "hard time," the hardest time to do so I'm through the worst. I'm over the shock, pain barrier etc. and I've adapted to my new surroundings. No worries!

It's quieter here so I can concentrate on writing. In the psychology book it said my type is good at writing fiction books. With all the stories I am hearing, I will write a book revolving around criminals, crime etc.

Claudia has sent me pics from her stay in England. I'm well pleased that she had such a good time. I've got pics of everyone in here now including Nan, Mo, Karen, friends etc. I look at them most nights before I go to bed. You seem planets away but I know eventually, hopefully soon, I'll be home celebrating with everyone.

I hope I get a positive break in the next few months.

Yoga month 6 is going good. I pulled some hand exercises from future months into the mix that include the tripod. I can only do the tripod for about one minute.

Claudia is such a love and she has kept me in the best of moods regardless of what has happened. If I can survive this I'll be able to survive anything for the rest of my life.

Thanks for all the books, love and continued support.

Love,

Shaun

CHAPTER 39

"Get the fuck out of our room with all that hair on you!" Joe says to Bullet who is fresh from the inmate barber. "I've just finished cleaning the room."

"Check this out, motherfucker. I'll kick you out of your own fucking room!" Bullet says. "You don't ever tell me that!"

Larry struts in behind Bullet. *It's about to turn violent.*

"Well, get to kicking then, you bad motherfucker," Joe says.

"I'll be right back 'cause I'm gonna put on my shoes." Bullet leaves.

"Shaun, Larry, you fellas mind stepping outside while I handle my business?" Joe says. For one-on-one disputes the routine is for everyone to leave the cell, so the men can fight.

I brush past Larry hovering in the doorway. "C'mon, Larry," I say, not wanting him to be near enough to intervene on Bullet's behalf. "If you stand there the guards will wonder what's going on." Reluctantly, he follows me to the nearest table in the day room, about ten feet from the door, almost ringside for the fight, which we can watch through the oblong gaps.

When Bullet returns, Larry says, "Hey, Bullet, it ain't worth going to the hole over. Forget it."

"Shut the fuck up!" Bullet snarls.

Joe and Bullet square off, gazes locked.

"You shouldn't have disrespected me like that," Joe says, shuffling forward.

"You ain't telling me what to do, motherfucker," Bullet says.

"You'll feel differently in about thirty seconds," Joe says. "I'm about to teach you to respect me."

Shuffling from side to side like heavyweights, they probe each other with jabs. Bullet feints a jab and wallops Joe's ear with a

247

right hook. Joe stumbles and only just yanks his pelvis back in time to dodge a kick. But he leans forward, exposing his head. Bullet punches Joe in the temple. The inner peace shining in Joe's eyes disappears – replaced by fierce concentration. Joe shakes the pain from his head and unleashes a series of jabs as if swatting a fly. Bullet dodges the jabs, drops into a crouch and tries to grab Joe. A kick to the hip propels Bullet backwards. He snags his leg against the toilet, losing his balance. Joe moves in with a perfectly timed punch to the jaw that sends Bullet against the wall. Bullet's legs go out. He clangs the steel toilet as he falls. Larry shoots into the room. I follow. Blood is trickling from Bullet's mouth.

Larry urges Bullet to get up. "Let's get back to your cell before the guard walks." Larry locks his elbows under Bullet's armpits and forklifts him onto his feet. They shuffle out unsteadily.

I can barely contain myself. "That was fucking brilliant! I thought he had you but you turned it around just like that." I click my fingers. "Where'd you learn to fight like that?"

"It was nothing," Joe says, panting. "Two grown men trying to hurt each other over dumb shit."

"So what'll happen now? Does this make you the head of the whites?"

"No. I ain't into all that. I earned a reputation in prison as an independent. That's why most of the guys in here know not to fuck with me." Joe splashes water on his face, takes a few big breaths and rests on his bunk.

"What's an independent?" I ask, taking the stool.

"A guy who keeps himself to himself, but'll throw down if disrespected."

"So how come Bullet messed with you?"

"Bad chemistry. I've never liked that dude since he came in here asking you about his case while I was trying to sleep. He thinks he's something he's not. That's usually the case when someone's always running their mouth, acting tough."

"Will he still have an issue with you?"

"The fight should squash the beef. He knows better than to

come back with a shank."

"I hope so." Proud of Joe, questions pour out of me. "What's your deal with the Aryan Brotherhood? It's like some of these guys are itching to fight you, but they're wary of you at the same time."

"I do a few things on the streets to make money. The Aryan Brotherhood know about these things and think they're entitled to a part of my action. But here's the rule: if I was doing something on the yard to make money, then yes, they would be entitled to twenty-five percent of the action, but since my action is done on the streets, they've got no stake to claim. So yeah, they get a little upset, but those are the rules. They respect me 'cause I've always stood my ground and don't let nobody punk me out. That's why they're wary of me: they know I play for keeps just like they do. I know a lot of them inside and on the streets, and they know I don't play no games. I know the guy who schooled the Aryan Brotherhood about the Aryan race when the High Wall Jammers changed to the Aryan Brotherhood."

"High Wall Jammers?"

"Back in the fifties and sixties, the blacks in the Arizona Department of Corrections used to rape vulnerable white guys all the time, so the whites started a prison gang called the High Wall Jammers and they started killing the blacks who were involved in the rapes. This was all going on in Central Unit, also known as The Walls. In 1970, the High Wall Jammers changed their name to the Aryan Brotherhood, the gang that started in San Quentin prison back in the sixties and spread across America. I've done almost twenty years and I've met a lot of gang members: ABs, Mexican Mafia, Warrior Society, Mau Maus, skinheads. There's very little I haven't seen or been through."

"I bet you've got some good stories."

"Check this one out. Back in '94, I was at Cimarron Unit in Tucson, serving eight for armed robberies on illegal-alien drug dealers. In Building 1, I knew three Aryan Brotherhood probates: Roy, Henry and Nate. All youngsters."

"What's a probate?"

"Someone aspiring to join the Aryan Brotherhood who hasn't put enough work in – killing, shanking – to get patched up. There was eight-hundred on the yard. Three-hundred whites. Thirteen Aryan Brothers. So, Roy and Nate are stepbrothers. Nate found out his celly was a chomo, and he figured killing a child molester would help him earn his AB patch. The Brothers didn't give him the green light on the kill. Instead they said, 'Beat the crap out of him, so he has to roll up from this yard.' Roy and Henry kept point at the cell door while Nate punched the chomo in the back of the head two times. The chomo collapsed and died. They decided to put him back on his bunk like he was asleep, cover him up and ride it out. It worked for three days: the guards thought he was asleep. But when he didn't show up for chow, they got suspicious. They lifted the sheet up and found a stinking bloated corpse. They locked the yard down. Someone snitched. The thirteen Aryan Brothers and Henry, Roy and Nate were sent to lockdown pending an investigation. Facing the death penalty, Roy and Henry cut a deal with the prosecutor against Nate. The prosecutor offered Nate a deal: twenty-five to life. Nate said no and asked for a trial. They put Henry and Roy in protective custody. The rest, they put in supermax, SMU1 in Florence. The trial went ahead and Nate was acquitted. They rehoused him at The Walls, also in Florence. The thirteen Aryan Brothers were sent back to Cimarron, and they offered Nate the AB patch for going the distance. Nate said, 'Fuck you guys and your patch.' So Nate was eating at the chow hall, and he chewed something in his food that turned out to be a hypodermic needle. He got hepatitis C and successfully sued the prison for two-hundred grand. The Aryan Brotherhood would have killed him, so they put him in protective custody. So the Aryan Brotherhood couldn't get Henry and Roy, they sent them out of state. Youngsters come in thinking it's cool to get in with the gangs, and this is what happens. The gangs just use them and often kill them when they try and quit that lifestyle. It's blood in, blood out."

CHAPTER 40

Three out of thirty of us collapse from heatstroke in July. An emergency medical team extracts each person. Our building conducts heat in the daytime, which it stores overnight, so the temperature hardly drops. With barely any recreation or religious services available in maximum security, we're trapped inside the pod. We circle the day room, dizzy, gagging on the hot foul air, clutching our chests, trying to stay alert so as not to be hospitalised next. My cooked brain feels like it is trying to expand beyond my skull. I get the same unpleasant swelling sensation in my chest around my heart.

On top of the heat, I'm lovesick for Claudia. We are depressed about losing our visits. She is upset over her charges. She turns to alcohol and is difficult to talk to on the phone. For the first time, I wonder whether our relationship will survive. She reveals she has a stalker. She hadn't told me previously because she didn't want to burden me with her problems. Her stalker read the article about me in the *New Times*. He threatened to shoot her and to visit me at the jail. He threatened Claudia's mother who called the police. Claudia is terrified. Trapped inside the jail, I feel helpless to protect her. Furious, I fantasize about him getting arrested, ending up in here with me and the bad things that might happen to him. When my anger subsides, I realise Claudia only has a stalker due to the crimes I've committed. Guilt eats away at me.

The heat and stress make it difficult to sleep, write and concentrate. Chest pains begin, accompanied by a tingling in my extremities. I submit a request to Medical, not expecting to be seen, but to document the condition in case I'm hospitalised. The pains usually come on when I'm reading. I have to put my book down and take deep breaths while clutching my chest until they go away.

Each day, I take multiple showers just to cool down for a few minutes. So does everyone else. The wait for the shower stretches to over an hour. Rather than stand in line, we place our towels and boxers in a row on the metal divide separating the shower area from the day room. Whoever's boxers and towel are at the front goes next. With the shower running constantly, the tiny black flies that live on the pond of scum and semen take to our towels. A quick belt of the towel against the wall gets rid of them. We have one towel each, which we illegally hang out to dry on string ripped from clothing and sheets. But the guards enjoy pulling our clotheslines down and threaten to ticket us for destroying county property. So our towels never dry. After each shower, I try to dry myself with a half-wet towel. Afterwards, I stink of an offensive mildewy odour from the fungus thriving in my towel. In our pod, the smell of mildew comes on slowly at first, blending in with the usual smells. Body odour. Bowel movements. Urine. Smoke. Mop water heavy on bleach. But by the time we are all taking showers every few hours, the mildewy smell dominates. After a few days of everyone complaining, the smell goes away. But not really. We are just so used to it, it's less noticeable. I only figure this out when I leave the pod and return. Re-entering the day room, I'm assaulted by the smell. It fades over the next few days as I reacclimatize. After showering and towelling, the smell of my body repulses me. Multiply that by thirty men and add it to the smell of the drying towels and all of the other smells and you can understand why the guards are reluctant to leave the control tower to do security walks. One guard says we smell like a health hazard.

Our skin does not take kindly to being treated in this fashion. There is the worst outbreak of skin infections I have seen. It looks like chickenpox until the bleeding starts. Nearly everyone has it. After dotting my body, it attacks my chest with a cluster of purple-red rashes. It travels, too. Not so much on my chest, but clusters shift on my limbs. I wake up amazed by their overnight migrations. It itches. I scratch my limbs constantly, but learn not to scratch my chest as the scabs detach and bleed too much.

"It's just a heat rash. There's nothing we can do about it," the guards keep telling us, ignoring our demands for cooler air.

Adding to Joe's discomfort is an inguinal hernia extending into his scrotum, trapping fluid in his scrotal pouch. Even though an inmate has died in the past year from a strangulated hernia, the medical staff decline Joe's request for an operation. The condition makes Joe urinate every few hours, disrupting our sleep. Whenever the roar of the toilet flushing wakes me up, I have to battle the heat, itchy skin and cockroaches tickling my feet to get back to sleep. I tell myself, *Don't itch. You'll only make it worse. Give yourself a good scratching when you wake up in the morning.* I look forward to scratching. The first scratch of the day is the best.

Joe teaches me how to get seen by Medical. Most inmates put in one medical request and await the outcome, but Joe likens a medical request to a lottery ticket. The more lottery tickets you enter, the greater your chances of winning. He puts in a daily request. I copy him. We run out of forms. We cajole our neighbours into requesting them from the guards doing security walks. I start to receive daily rejections from Medical until a positive response proves Joe's theory.

A guard extracts me and escorts me up several flights of stairs to Medical, where the air is mildew free and cooler than in the bowels of the jail.

A jovial 400-pound black nurse weighs me. "I really dig your accent. Will you say something for me?"

Amused, I dip into my repertoire of English phrases. "The rain in Spain falls mainly on the plain."

"No! Not that. Will you say, 'Do you think I'm sexy, baby?'"

I giggle. "Do you think I'm sexy, baby?"

She laughs hard. I hope she's done with me, but she insists on us touring the Medical Unit. In each room, she says, "Listen, everybody! Go on. Go on, Attwood."

"Do you think I'm sexy, baby?" I respond for about the sixth time, bracing for her laughter.

She can't get enough of my accent. I'm glad when she runs out of staff to exhibit me to and deposits me in the Plexiglas holding tank for sick prisoners.

I wait two hours to see Dr Jean. All of the previous doctors were abrupt and discourteous, but I've been told that Dr Jean is fun and frisky. I find a thin man with short blond hair, wearing rectangular glasses. Smiling, he is holding a stack of my medical-request forms in a three-ring binder.

"So you've been having a variety of medical issues?" he says in a chirpy voice.

I tell him about the bedsores, the skin infection, the persistent itching, the chest pains, my insomnia. He compliments me on my accent. I half-expect him to ask me to recite some Austin Powers' lines, but he doesn't. He asks me to remove my top. I show him the rash on my chest. Having lost twenty pounds, I'm embarrassed by a torso reduced to a tangle of matted sweaty hair on protruding ribs.

"These things happen while it's hot," Dr. Jean says, examining the rash. He grabs a tube off a shelf. "Here's some hydrocortisone cream to relieve the itching. I'll put you in for an EKG for the chest pains. Let's take a look at the bedsores shall we?"

I drop my pants and boxers, embarrassed by the vinegary stench of genitals marinated in sweat, and turn around.

Dr Jean crouches to inspect the bedsores. "Heat, sweating, sitting around. Nothing we can really do," he says with pity. "I bet you wish you were in the cooler climes of England."

I pull up my pants and turn around. "Yes, it's much cooler. But it rains too much. Kind of like Seattle weather."

"Whenever I see it on the TV it looks so green and wonderful. All those castles and countryside."

"We've got loads of castles. Especially in North Wales, near where I'm from…" To extend my stay in the cool air, I elaborate on the scenery in my motherland. Before I leave, he surprises me by offering a handshake. Starved of human kindness, I'm overwhelmed with appreciation.

Back in my cell, I'm applying antifungal cream to my behind when Joe rushes in to say that his friend, a crystal-meth chemist in his late fifties, has collapsed in the shower.

I pull my pants up and rush down the run. We join the group of whites standing over a podgy man with a wizard's beard and friendly piggy eyes. "It's my lungs," he wheezes, his face corpse-pale. "I ain't got much longer to live."

"You want us to yell 'Man down'?" Larry asks.

"It's probably the only way I'm ever gonna get to Medical," he replies.

Half of the whites pound on the Plexiglas at the front of the day room, yelling "Man down!" at the guards. Inmates all over the pod join in. Prisoners in neighbouring pods flock to their windows to watch us. "Man down! Man down!" It's good to see everyone chanting together.

"Lockdown!" a guard announces. Guards from neighbouring housing units dash down the corridor and into our pod. They swarm around the chemist, quickly joined by medical staff who extract him on a stretcher.

An hour later, they take us off lockdown and an old-timer suffering from heat exhaustion collapses on the toilet. They lock us down again. As they stretcher him out, the prisoners yell:

"How many more of us have to fall out before you get us some fresh air in here?"

"Turn the fucking air up!"

"It's got to be cheaper to give us some air than put us all in hospital!"

"It's not hot enough in here! Can you please turn the heat up?"

"Where's our ice cream?"

The chemist returns, disorientated, with a heat-exhaustion diagnosis and a pink slip of paper. "They gave me a ticket for passing out in the shower!"

None of us believe he has been ticketed for being ill. We assume he is delirious until he shows us the paperwork.

DISCIPLINARY ACTION REPORT

On 7 24 03 at approximately 1647 hours at 225 W. Madison Street jail, Phoenix, AZ 85003 2-3 D-2 inmate A927117 was taken by wheelchair to medical where R.N.B. diagnosed him with heat exhaustion due to too much activity. This disrupted the operation of this institution by having to cover (3) security walks and delaying medical pill call.

For collapsing in the shower, he receives thirty days full restriction. No commissary, visits, phone calls…

July 03

Dear Love,

I'm writing this in the dark, so I really can't see it. Apologies for the handwriting. I'm trying to dry off (sweat) before I put my antifungal cream on and go to bed. I ate my Benadryl and I'm sleepy.

I've been thinking a lot about your depression and drinking. It must be hard, waiting for me. Drinking vodka almost every night may make you feel good temporarily, but eventually it will turn into a problem. Balance is the key! Go out and have fun on the weekends, but don't throw away your goals and plans. Be strong, and try to do positive things.

I did another mammoth yoga session. Three hours. Medical sent me an extra blanket and I was happy to start doing my yoga with it. I now do the bridge and the tree. Month 6 is a long workout. 1½ hours because there are so many exercises to do. It feels absolutely fantastic though. It's pretty strenuous. I'm holding all these positions for minutes now.

I'm tired but still sweaty, so I'm just going to have to mix the antifungal cream into my sweat.

I think about you constantly. You drive me wild with your amazing beauty.

Goodnight sexy arse!
Shaun

In August, one of the regular outbreaks of food poisoning affects dozens of men. As converts to vegetarianism, Joe and I avoid it. The prisoners blame the green baloney for their vomiting, diarrhoea and dizzy spells. They use up their toilet-paper rations and the guards refuse to provide any more.

Another jail hazard is the filthy rusty metal. Bullet, extorting someone, cuts his thumb on a cell door. His thumb balloons to twice its size, but the guards refuse to take him to Medical. When it turns black and fungal, the guards assure him he'll be seen by Dr Jean, but no one comes for him. The stretched skin eventually splits open and leaks pus. The guards escort him to Dr Jean, who hospitalises him. A surgeon slices Bullet's thumb down the middle to drain the pus out. The inmates make bets as to whether he will lose it.

"That's called boomerang karma," Joe explains.

Bullet returns from hospital angrier than usual. "This motherfucking bread's way too fucking mouldy to eat!" he yells at the guard serving Ladmo bags at the foot of the metal-grid stairs.

"What do you want me to do about it?" the guard says.

"You try eating this shit! Would you feed your family this fucking crap?"

To denounce the food or a guard even is one thing, but it's never a good idea to bring a guard's family into it. The guard snatches the Ladmo bag from Bullet. Bullet grabs a fresh Ladmo bag from the guard and rushes away. The guard gives chase, catches up with Bullet halfway up the stairs and seizes the Ladmo bag. Bullet throws a carton of milk at the guard, which hits the guard's neck and splatters open.

"Lockdown!" announces the guard in the control tower.

Ten minutes later, four goon-squad guards march to Bullet's cell. Keys jingle at his door. A body thuds against the floor and boots slide as kicks are launched. Bullet appears with a brown leather harness around his body and arms, a chain attached to the back of it held by a guard walking him down the stairs like a dog. He doesn't return.

Guards escort me to Medical for the EKG Dr Jean ordered. The nurse attaches the EKG sensors to my legs. Her eyes bulge at the equipment.

"What is it?"

"The reading."

The jail's finally done me in. I'm probably about to a have a heart attack.

She disconnects the sensors and retries but gets the same reading. "I'd better get the doctor!" She rushes away as fast as she can carry her great mass, as if any delay might be fatal to my health.

The prospect of there being something wrong with my heart makes it beat louder.

The nurse bursts into the room, eclipsing the doctor behind her.

Dr Jean works his way around her and gazes at my legs. "They're not supposed to go on his legs. Put them on his chest."

"Thank goodness! You had me worried," I say.

"With that sexy English accent, you're my favourite inmate." Dr Jean winks at me.

The next EKG reading is fine. I return to the holding cell, where two men are comparing spider-bite wounds so infected Medical has actually agreed to see them. Looking at their wounds leaking pus – raised reddened areas threatening to erupt – the bleeding rash on my chest seems trivial. Yes, my chest is itchier than ever and a splinter group of pox-like sores has been travelling up my legs as if it's a living thing homing in on my groin, but I wouldn't trade my rash in for their zombie wounds. No thanks.

August 2003

Oh Claudia,

I just spoke to Alan Simpson and he said Wild Man got 8 years, almost the maximum sentence in his plea bargain, and that doesn't bode well for me. I'm very nervous. This is such an awful bloody never-ending mess! He didn't give me the impression that I'll be getting out anytime soon, so that leaves marriage as the only way of getting our visits back.

We've had constant lockdowns. It's excellent suffering. No showers for days on end. I itch all day now like a wild animal. We've had no toilet paper for over 24 hours, so we're using the Financial Times! I'm hanging out in my pink boxers all day to try and minimise the heat.

I told you that I help the whites out with cookies if they get no store. It costs me nothing, keeps me in their good books and puts me at less of a risk of violence. How do I do it? I lend out 2 for 1 commissary items to the Chicanos. For example, if I lend them $4 worth of store then they pay me back $8. I use the entire profit to pay for cookies for the whites who get no store (and sometimes Chief – the lone Native American). Most people greedily eat all of their store within days, so it's easy getting the Chicanos to do 2 for 1 deals. I've also allowed some people to put money on my books for them to spend. If you're getting money on your books from people you stand less chance of getting attacked because if you get attacked, you end up getting moved, taking their money with you.

There are some heavy hitting criminals in here. My new neighbour in cell 5 is bigger than Wild Man. In his 40's, he's the head of the Hell's Angels' chapter that were in the Laughlin shootout, which he was in, and he was bonded out for $1.7 mill! His name is Chico. Another new guy in cell 7 is about 6 ft 4" and 300lbs, he has a big scar on his face and looks like a classic con.

Chow is in the house. I'll write more later.

Yours always,

Shaun XXX

Dearest Claudia,

I am itchy and waiting for the shower as I'm writing this. Tis very early in the morning and chow is in the house. I am going to have 1 granola bar, 1 pack of mixed nuts and 2 milks. That's as healthy as I can get it.

It was nice to do yoga after the 3 day lockdown. My body feels liberated, and it helps me cope with the stress. I love doing exercises stood on my head. I can't wait to show you what I am now capable of. I am officially Plastic Man as I can bend in so many different ways.

They turn our lights out at 10:30 now. I guess they're trying to save on the electricity bill, so I listen to my radio from 10:30 till about 11:30 or 12 then I try to get to sleep. I listen to Radio Unica (Dr. Isabel's problem page in Spanish) or Coast to Coast with Art Bell. I like the political stuff.

I'm going to try and get back to sleep now that our mopped floor has dried.

Have a good weekend.

I L U

Shaun XXX

CHAPTER 41

In September, I read a book by Arnaud Desjardins, a student of Eastern spiritual traditions. I learn about monks who, from time to time, do horrible things such as eat their own crap as a show of mental stamina. According to Arnaud, "To appreciate a painful situation is to be at one with it, to be at one with the suffering. It is only in this way that we can learn something." Thanks to books like Arnaud's, I make progress on how I view my incarceration. I put myself in jail, so I'm ultimately responsible for my suffering. I must accept my karma cheerfully no matter how bad things get. I must learn as much as I can from the situation.

Discussing karma with Joe, he says that it's up to us to put happiness into our lives and the lives of others, no matter how bad the jail conditions are. That's why he always allows time for inmates to unload their grievances on him, no matter how petty. Even though our belongings are meagre, Joe is constantly coming up with novel ways of giving people little gifts. One of his favourite sayings is, "Giving is good." He describes every new crisis as good suffering, which is necessary for our learning. Although his attitude is alien to my belief system, it's working so effectively for him that I adopt it. Whenever I'm struggling to spend time with certain inmates whom I fear or dislike, Joe insists I especially make time for them and jokes that it's good giving.

Hoping to get off the sleeping pills, I gradually increase my meditation time from ten minutes to a few hours. To remain undisturbed, I wait until the cells are locked-down. I put pink socks on and tuck my pants into my socks so that the cockroaches can crawl on me without gaining access to my legs. I place books on the floor, so I can elevate my behind above the cockroaches. With my back parallel to a cement-block wall patrolled by cockroaches,

I sit cross-legged and close my eyes.

At first, I'm intimidated by the prospect of calming my mind for longer than ten minutes. I start out concentrating on my breathing, counting breaths when I have to. Eventually, the thoughts stop. Every now and then a thought intrudes, but I refocus on my breathing. Thirty minutes in, I'm struggling to ignore aches and pains and pins and needles. I stop, but try again the next day. Over time, I learn to alternate crossed-leg positions to prevent my legs from turning dead and to ease the discomfort. After an hour of meditating one night, my thoughts are barely there. I enter a deep state of relaxation as if all that exists are my breath, pulse and the movement of blood and energy throughout my body. Sensing areas of facial tension, I concentrate on allowing those subtle muscles to relax. My previously tense fingers open like flowers blooming until my hands are as flat as spades. I want to meditate forever, but my cellmate using the toilet snaps me out of it. After meditating for a few hours every night for two weeks, I feel less stressed. I stop the sleeping pills. My clarity of mind returns. I'm surprised at how easily I sleep after meditating even with cockroaches tickling my extremities. Some nights, I meditate for so long that images materialize in my brain. Meditation is saving my sanity.

Lying down after meditation, I wonder why I committed so many crimes for so long. Are there any criminals in my family? Definitely not my parents. As far as nurture is concerned, my sister is a model citizen. I had all of the advantages in life not afforded to most of my neighbours, which makes me feel guiltier. I put my crimes down to the selfish pursuit of pleasure by a man with more money than common sense. Considering the dangerous situations I put myself in, I wonder how I'm still alive. *Getting caught may have saved my life. I'll never do drugs again.*

I incorporate new yoga postures into my routine. I'm in the canoe pose – belly down, alternate arms and legs slightly raised – when a Lindo Park Crip gang member facing the death penalty for murdering several people walks in. He shot a woman in the face who was holding her four-year-old son as a protective shield. Shortly after that, a witness was found floating in a canal. He says, "You look like one of my victims trying to crawl away." Energy flutters from my solar plexus and bursts through my chest. I'm tongue-tied. Afterwards, I tell Joe, who responds nonchalantly, "He's all right when he's not murdering people. I get along good with him." Joe's answer enables me to talk to the Lindo Park Crip without hyperventilating. He takes a liking to me because we've both made the cover of the *New Times*.

A gaunt freckly redhead from South Carolina limps into my cell. I ask what's wrong. He says he has a year to live because of stomach cancer. He has syphilis, hepatitis C and herpes. Urinating is agony and he hasn't passed a solid stool in three years. The metal screws in the steel rod in his leg have unloosened, causing constant pain. I ask him what he's in for. He says he took a foot-long knife to the woman who gave him syphilis, repeatedly stabbing her in the stomach. Facing a life sentence for attempted murder, he's going to die in here. Hearing his story, I realize things aren't so bad for me.

The extent of my neighbours' problems puts mine into perspective. Throughout my life, I only cared for myself and a close circle of friends, often neglecting my family. I realize that must change. In the spirit of Joe, I aim to make the most of the situation and put a little meaning and humour into our lives. I start a competition called sufferer of the week. I offer a Snickers to the winner as voted by the rest of the prisoners. As we barely get fed, a Snickers is equivalent to a meal. Joe contributes a honey bun. The competition takes off, delighting my neighbours. An early winner is a prisoner bitten by a spider. Daily, he begs the guards to take him to Medical, but they decline, informing him that it's the policy of the jail not to treat insect bites. Over time, his pus-filled thumb turns fungal and black. By the time it's so bad they actually take him to Medical, he's rushed to hospital to have the thumb amputated. He says it was all worth it to get the Snickers.

Many of the prisoners can't read or write, never mind comprehend the legal terminology on their case paperwork. I start reading their cases and interpreting the jargon for them. The Mexicans have the most difficulty with their paperwork, so I offer to start an English class for them. If the jail doesn't want to educate prisoners, maybe I can make a small difference.

The class is in a cell upstairs. I'm surprised and delighted when half of the Mexicans show up. I have five students. Four murderers and one charged with attempted murder. Secluded with them, I could easily be grabbed and hurt, and no one would come to my rescue, but I believe that by trusting them, I will earn their respect. If I show fear, they will behave accordingly. I teach them the basics from a text book. In their eyes, I see friendly curiosity and a thirst to learn, not danger. One of the murderers is a midget with a thick beard and a boyish happy face. Mid class, he stands up, flexes his muscles like a strongman and chuckles.

Some of the whites disapprove of my helping another race, which scares me because a female guard is smuggling drugs in and the men have been up for days and are looking for someone to smash. Joe intervenes with the whites and tells me to continue. That I've gone against my own race to help the Mexicans surprises the Mexican gang leaders, who tell me that if I ever have any problems, they will back me up. Individual Mexicans ask me to tutor them one-on-one in their cells, mainly to help them compose letters in Spanish for their loved ones. Helping read their court papers, I'm flabbergasted by the amount of time they are facing. Teaching them gives me a sense of purpose and it feels great to help others. I'm frustrated at the jail for not offering any classes to the Mexicans. An ideal opportunity to intervene in their lives is being wasted.

Sept 2003

Dearest Claudia,

You asked how I am feeling. Sick. I feel sick because we have no visits and deep inside a voice says you are slowly forgetting about me. I have spent hours writing you letters and you have not responded to any of them. I get no mail from you and I can feel you drifting…drifting…drifting away from me. And when I call you, I hear so much pain in your voice, I wonder if my happy Claudia will ever come back to me. I know it's hard for you, and this mess is all my fault, and that is making me feel even worse.

We're suffering lockdown after lockdown. This lockdown run has no amount of days on the notice, and the reason given is "INVESTIGATION." They have paraded us out of our cells twice and searched the whole pod. This morning the goon squad strip-searched all of us. I took the pictures of you down just in time before the goon squad came. In the pits of hell I am, but I am constantly thinking about you. As you have stopped writing to me, I reread your old letters during these lockdowns.

You are my world and my biggest fear now is losing you. We have been through so much, it would be such a shame. If you continue to not write to me, then I shall be forced to write enough for the two of us combined.

Devotedly,
Shaun

Dearest Claudia,

Sorry about the previous sad letter. It's so hard being separated from you. Please try and understand how it is to be in jail. The kinds of thoughts, worries and stresses that run through my mind, and how helplessly, hopelessly trapped I am. I apologize to you for sounding down on the phone. You are feeling depressed and that explains your behaviour. I love you so much. I just want it all to end and for us to begin our family. We should be snuggling, spooning and having unprotected baby-making sex!

Please be strong for us. Your strength is my strength.
Shaun XXX

Darling Claudia,

It is the morning after I just listened to your sweet voice. Talking to you is the highlight of my day, and I appreciate you taking my calls even if you are not up to writing.

I did my yoga workout and now I'm waiting for the shower. South Carolina "sufferer of the year" is in the shower right now. He takes about 7 showers a day to soothe his ailments. They gave him little cups to poop in today so they can check his stool. This morning he asked me if yoga would help him, so I showed him month 1 in the yoga book.

Chow has been rotten spuds and carrots every single night! I'm getting fed up with spud-carrot sandwiches 3 months in a row. My only meal of the day!

Luv you loads!
Shaun XXX

CHAPTER 42

I'm in a packed court holding cell when two Tempe transportation guards stop outside. They keep glancing at me, rousing my suspicion because Tempe Police Department initiated my case.

"Which one's the snitch in this cell?" one asks.

"Attwood's the snitch," the other says.

My ears twitch. *Was that my name? No. Surely, I'm hearing things again.* I concentrate.

"Attwood's the snitch."

I shudder. An electrical current travels across my skin, raising the hairs on my arms. *That was my name. Holy shit! They're setting me up to get killed. How can they get away with this?*

When they know everyone has overheard, they walk away. They've "jacketed" me. In the sixties, federal agents jacketed the leaders of radical student groups. By giving the impression that the leaders were cooperating with the authorities, they turned the group against their leader or at least flipped those members who fell for the ploy. In here, the gang rule for snitches is KOS: Kill On Sight. Snitches are as hated as child molesters. If the prisoners believe the guards and figure out I'm Attwood, I'll be attacked.

"They're just trying to cause trouble for Attwood," an inmate says.

Thank God for that! Relieved, I'm about to volunteer my name and explain that Tempe police are out to get me because they don't have much of a case, but a much larger prisoner says, "If we've got a snitch in here, we need to handle it."

Fuck! Now what should I do? As if to prevent me from speaking up, the muscles in my face tighten. Other prisoners side with the big prisoner, clamming me up even more. All eyes roam the room for Attwood. Blushing, I pretend to look for Attwood. *Is my*

267

red face giving me away? I blush more. The more vocal prisoners debate what to do, mainly expressing enthusiasm for smashing Attwood. *I'm about to pay for all of the violence I've dodged since my arrest. The guards who started it won't be in a hurry to stop it.* Motionless, I say nothing, convinced opening my mouth will invite disaster.

Five minutes later, a guard yells, "Attwood, come out!"

Everyone looks at everyone else, as if ready to pounce on Attwood. My pulse skyrockets as I wait for the door to fully open. I step out fast and breathe easier.

"You're not going to believe this," I say to my attorney. "Two Tempe cops just told the inmates in the holding cell I'm a snitch."

"You cannot be serious," Alan Simpson says.

Still rattled, I describe what happened. He tells the prosecutor. The prosecutor guarantees a full investigation. The inmates in the cell will be interviewed. I'll have to identify the officers in a line-up and they'll be reprimanded. Suspecting the prosecutor is in on the plot, I doubt anything will be done.

In a holding cell afterwards, I can only think of one person capable and motivated enough to jacket me: Detective Reid. He led the investigation, said disturbing things while arresting me and attends nearly all of my court appearances with the devotion of a stalker. He reacted emotionally when no drugs were found at my apartment and threatened me over the keys to the safe. *It's more like a vendetta.*

When I return to my floor at the Madison Street jail, the guard in the control tower says, "Attwood, you've been rehoused upstairs for your own protection."

I'm not allowed into my pod to collect my property. A porter brings it out in plastic bags packed by Joe. Realising I might never see Joe again, I'm sad, and fearful of new cellmates. My books and stacks of legal paperwork slowly tear the bags open as I wearily follow the guard to the elevator.

"Where we going?" I ask, shuffling slowly.

"Wherever I take you," he says.

The elevator stops at the fifth floor. I follow the guard down a series of corridors. We arrive at a control tower overlooking four pods. All of the prisoners are locked down except for in one pod, where the men are watching me, some smiling. Many of them are older men, clean cut, a breed apart from the regular prisoners. The guard in the control tower instructs me to go to a cell in a pod that is locked down. He activates the sliding door. As I approach the cell, one of the rips in the bags containing my property expands and sheds a few golf pencils, which clink on the floor. The control guard hits the button to open the cell door. The door slides open, groaning mechanically. I enter.

Inside, a startled black man in street clothes is hiding a glass pipe in the toilet. "What the fuck!" he says, echoing my thoughts. The trapped crystal-meth smoke reeks like cat urine with a twist of lemon.

"Who're you?" Wincing, I put my bags down. The door slides closed. *Am I being set up for this guy to attack me?*

"Who the fuck are you coming in here making me flush my motherfucking dope?"

"They just moved me up here." I don't appreciate him talking to me as if I'm new to the jail. "I've been in the county jail for almost a year and a half."

"A year and a half! What the fuck for?" he asks.

He might be a snitch or undercover cop assigned to pump me for information. "Drugs. It's a complex case."

"Mine's a complex case, too." His eyes find my commissary bag. "Got anything to eat, wood?" Addressing me as wood means he assumes I'm a gang member.

"Not much. Just enough for me. Why the street clothes?"

"Getting released at midnight. Girlfriend's bonded me out."

At least he'll be gone soon. I can't sleep safely around him.

"Give me something to eat, wood."

I don't mind giving him a snack as he won't be around long enough to demand more, but I feel disrespected by his tone. *He is testing me. I must establish boundaries.* "Where's your manners at? If you ask politely, I'll consider it." *If we're going to fight, it'll happen now.* I gaze as if crazy from starvation and willing to fight to the death to defend my food. He has a weight advantage. Even though I'm skinny, I've been working out with Joe and I feel a ropey strength. He has sneakers on. I have deck shoes acquired from a diabetic, not slippery shower sandals. Tense and ruffled from being moved, I have no patience left. *Showing I'll fight might make him back down.*

"All right, man, can you at least hook you celly up with a little somethin'-somethin'?"

Knowing he's playing on the rule that cellmates look out for each other gives me a sense of control over the situation. "I've got Snickers, MoonPies. I ain't giving up any of my peanut butter."

"Oo, a MoonPie."

His response pleases me. A MoonPie costs half the price of a Snickers. I only bought them for barter. Giving one away will not cut into the commissary I've allocated to eat. I hand him a MoonPie. He flushes the wrapper down the toilet and crams the whole thing in his mouth.

Realising the top bunk doesn't have a mattress, I fume. "No mattress!"

He stops chewing loudly. "You got mine when I leave."

"I ain't lying on that steel. I'll flag a guard down when he walks."

"He ain't gonna give you no motherfucking mattress. They just ignore you up in this motherfucker."

"What is this pod anyway?"

"Temporary lockdown housing."

"What the bloody hell's that?"

"They put people here they don't know what to do with till they decide what to do with them."

"So you saying I won't be here long?"

"No one's here long."

I hate being in transit, having nowhere to settle, uncertain where I'll end up. "What's our neighbours like?"

"Got none. This pod's mostly empty."

"How about that pod over there with all those guys hanging out?"

"Them's all chomos and rapos."

"What?" I ask, shocked. Having never seen a pod full of sex offenders before, I press myself to the cell door's narrow window to get a better look. None of them have tattoos. Many are old or middle-aged, fat, bespectacled, meek-looking. I don't want to imagine what they've done.

"Some high-profile Catholic-priest motherfuckers over there," he says, shaking his head.

I don't doubt it as Catholic priests have been on the news. I put my commissary bag on the top bunk to use as a pillow and to prevent theft. I climb up and read. The metal punishes my back. Every so often, I have to shift my position due to the discomfort. Hearing the day-room door slide open, I jump down and bang on the window at the guard and yell for a mattress. The guard passes as if I don't exist. My cellmate laughs. I curse the guard, return to my bunk and read for hours, unable to absorb much or let my guard down in case my cellmate tries anything.

Come midnight, I want to sleep but my cellmate hasn't left. By 1 a.m. I assume he's lied about getting released and I'm stuck with him and no mattress. My disappointment ends around 2 a.m. when the guards collect him. When the door shuts behind him, I finally start to unwind. I jump down, convinced watching him go will prevent him from coming back. When he is out of sight, I luxuriate in being completely alone for the first time in ages. My mind is briefly happy but my body aches all over from the steel. I move to the bottom bunk. His mattress stinks of sweat and the lemony-urinous odour of crystal meth. Drifting into sleep, I wonder what kind of person the jail is turning me into.

CHAPTER 43

The next afternoon, the noise *step-squeak-slide step-squeak-slide* interrupts my reading. It's coming from the day room. *A sound I'm unfamiliar with. How odd.* The *step-squeak-slide* gets louder. I roll off my mattress and go to the cell-door's narrow window. Someone is approaching. To avoid getting caught staring, I back away.

A tall frail young man in bee stripes limps past. He has cropped copper hair, a gaunt freckled face and a shrivelled left arm sticking up uselessly in the air. After he circles the day room, I move closer to the window to get a better look. Dragging his lame left leg behind a strong right step, he passes by, his face streaked with rivulets of perspiration, his eyes sad. Watching him do laps, I put my face closer to the window. Eventually he sees me and flashes an uncertain smile. Feeling guilty for watching him, I smile back. I return to my bunk and try to read, but my mind keeps returning to him. *How hard it must be to be disabled in jail.* Wanting to know more, I plan on talking to him at his cell window when I'm allowed out for a shower. By law, prisoners in lockdown have to be let out for one hour each day to take a shower, make a phone call and walk around the day room, but inmates in lockdown are prohibited from loitering outside of each other's cells. He is housed in cell 1 next to the shower, so my best bet is to talk to him by hovering near the entrance to the shower, which hopefully won't be so obvious to the guard in the control tower.

Every day my hour out is an hour later than previously. For the next three days, I'm disappointed to see him asleep in the foetal position. At 9.30 a.m. on the fourth day, I catch him awake but forget what I want to ask him.

"Hi! I'm Shaun!" I shout at his window.

"Hi," he says, sitting on the bottom bunk, barely audible be-

272

hind the Plexiglas. "I'm Chicken Wing."

"Do you have any deodorant?" I ask, assuming he is indigent.

"No."

"Need some?"

"Er, yeah, yeah, sure." He seems confused.

"I'll be right back then." I fetch him a deodorant from my cell and push it through the gap below the bottom of his door.

He scrambles from his bunk, crouches down and grabs it. "Thanks," he says in a weak voice, staring at the deodorant as if he doesn't know what to do with it. "Got any crackers? I'm hungry!" he yells, his face lighting up and shaking.

"Sorry," I say, disappointed. "Haven't any left."

"Oh, well. Never mind. Thanks for the deodorant." He turns around, ending my plan to learn more about him.

The next day an announcement comes: "Attwood! Cell 4! Roll up!"

Nervous about being moved, I gather my property.

A few minutes later, a second announcement: "Miller! Cell 1! Roll up!" The only person in cell 1 is Chicken Wing.

Glad Chicken Wing is rolling up, I hope to talk to him. I coil my mattress, place my books onto a bed sheet and make a carrying sack. When the sliding door opens, I follow the guard's instructions to wait in the corridor next to the guard tower. A guard arrives, handcuffs me and leaves. Chicken Wing is called out but not handcuffed. We stand together, awaiting instructions.

"How're you?" I ask Chicken Wing.

"I dunno. OK, I guess," he says.

"Pleased to meet you again," I say, offering him my handcuffed hands.

The tower door clicks open and a Mexican American guard emerges.

"Where we going?" I ask the guard.

"Dunno. It's up to the guards in 5-4," the guard says.

Chicken Wing can't be handcuffed in the usual fashion. It's impossible to cuff his good arm to his handicapped arm, but security protocol demands he be cuffed somehow. The guard straps a thick brown belt around Chicken Wing's waist and handcuffs his good right arm to the belt buckle, rendering him unable to carry his mattress. Reluctantly, the guard picks it up. Shackled and carrying my heavy belongings, I struggle to 5-4. Instructed to wait at the foot of the control tower, we sit on our mattresses.

"What's your accent?" Chicken Wing asks with a curious smile.

"English. I'm from England."

"England! You Scottishman, Englishman, Londonman you!" Animated, he stutters: "S-S-S-S-So t-t-tell me, wh-what's it like in England?"

"Cold and wet most of the time. Very green 'cause all the rain. The people are friendly. I think you'd like it."

"I-I d-d-don't like the cold. W-W-Well d-d-do they have car races in England?"

I pause. "I don't follow that. They have the Grand Prix in Europe. A lot of it goes on in France, which is next to England. There's some motorbike race on the Isle of Man, a small island off the coast of England and people are always getting killed."

"D-D-Did you see them get k-k-killed?"

"No, I never went. I only saw bits on the news. I had a nice little Japanese sports car before my arrest."

"D-D-Did it have gears?"

"Yes. Up to fifth and a twin-turbo engine."

"I-I-It went fast! It went faster! It went fastest!" Chicken Wing yelps. He makes a low rasping sound, mimicking an engine revving, while shifting gears with his good arm. As his euphoria expands, he turns up the rasping noises and starts rocking. Perched hazardously on his rolled-up mattress, he loses his balance, topples backwards and bangs his head against the wall.

He touches his head. "B-B-Blood? Am I bleeding?" Rubbing the back of his head, he howls, "Will I die?"

I assure him he's neither bleeding nor going to die.

A guard emerges from the control tower. "You lot are going to

B pod. Miller, cell 1. Attwood, 14."

Glad to be housed in the same pod as Chicken Wing, I aim to get to know him better. I watch him approach cell 1. His new cellmate, a tattooed youngster, fetches his mattress.

CHAPTER 44

My cellmate, Squeegee, has the wide eyes of a zombie and a weatherworn animal-like face. In the throes of heroin withdrawal, forty-one-year-old Squeegee has straw-like shoulder-length hair and abscesses the size of emu eggs on his tattooed arms, some of which are hatching into open sores.

"I was arrested on October the third for the seventy-seventh time," Squeegee says in a soft-spoken Texan accent.

"How can you be arrested that many times?" I ask.

"Forty-seven of them were misdemeanours. I've been in prisons and jails across Arizona and Texas and I can honestly tell you this place is the worst. Sheriff Joe's jail is hard time, dog. It's even worse than death row."

"What did they charge you with?"

"Weed. But it's a bullshit case. The cops pulled us over for a traffic violation. I was in the passenger seat. The cops became suspicious and searched the vehicle. They found a roach with a tiny bit of weed in it."

I explain my charges and ask about his drug history.

"I lived in Tyler for twenty years. At nine, I started smoking weed, boozing and burglaring. I dropped twenty hits of acid at fourteen. I was twenty-one when I moved to Phoenix and got into crystal meth. Five years later, I was slamming it. I was thirty-eight when I got into heroin. In '98 I shot up some coke and fell out in the bathroom. My dad found me and called the paramedics. In June of 2000, I shot a dime of heroin, went outside and collapsed on some bushes. My sister found me and called the paramedics who revived me. Up until this arrest, I was shooting a gram of heroin a day. That's three hits a day for three and a half years. Three times a week, I treated myself to a special high. I'd cook a quarter gram of heroin, melt a quarter gram of coke into it and add half a gram of speed. It all dissolves nicely in the spoon. There's nothing like it. It's the best high there is. It makes your body warm, gives you an instant erection and makes your asshole tingle."

I laugh. "When were you last employed?"

"I worked construction – roofing, cement, clean-up – for fifteen years. My girlfriend of nine years broke up with me in 1990 'cause of my habits. Since then I've hung out on the streets."

Squeegee passes the time wriggling on his bunk, his eyeballs rolling around non-stop as if projecting figure eights and loop-de-loops on the cell walls. Sometimes, I catch him gnawing on the abscesses on his arms. When he attempts to eat, he suffers chronic farts. He fills out a medical request: *I need to see a doctor. I have been here 10 days, and my heart just keeps racing. I can't sleep. I toss & turn every 30 seconds. I need to see someone.*

The lack of human contact in lockdown can send prisoners crazy, but I view it as an opportunity for uninterrupted thinking. I read like never before. My mind begins to skirt around the big questions in philosophy. *What are we? Where are we? Why are we here?* My father mails me *On the Origin of Species*. Reading the book that shook the foundations of many religions raises more questions. I wonder why Darwinism and creationism can't be reconciled. *What if a creator made a species that evolved? What if a creator is some kind of cosmic scientist and we are just bacteria in a petri dish? But who created the scientist? Or God?* Boggled by how insignificant humans seem to be in relation to the vastness of the universe, I strain my mind on these questions, only to conclude I'll never know the answers. On religion, I decide that most people need some form of spirituality to flourish as well-balanced beings – especially during difficult times – and that's why I do yoga. After Adam Smith's *Wealth of the Nations*, I move on to Karl Marx's *Capital*. I learn that at the height of the cotton industry, the people living in the region of my hometown were worked so hard that they only lived thirty to forty years. The chapters on child labour and ailments appal me. The people from my region became so haggard from overwork that some married Germans to try to restore a normal appearance in their children. Obsessed by history books, I range from World War II back to the Sumerians. Fascinated to learn how much knowledge they had in areas such as astronomy, geometry and trigonometry as far back as 6000 BC, I wonder why I was taught that Westerners had discovered most of these things in recent centuries. Reading is transforming my world view. Things I've been conditioned to believe all of my life start to dissolve. I realize that the corruption in the legal and prison systems is a small part of political and corporate corruption throughout many industries worldwide, a subject I pledge to research more and write a book on. I read for over fourteen hours a day, until my brain and eyes ache so much I can't continue. Every word I don't understand, I look up in a dictionary: metaphysics, inchoate, caprice, solipsism, empiricism, acrimony, abstruse, irascible, phlegmatic…

"How're you liking the fifth floor, English Shaun?" asks a tall grinning twenty-something with a handsome Hawaiian-looking face and a snake tattooed on the side of his neck. He is stood outside of my cell, yelling at the narrow window.

I approach the window. "How do you know who I am?"

"I've been to your raves. Name's Mack. You gave me some Ecstasy one night. Tempe cops even offered to cut me a deal if I'd provide information on you, but I told them to fuck off."

"They did!" I say, surprised, until I think of Detective Reid.

"Yeah, we both know a lot of the same people. Glad you finally made it upstairs. I read the *New Times* article on you. We've got a few high-profile cases up here."

"Like who?"

"Let's start with the Native American living next door to you. Remember the Rodeo fire up by Show Low and Heber that was on CNN every day?"

"Yes. It was all over the news. The biggest fire ever in Arizona. It destroyed hundreds of homes."

"Your neighbour in 15 is the Rodeo Arsonist."

"No way!"

"Don't get too excited. He's just some brain-damaged dude the Feds found for a fall guy."

"You saying he didn't do it?"

"Who knows? But if you talk to him, you'll see what I mean."

"Who else is up here?"

"The 101 Slayer."

I'd heard a news report about the 101 Slayer. He'd run people off the Interstate 101. The police thought only two cars were involved, but a third was found three days later with more dead people in it. "What's he like?"

"He's cool, man. He's from a rich family. He used to go raves."

"Any more up here on the news?"

"In 11 is the skinhead who made the news for spray-painting a swastika on a mosque. The guys in that pod over there only get the loaf to eat. It's a disciplinary-segregation pod. They just moved two guys from the Mexican Mafia in there for soaping off the American flags painted on their cell walls. That was on the news. Sheriff Arpaio made PR out of it. In that pod over there is the abortionist, Dr Ross, who the *New Times* ran a whole series on. They say he molested his patients."

"He's all over the news. He's got no chance."

"He says he didn't do it, and I kind of believe him 'cause he refused to sign a plea bargain that would have set him free and he's taking it to trial. If he loses, he's gonna get a life sentence. My celly was on the news. His girlfriend dumped him, so he figured he'd commit suicide by doing a bunch of robberies and getting shot by the cops. He did the armed robberies, but they just ended up arresting his dumb ass. That guy yelling to you down the vent from the sixth floor is a maniac who killed a bunch of people."

"How do you know what all these people are accused of?"

"You find out when you go to court with them and see them on

TV. The last time I went to court, a chomo teacher was sentenced to 400 years: fifty for each victim. The news channels filmed us spitting on him. Some soldier got four years for statutory rape. The seventeen-year-old daughter of his colonel seduced him at his barracks, but he goes to prison 'cause she's underage."

"I just saw they gave the death penalty to that guy who killed the Sikh right after 9/11. The Sikh was the uncle of two of my friends who own an Indian restaurant. How much time you facing?"

"Forever. When the prosecutor brought up how much time I'm facing, I told her, 'I'm going to fuck your dad in the shower and then have a little snack afterwards.' She said, 'I'm gonna see to it that you never see the light of day.' The goon squad escort me to court now in all kinds of shackles and chains."

Later on, an inmate shoves a note and a book by David Icke under my door:

Shaun,

This is Mack in B12 again. This pod is cool. Every day we get a comedy hour when certain inmates are on their hour out. It's some pretty hilarious shit. So have some laughs. Tell me, do you have a radio? I have 2 if you need to borrow one let me know.

I am in here on 54 felony 2's. Shitty deal. I have a real good lawyer though. I am lookin' at 540–775 yrs. However, I am innocent, and I will only be convicted on one Attempted Murder from 2001. I gave my lawyer $40,000, so hopefully I won't serve more than 8–40 yrs.

If there is anything you need let me know.
Mack

Oh yeah, here's a list of shit you might hear people yell at nite.
  Who shit in the shower.
  There's roaches in the ice.
  I'm going home tomorrow.
  Take a fucking shower.
  Ya got any oranges.

What are ya gonna do for me.
You ain't gotta lie to kick it.
I was teabagged in the army.
I've seen so many balls.
Hook me up with your sister.
Your sister's got a pretty mouth.
Why don't you look at some balls, ballgazer.
Sweet.
We're gonna shank that little fuck.
Shut the fuck up Leprechaun.
If I was in Durango I'd smash your ass.
I wanna go home.
I would fuck the shit out of your grandma.
Last call for alcohol.
I'm not supposed to be here.
This is all a big mistake.
Does anyone have a Honey Bun for Ramon.
Do that shit in the shower.
You shit eating pole smoker.
Gentlemen, times up, times up, your hour has expired. You need to go back to your cell and lock down.
Look at these haters surrounding me every day.
Don't smile at court tomorrow you'll get another charge.

CHAPTER 45

At a legal visit, Alan Simpson says four of my co-defendants have agreed to testify against me, including Wild Woman. Due to these witnesses, I'm facing a minimum of nine years if I sign a plea bargain and the judge doesn't aggravate my sentence and a maximum of over a hundred years if I lose at trial and the judge gives me the aggravated sentence for each of my twenty-three felonies and runs them consecutively. If I hold out for much longer on signing a plea bargain, Alan warns, each additional witness found will increase my sentence. The news shell-shocks me.

Wild Woman has signed a cooperation agreement with a sentence ranging from four to eight years to avoid the hundreds of years she is facing on over 150 felonies. Her public defender – who has barely done anything for her throughout her incarceration – has frightened her into cooperating by stating that Wild Man and I are setting her up to take the fall for my crimes, and that most of the evidence would go against her. He said she would get anywhere from 25 to 99 years if she didn't cooperate. After agreeing to cooperate, Wild Woman was told that her life was in danger from me. She was whisked off to Payson jail, where the police booked her in as "Missy" and prohibited her from writing to anybody, including her dying mother.

Wild Man writes, urging me to sign a plea bargain, so Wild Woman won't have to testify. Angry, I refuse to sign a plea bargain. Against Alan's advice, I demand a trial. Wild Woman sends an apology.

Hey now! Hi Shaun,
    I hope this letter has found you in good health and that you are doing ok. I have wrote and re-wrote I don't know how many letters

to you but no matter how I write it I just can't find the right words to tell you how sorry I am about everything and all the trouble I might have caused you. I never meant to do you any harm. I really didn't. I am so sorry Shaun and I mean that from the bottom of my heart. I am sorry for being weak and letting everything get to me. I should have stood by you and I didn't and I hate myself for that. It's something that I have got to live with for the rest of my life. I feel I got pushed into doing something that was against all that I believe in and I was at a low point in my life. I was not thinking straight. I had been told that my mum did not have long to live, sad to say she passed away, and I was told that it was getting pinned on me and if I did not stand up for myself then I would lose. They also said it would get me home to my mum but it didn't.

To tell the truth, I was scared shitless and I didn't know what to do and I was in a mess for the longest time. I could not sleep, eat or anything. I was so upset and confused by it all. I just kept thinking that I had to get home to care for my mum and that I had to put our friendship on the line. It was the most horrible choice I have ever had to make. If I could turn back time, I would. I never meant to hurt you or make a mess of things for you. Please believe me that I love you with all my heart and it hurt me so bad knowing what I was supposed to do, it all made me so ill. I only hope that you will forgive me one day. You are a great guy, you were a great friend to me and I thank you for being there when things went crazy with Wild Man.

I received your article last week. It made me cry. I hate the thought of you going through that shit and believe me I know what it was like. I am not doing too badly now. I tried to kill myself twice, stupid I know but I was in a bad way for a while. I have since become Muslim and I started to study Islam. It has changed my way of life. I meditate every night. It helps me to focus and it takes me to another level, a higher state of mind and I feel more at peace with myself. I would love to do yoga but I don't know if I can do it as I still have a lot of back pain. I used to read my Koran a lot but I don't have one now and I am trying to get one. I don't smoke anymore. I don't curse and I pray to god as often as I can. I don't eat pork or ham. I hope I can be a better person.

Anyways, I will close this letter for now, please forgive me for all the trouble I may have caused you, you are always in my heart.

I hope to hear from you soon.

Please take care and stay safe. I worry about you.

Stay strong. Peace. All my love always,

Wild Woman

October 2003

Dear Claudia,

Now I've been moved upstairs, it didn't take long to be recognised. Just like at Towers when I met Billy the Hippy who I'd taken really good care of one night, well Mack in cell 12 here was at some apartment in Tempe when I brought my party friends over. I was v. nice to Mack and he's offering to help me however he can. He already sent me a tub of peanut butter, which is good because I'm now 5 days without the veggie diet. They've been trying to give me white sliced cheese with grey speckles in it and it is foul. We've been getting stale pita bread lately and genetically modified plums that went to the size of grapefruits and suddenly stopped. Now we're getting 2 slightly rotten oranges in the mornings.

Last night Chicken Wing was walking around on his hour out, and someone asked him to go to cell 7. Chicken Wing stumbled over there and went hysterical, and started running around the pod shouting, "They're fucking sucking! They're fucking sucking! He's eating sperm! He's eating sperm! He's eating sperm! Fucking sucking! Fucking sucking!" for about 10 minutes and cackling like a possessed Rain Man. It was pretty funny. Maybe #7 is a gay cell! I've saved my dessert, a donut, for Chicken Wing. I'll stick it under his door on my hour out. Good "giving." I feel so sorry for him because he is in here and disabled.

The maniac above me is losing his voice from shouting:

"Shut the fuck up, punk!"

"Punk ass, bitch!"

"Get away from my door, punk ass!"

He also makes noises that sound like he's digging through the ceiling, which is of concern as he's supposed to have murdered a bunch of people.

In the next pod is David, an all American lad with a good job, no drugs, and a beautiful young Spanish wife. He got sentenced to a flat 21 years. He came home from work one day and his wife was having sex with another man in his bed. David told the man to quickly leave and he went to the bedroom closet, pulled out a fully loaded shotgun, and blasted his wife in the head. The shot removed most of her head, killing her. Yikes!

I drew a picture of the view from our cell's skinny window located above the top bunk near the ceiling. Looking east, I can see the stadium directly in front of me. Looking down, I see the parking lot roof and street. I think it's Jackson because I can see a grey building which looks like the Jackson Hole bar where I threw the rave Mechanism. I can view it at any time, so it's easy for me to see you on the street. I just need a time.

That's my update. I'll write more later on.

Love you,

Shaun XXX

ps) I discovered that I had brought the cockroaches upstairs with me. They had nested in one of my brown envelopes. I wondered where they were coming from. Hopefully that was the last of my run-ins with them.

Love,

Today's gone pretty fast. I read Darwin all day. Chicken Wing ran around making fake orgasm noises and shouting "runny poop." Someone left poo-stained pink boxers in the shower. I suspect my celly. He sneezes and itches all day and his long hair is falling out and decorating the room. He's ill from the heroin come down. At least he's quiet though. He naps with his eyes open. Quite odd, eh?

I've started talking to 2 Arab fellows downstairs, and they are both a good laugh. They sneak upstairs on their hour out to talk to me.

I did get to meet some interesting people at the weekend. On Saturday, a downstairs neighbour, Leprechaun, went to Visitation and I finally got to meet him at close range. He is short but stocky. He looks like he is in his mid-40s and he has long straggly hair and a beard. He has Irish features and long nails on his hands and feet. His toenails curl down over his toes. So upon closer examination, he fits all of the leprechaun criteria, but I guessed that his leprechaunness probably ended there, he was probably a nice guy to talk to, and probably didn't act like a leprechaun. The guard escorting us to the elevator was 6 foot 4" ginger-haired with Elvis style sideburns. We got to the elevator and Leprechaun talked:

"I was on TV. I pulled me pants down. I was alright. She thought I was attractive. She called me mother." He grunted.

The guard shook his head and looked at Leprechaun like he was crazy.

Then Leprechaun yelled at the guard, "You've never smoked!"

At this point I concluded that he was a genuine leprechaun. The guard couldn't believe what he was hearing. The angry Leprechaun continued:

"She saw me on TV and called me mother. She said I was very handsome. I said I didn't want anything to do with her. I was trying to light a cigarette and my pants dropped. Then there was a big light. It was all on the TV."

I've finally met a leprechaun!

Then on Sunday I went for a hair trim and the tall skinny Chicano/Italian inmate barber starts cutting my hair and telling me that he had been peeping at me in the shower from the pod opposite. He said he saw me with an erection, and he was wondering if I needed a new cellmate. Yikes! He'd done 8 years in a prison which was "nothing nice" and he was now bisexual. I told him that I threw raves and that most of my friends were bisexual but I was a max inmate (he was medium) so that he couldn't move to my room.

I love you more than garlic naan,

X Shaun X

November 2003

Dearest Claudia,

It's chilly in here now. Last night I slept in my full clothing with a skinny sheet over me. The chow was yellow rice last night, and my celly didn't want his so I purchased it for a bag of snack mix.

I've also been writing some expose-style stuff for my jail book, and yesterday I wrote a big chapter on the food. Squeegee used to work in the kitchen in '99, so he told me about what goes on in there. Some of the food he helped cook (boil) was 15 years past its sell-by date. It was canned vegetables. Squeegee gets sentenced soon, and he is stressed out about whether the judge will give him 1 year or 1½ years. I wish I could trade places with him.

The inmates say the madman in the cell above me is James, a mass murderer. He is growling and yelling at the people in his pod. His voice travels quite loudly through the vent:

"Punk arrrggghhhhhh! Punk snitch hideout bitch arrrghhhhhhhh!"

I talked to him through the vent the other day. I pretended to be Mike, one of the 9/11 detainee Arabs downstairs who was in the shower, and James proceeded to tell me about stabbing someone 60 times, and he gave me some names that he wanted killing. "Kill all of 'em and take care," were his parting words. He thinks he's getting 75 years, and claims to have murdered his own daughter.

Leprechaun is hassling people downstairs, and telling the young gay lad in cell 7 that he knows that he "hangs out in the streets with his ass in the air," and "he should try fuckin' his mom 'cause she hasn't had any dick in 20 years." He's being a crude little leprechaun this weekend.

It'll be almost 2 years of jaildom soon. Unbelievable! Even Alan Simpson said the case would take less than a year to resolve. It's so unreal. I can handle doing this time but it kills me to be putting the people I love most through it as well.

See you in court,
Shaun XXX

Hello precious,

It's almost lights out time, and I'm pretty exhausted. The philosophy and thinking books that I've been reading have sapped my brainpower. I'm back to writing again, and I'm currently writing about my first month at Towers.

Thank you for taking 3 calls this evening. I imagine I sounded pretty mental on the phone. You made me feel a lot better. I was worried about a number of things. When Alan talked to me in court, I was doolally nervous and I did not fully understand what he said to me. I did hear him say 10 years and then my mind started worrying. I figured the Tempe cop who lied to the inmates that I was snitching and tried to get me smashed was part of a bigger picture of them just wanting me to die or to be locked up forever. Plus with Wild Woman cooperating, everything at once has just hit me again when I expected the madness to end. It just gets madder.

I dreamt that I got many years and that for you to wait would ruin your life so I ate a gram of heroin and killed myself so you could go on with your life. As I did it I knew how much it would hurt my mum and it made me hysterical, but I knew that I had to do it and I did it anyway. It's hard to get these negative thoughts under control recently. I hate being weak like this and I don't like to burden you.

Sometimes I feel like I am going mental and I try and disguise it by being positive all the time but it's so hard. Getting deeper into yoga and meditation certainly helps. My usual worries are trial, sentencing and what is going to happen. I can be sat reading and then a silly little thought will just pop into my head and then my mind goes and I'll have to reread what I just read. Not knowing what is going to happen to me for this long is utter torture. Squeegee says anyone else would be on meds or mental by now for being in jail for so long. My efforts to stay sane are exhausting me. I miss simple stuff like us buying smoothies and going grocery shopping at nights.

I am sorry for putting you through this, and I constantly feel guilty for letting my family down. I can't believe they are trying to give you a felony for a few prescription pills. Squeegee is an expert on misdemeanours. He has 40. He thinks that they'll end up offering you a misdemeanour to avoid trial. He said a felony will really hurt when it comes to job applications and stuff like that.

Tonight's been a wacky night. Mack intercepted a love letter from a guy in another pod to cell 8. It was news to everyone, and now the whole pod is singing YMCA. I joined in on my hour out and sang a little bit of "I'm too sexy for the jail...too sexy for the jail," and some Relax by Frankie Goes To Hollywood. All of the excitement gets me going and then I feel sad because I wish I were enjoying life with you.

All my love,
Shaun XXX

December 2003

Dear love,

It's all so terrible. Today the judge said that I would get life if I lose at trial. I would definitely kill myself if that happened. Nobody here has ever heard of a first time drug offender getting such a high plea. I am getting so screwed if I sign this deal now.

I've had to increase my meditation time. I've started meditating first thing in the morning to begin my day on a positive note. I think about the people I love, including you and my family members.

Love you loads,
Shaun XXX

Claudia's public defender refuses to prepare a defence and urges her to sign a plea bargain for three years of probation, two years of drug counselling costing $50 a month and a $5,000 fine. She can't pay the fine and fears a felony will ruin her career prospects.

Claudia visits her attorney to tell him no. The meeting snaps her out of a depression. He says we'll get our visits back if she signs for a Class 6 felony – conspiracy to sell or transfer prescription drugs – and pays a $200 fine. She happily agrees. Her sentencing hearing is set for December 23. She says getting our visits back is going to be the best Christmas gift she could possibly ask for.

Out of love for me, Claudia pleads guilty to a crime she hasn't committed. When I call, she is the happiest I've heard in months. She says she's coming to see me. When the visit we are looking forward to isn't announced, I worry something is wrong and call her.

She answers sobbing.

"What's wrong? What's the matter?"

"They…wouldn't…let…me…in."

"Calm down. Try and tell me."

"I…I…again, I just lost the one thing I used to look forward to three times a week, coming to see you. I just signed my life away 'cause I was lied to." Her tone turns angry. "I stood in front of a judge and said yes, yes, yes all because my public pretender, that Dick Tosso, that motherfucker–"

"Try and calm down," I say, containing my outrage. *Are there no limits to the dirty tricks lawyers play?*

"He was never nice to me. He was always trying to get me to turn and talk against you. The first thing I asked him was, 'What can I do to get visits back?' He called me and he was shouting, implying I was being an idiot for not taking a misdemeanour and up to three years' probation. But if you're on probation, you can't visit the jail. He said if I pled guilty to a felony, I'd get visits back. The judge said, 'A felony will impact you for life. It will impact your right to vote and any civil rights you have. Certain jobs you'll never be able to get.' And just at that moment and with a confident smile, I said yes 'cause all that was important to me at that moment was getting our visits back."

"I can't believe this! I didn't know an attorney can just lie to you like that. You need to put a complaint in to the Arizona Bar Association."

"That's not gonna get our visits back!"

"Maybe I can get Alan Simpson on it."

"When? What are we gonna do in the meantime? I'm so sad." She sobs. "I don't think I'm ever gonna be able to see you again until you're out. They haven't even tried you. They're moving so slow."

Fearful of losing her, I strain to sound calm. "We've come this far and it hasn't been easy. We can make it through the dirty games these attorneys are playing. Look, I love you. We can get through this."

"You're always so positive. Maybe too positive."

Without the visits, I fear for our relationship. That Claudia is the victim of my mess recedes into the background as my anger erupts at the prosecutor and Claudia's public defender for tricking her with more injustice than she can bear.

For the first time, I do a ten-minute headstand. I discover Greek philosophy and become obsessed with Plato's *Republic*. Biographies take up much of my time: Timothy Leary, Howard Hughes, Aldous Huxley... From David Icke's books, I learn about corporations such as Halliburton that are profiting from George W. Bush's response to 9/11. I grow fearful about the direction both UK and USA politicians are steering the military. Meditating, I visualise being inside various shapes: spheres, tetrahedrons, spinning Platonic solids... I imagine light running down my spine, grounding me with the earth. I sit in the lotus position for twenty minutes staring at a mandala pattern and when I close my eyes, the glowing image of the mandala remains. I discover higher states of consciousness without poisoning my body with drugs. I long to visit an ashram and read Sanskrit texts. I write letters about parallel universes, sunspots, supervolcanoes and the illuminati. I move onto an advanced Spanish text. Attempting to learn Mandarin, I sketch Chinese characters. These activities take my mind off the time I'm facing.

CHAPTER 46

Inmates in the upper-tier cells coax Chicken Wing into climbing the metal-grid stairs that rise from the front of the day room up to the balcony.

"I've got crackers! Come and get them!" a prisoner yells as if talking to a dog.

"Cookies for you over here, Chicken Wing!"

"You can do it, Chicken Wing!"

Chicken Wing looks around for his cellmate to get the food, but his cellmate is in the shower. Chicken Wing attempts the first stair, but stops when he almost falls.

He's going to hurt himself. I must stop this. On my hands and knees, I yell through the gap under my door, "Don't do it, Chicken Wing!"

"I can't come up the stairs!" Chicken Wing yells.

"Come on, climb the stairs!"

"*Cookies,*" a man shouts in the Cookie Monster voice, shaking a rack of cookies.

Chicken Wing tries again. The inmates stood at their doors cheer. He makes it to the second step, swaying, hanging onto the railing with his good hand. They cheer again.

"Go back down, Chicken Wing!" I yell.

He almost falls forward onto the third, but rights himself to more cheering. Pausing, he looks over his shoulder at the distance he's travelled and shudders.

"Don't give up now, Chicken Wing!"

"You can do it!"

"You better get your ass up here if you want these cookies, dog!"

"*Cookies,*" comes the Cookie Monster voice.

Watching through the Plexiglas, I shake my head.

Using the railing, he pulls himself forward, but falls to one side and collapses on the stairs. The inmates boo, laugh and mock him.

Emerging from the shower in pink boxers, his cellmate finds Chicken Wing sprawled on the stairs. "You shouldn't fuck with a cripple like that!" he yells at the men upstairs. "I'll be right up there when I get dressed to get those cookies from y'all!" He helps Chicken Wing up, gets dressed, charges up the stairs and demands the cookies.

Chicken Wing's cellmate is sentenced and rolled up a few days later. The guards cell Chicken Wing with a schizophrenic old man who urinates on the walls. Chicken Wing spends most of his time on the bottom bunk at exactly the height the old man urinates at. Living in constant fear of being urinated on sends Chicken Wing into a depression. He stops badgering us for crackers.

On my hour out, I watch the old man accost a guard. He is stood at his cell door, gazing at a Mexican American female through the window. "Why am I here?"

"What do you mean: why am I here?" she replies.

"Why am I here?"

"'Cause you've got charges."

"I'm not here for the good of my health you know! Why am I here?"

"You have charges," she says sympathetically.

The old man dances around the cell, twisting his head from side to side as if seeking something. He stops as suddenly as he started and stares at the guard with a crazy expression. "I don't see my charges! I definitely don't see them! My charges aren't in here! Why am I here?" It's more than she can take. She abandons him ranting.

The old man's behaviour devastates Chicken Wing. He stops speaking to us and barely leaves his cell during his hour out. Whenever I peer into his cell, he is on his bunk rocking dementedly, his face blank.

After taking a shower, I visit him. "Come and talk to me, Chicken Wing."

"No! Go away!"

"Look, if you tell me what's wrong, maybe I can help you."

Silence.

"I'll get you anything you want off the store list."

His remote expression fades. "Anything?"

"Anything."

"Cookies?" He grins like a child.

"Lots of cookies."

He raises himself awkwardly and stumbles to the window.

"What's the matter?"

He glances over his shoulder at the old man asleep on the top bunk. "He's gonna pee on me. He already peed on my mattress."

"How about I fill out an Inmate Request Form, asking they move you to another cell and you sign it."

"I'll do it! I'll do it! I'll do it!"

The guards move him in with Leprechaun. Chicken Wing's mood improves for a few weeks, until Leprechaun announces that Chicken Wing is wetting the bed, leading to cruel jokes on Chicken Wing's hour out.

Squeegee's public defender dupes him into signing a plea bargain stipulating a minimum sentence of four months, a presumptive sentence of one year and a maximum sentence of two years. Reviewing the police reports, Squeegee decides the police conducted an illegal search and have no case against him. Insisting he stick to the plea bargain, his attorney refuses to prepare for a trial. After consulting his family, he petitions the court to revoke the plea bargain and replace his attorney. The judge denies both requests and sentences him to nine months.

During his last week with me, Squeegee mentions Bonzai.

"Throughout the jail, I've heard so many people talk about Bonzai," I say. "Is he the bogeyman of the Arizona prison system or what?"

"I served time with Bonzai at Florence," Squeegee says.

"You knew him?"

"Yeah. Robert Wayne Vickers."

"What's his story?"

"He was just some tall skinny kid arrested for doing burglaries in Tempe. He was only sentenced to do a few years. He came in in the late seventies. He was real quiet, not considered a threat at all, so they housed him with the general population at CB4, all two-man cells. He snapped 'cause his celly drank his Kool-Aid and didn't wake him up for chow. He waited for his celly to go sleep and killed him with a shank made from a toothbrush. He carved the word Bonzai on his celly's back. To show the guards his celly was really dead, he put a cigarette out on the corpse's foot. After that they called him Bonzai or Bonzai Bob.

"They charged him with murder and moved him to a single cell in CB6 – super-max housing for death row, gang leaders and the most violent prisoners. In CB6 they were locked-down all day except to come out for showers. They said you couldn't escape from it but Bonzai managed to get on the roof.

"Another time, he picked his cell-door lock, waited for one of his neighbours to come out for a shower, came out and almost shanked the guy to death, but the guards stopped it. So he got attempted-murder charges for that one.

"Back then, the cells had power outlets, and you could heat up food in your cell, like plug-in hotpots from the store. In '82, Bonzai boiled up some hair gel and took it with him when they let him out of his cell. He told his neighbour to come to the front of the cell and threw it on him. He used toilet paper to set him on fire. His neighbour died and a bunch more nearly died from the smoke."

"Why'd he kill that guy?"

"He'd talked some shit about Bonzai's niece. They transported him to Florence for a court appearance. In the holding cell, he picked the lock on his handcuffs, but made it look like he was still cuffed when they took him into the courtroom. He waited for the judge to start, then jumped up and attacked the people in the gallery. It was on the news. When the guards were about to cuff him for another court appearance, he pulled out a shank and stabbed one in the stomach and the other in the shoulder and armpit. He was so dangerous, the warden had a shower installed in Bonzai's cell and had the door welded shut. They considered him the most dangerous inmate ever in Arizona. In '99, they finally let him out of his cell – to give him a lethal injection. The guards said in his last years his crazy eyes made him look like he was possessed by the devil."

January 04

Dear Mum and Dad,

I am sorry about recent stressful events in court. I suspect, as usual, there will be no March trial. No hearings to listen to the calls have been set, and I'm expecting a better plea bargain. The current plea was tinsel wrapped to entice me. When in reality the judge could sentence me to 12 years of which the Department of Corrections would make me serve 85%, and I calculated I'd be 44 when I got out! Nothing is as it seems in this game that the prosecutor and Detective Reid play with people's minds and lives. In my 20 months in jail, I have never witnessed a 1st time offender with like charges get offered so much time. They are hell-bent on making an example out of me. Look how they took it to the media immediately to make a splash and to get public opinion against me. People with more serious charges than me generally get probation or less than 5 years if it's their first time in trouble.

I am deeply sorry that by prolonging my legal fight I am also prolonging your agony. Sometimes I feel like I should just give in, and sign the plea, and let them do what they want to me. Just to end the uncertainty and stress and costs. It's a horrible situation I've put myself in. Sometimes I cannot concentrate on my studies because I fear I am about to lose the prime years of my life. This is the end phase of extremely high stake negotiations, and that's why our stress levels are peaking. I honestly think that things shouldn't be dragged out too much longer. My goal is to be in prison before the summer heat starts to cook us alive.

All my love,
Shaun

Darling Claudia,

Today was weird. We have been on security override since last night because of a riot on the 2nd floor, and our water was turned off all day for repairs. The riot happened because 2 pods got out of their pod doors and fought a bloody battle. We heard reports of an inmate smashing a fire extinguisher into other inmates' heads. It sounds like the jail nearly lost control.

They took my celly, Squeegee, to Alhambra, which is the processing centre on 24th St and Van Buren where we all go before going to prison. Then they gave me a new celly from the 2nd floor. He was a Chicano caught with a needle, and he was quite a thug. They moved him out pretty quickly. Then the female guard said that she was moving some crazy old crackhead up to my room from room 3. I pleaded with her not to, and Jack, one of my neighbours, pleaded with her and now he is my new celly. Jack is nice. We've played chess and he likes my books.

Leprechaun has a new celly again after his old celly rolled up within a few days claiming to the guards that Leprechaun had put a curse on him.

Some poor sod in cell 2 got sentenced to 26 years today. He was convicted of armed robberies and had prior convictions. Ouch!

Sorry I am unable to call you because of the security override. I hope to hear your sweet voice soon.

All my love forever,
Shaun

CHAPTER 47

"How does Arpaio get away with these jail conditions?" I ask a guard.

His reply, "The world has no idea what really goes on in here," makes me want to tell the world. *But how?* I'm limited to describing the conditions in the letters I write to my family and friends. *If I can draw media attention to the conditions things might improve for those stuck in here after I've left.* I've gone from being afraid of some of the prisoners when I was first arrested to bonding with them through our shared endurance. I've gained an understanding of their backgrounds. The majority never had the advantages I had in life, so I feel it's my responsibility to articulate their sad situations. Many have addiction issues and are from broken homes and are victims of abuse. The jail offers nothing to rehabilitate them. The horror of this place pushes them further into drug use, which offers them a temporary escape.

Since 1982, Sheriff Joe Arpaio has won multiple elections by proclaiming that he is the toughest sheriff in America. He's got away with decades of human-rights violations because most people don't care about prisoners – which I understand because I didn't either until after my arrest when I discovered that society's most vulnerable people are in here, including the mentally ill. The media led me to believe that jails are full of serial killers and child rapists, but they are only a small percentage of the population. The disproportionate amount of stories about killers and rapists keeps the public in fear of all prisoners and feeds the lock-them-up-and-throw-away-the-key attitude. Most of the prisoners I've met need counselling, mental-health care, education and job skills yet they are treated like animals, which sometimes creates monsters like Bonzai in Squeegee's story. Going on two years in here, I no longer recognise my former selfish self. I want to do something that will benefit the prisoners more than sufferer of the week.

My mother writes to a member of the UK parliament about the conditions and requests he demand a resolution to my case. He says that if you commit a crime overseas, you must abide by their rules. She writes to Amnesty International and finds out they are documenting the human-rights abuses but are powerless to intervene.

My father reads *The Clandestine Diary of an Ordinary Iraqi* by Salam Pax. It contains the blog entries Pax wrote as the bombs rained down on Baghdad and what it was like during the early days of the war. My father thinks it will be a good idea to post my descriptions on the Internet as a blog. He sends me a copy of Pax's book. Awaiting it, I wonder if a blog is the tool I've been searching for to expose the conditions. After reading the book, I agree with my father that we should start a blog. (The prisoner who reads the book next is an ex-pilot of Saddam Hussein's who lives below me.) Prior to my arrest, my knowledge of blogs was limited to one written by a friend of Claudia. Blogging seemed trivial, but Pax's book demonstrates that it can be newsworthy. Part of me relishes the opportunity to get back at a system that has pulled so many dirty tricks on me and Claudia. Yes, as a criminal I deserve to be punished, but things like trying to get the prisoners to kill me by using a snitch jacket and criminalising Claudia to prevent her visits have overstepped what I can reasonably accept by those who are supposed to be upholding the law. I want to expose Sheriff Joe Arpaio and other criminals working in the justice system.

My mother is aware of news stories about Arpaio's guards being responsible for the deaths of inmates such as the partially blind Charles Agster and mentally ill Scott Norberg. She is worried about reprisals against me for exposing the conditions. With things deteriorating on the legal front, I don't want to put anything online that might hurt my case. To avoid repercussions my father suggests we start the blog under a pseudonym. My parents come up with Jon's Jail Journal. Jon because the Irish spelling of

Shaun is Sean, which means John, and Jail Journal tacked on for alliteration.

The riskiest part for me is getting what I write out of the jail undetected. Mail can be opened at any time to be inspected for contraband or if a guard suspects that a letter contains details of crimes that have been committed or are in progress. If the mail officer opens my letters, I will be discovered. My aunt Ann is still visiting every weekend. *I can stash my blogs in the personal property I release to her. A few sheets of paper among many will surely get through unnoticed.* After sharpening my golf pencil on the door, I start writing.

Feb 19 04

The toilet I sleep next to is full of sewage. We've had no running water for three days. Yesterday, I knew we were in trouble when the mound in our steel throne peaked above sea level.

Inmates often display remarkable ingenuity during difficult occasions and this crisis has resulted in a number of my neighbours crapping in the plastic bags the mouldy breakfast bread is served in. For hours they kept those bags in their cells, then disposed of them downstairs when allowed out for showers. As I write, inmates brandishing plastic bags are going from cell door to door proudly displaying their accomplishments.

The whole building reeks like a giant Portaloo. Putting a towel over the toilet in our tiny cell offers little reprieve. My neighbour, Eduardo, is suffering diarrhoea. I can't imagine how bad his cell stinks.

I am hearing that the local Health Department has been contacted. Hopefully they will come to our rescue soon.

I received a card from Claudia saying she is going to stick with me no matter what happens. Through her brother, I was able to coordinate a delivery of roses for her on Valentine's Day.

Feb 20 04

My cellmate couldn't hold his in any longer. He pinched his nose and lifted the towel from the toilet. Repulsed by the mound, he said, "There's way too much crap to crap on, dog. I'm gonna use a bag." So as jail etiquette demands in these situations, I rolled over on my bunk and faced the wall. I heard something hit the rim of the seatless toilet, and him say, "Damn! I missed some!" When he was done, he put the finished product by the door and the stink doubled. He had no water to clean where the piece had fallen on the toilet, so it remained forming a crustation on the rim. We were hoping to be allowed out to dispose of the bag, until a guard announced, "There will be no one coming out for showers and phone calls as we have to get one-hundred-and-twenty inmates water from an emergency container!"

The water came back on in stages. In our toilet, its level slowly rose.

"Oh no," I said. "It's about to overflow, and we'll be stuck in here with sewage all over the floor."

"One of us needs to stick his hand in the crap to let the water through," my cellmate said. "And you're the closest."

The brown soup was threatening to spill from the bowl, so I put a sandwich bag on my hand. "I can't believe I'm doing this," I said, plunging my hand into the mound. The mound took the bag from my hand. Almost up to my elbow in sewage, I dug until the water level sank.

"I owe you one, dog," my cellmate said.

"It's your turn next time," I said.

Because the tap water hadn't come back on, I couldn't wash my arm. Not wanting to contaminate anything in the cell, I sat on the stool until a guard let us out for showers hours later.

Feb 26 04

At 7 a.m, I awoke to a cockroach tickling the palm of my hand. Like everyone else in the jail except for the staff, it was probably hungry. I flicked it towards the door. It took the hint and headed west.

The excursion of the week was to the Medical Unit for a "general wellness check-up." Four of us were summoned from our pod. At the nurse's desk we were interviewed one after the other:

"I slept with a woman from a trailer park just before I was arrested," said one of my embarrassed neighbours as the nurse diagnosed him with scabies.

Next up was our chow server. I was shocked to overhear that he has had infectious tuberculosis for the duration of his stay.

The third inmate complained that he had gone two days without his seizure medication and as a result was unable to sleep.

When it was my turn, the nurse insisted I should take a TB test. I protested that I had been tested twice already. She looked at my medical history, and snarled, "Well, you'll have to take another test before June, so you might as well have it now."

At least our water is flowing again. Inmates are still trading stories about crapping in plastic bags and urinating in pop bottles. The 101 Slayer boasted he was able to hold his business in for the entire three-day outage. It was also his mum who called the Health Department. Hopefully, our toilets will continue to function normally, at least, until we are moved to the new jail facility, which should be this summer.

As my cell can be searched at any time, I stash my blogs into a manila envelope containing mail I've received. *It would take the guards hours to read through everything in the envelope and they just don't have the time.* I fill out an Inmate Request Form: requesting a sergeant's approval to release excess cell property (old mail and books) to my aunt Ann at Visitation on Saturday. The next time a guard does a security walk through the day room, I hand him the form. He reads it and signs off on it as the receiving officer. Two days later, during mail call, I receive the form back signed and approved by a sergeant. *So far, so good.* As Saturday approaches, I'm equally nervous and excited. I'm worried about the Visitation staff detecting the hidden blog entries and the risk my aunt is taking smuggling the blogs out. On Saturday morning, I sandwich the manila envelope containing the blogs in-between manila envelopes containing legal papers. It is illegal for guards to read legal paperwork, so hopefully they'll assume that all of the manila envelopes contain legal papers and leave them alone. To add to the illusion, I put five books onto the pile. Hand-cuffed, leg-cuffed and belly-chained, I shuffle into Visitation, carrying my property pressed against my torso. The blogs are well hidden, but my pulse keeps climbing.

"You got a form approving that property release?" a guard barks.

"Sure do." I extract the form from my property.

He examines the form and takes my property. He looks in each of the manila envelopes, pulling pieces of paper out here and there. My brow and palms moisten. When he's finished, he puts my property on his desk. *Phew!*

My aunt is sitting at a table behind a Plexiglas screen. A guard chains me to a table and frees one of my arms, so I can speak to her through a phone. As soon as he moves onto the next prisoner, I give my aunt a sly smile and nod, which she returns, confirming that my parents have briefed her. I can't discuss the blog with her on the phone because the guards can listen. As we talk, I'm concerned that a guard might search my property again. I'm glad that out of the corner of my eye I can see my property on a desk and the guard overseeing it. I'm facing my aunt, but my main focus is on the guard. A thirty-minute visit usually goes fast, but my dual focus and the sense of danger combine to prolong time. Sweat streams from my armpits and trickles down my back. While my aunt is talking into her phone, I use my free hand to wipe sweat off my brow. Aware that my body language is betraying what I'm doing increases my nervousness.

When the visits are terminated, I'm usually sad to say goodbye, but this time I'm relieved. The guard un-handcuffs me from the table, but doesn't give my aunt my property. It's still on his desk as if forgotten. My aunt exits the visitation cubicle to a corridor, where she shrugs her shoulders at me. Not wanting her to leave without my blogs, I remind the guard about my property release. He instructs me to line up with a group of prisoners at the back of the room. The prisoners are smiling at the departing visitors and waving at torso height due to the restrictions of the handcuffs. The guard meets my aunt at a security door and hands her everything. She winks at me and leaves. With the day's tension melting away, I float back to my cell, smiling to myself, imagining my aunt leaving the jail with my blogs. Outsmarting the guards puts me on a natural high for the rest of the day. *It's for a good cause if the blog succeeds in exposing what's going on.*

At home, Ann types up the blogs and emails them to my parents, who post them to Jon's Jail Journal. The first week, only family and friends circulate it, so it doesn't get many hits. While appreciating that people are taking the time to visit my blog, I dream that it goes viral and there are mass protests outside of the jail, demanding the observance of human rights, with some protesters even burning effigies of Sheriff Joe Arpaio.

CHAPTER 48

The hardest part of being un-sentenced is not knowing how many years I'm going to get. It is a stress like no other. It gnaws at me constantly, haunts my dreams and overwhelms me during moments of weakness to the point where I contemplate suicide as a quick exit. And there's nothing I can do about it. It's not like work stress where I can change my job, or relationship stress where I can break up with my partner. The stupid decisions I made when running around on drugs are irreversible. Now my fate is in the hands of people vested with the power to put me away forever. That such few people have this power over me makes it even more terrifying.

Prosecutors' promotions and salary advancements hinge on performance measures such as conviction rates, sentence lengths and the size of financial forfeitures. It reflects better on the prosecutor if I get a long sentence. Ditto for Detective Reid. That's why some people end up getting hundreds of years. With the prosecutor obtaining witnesses, and each witness adding length to my sentence, the stakes are so high that my mind is starting to snap again like when I was moved to maximum security.

In a courtroom conversation with her boss loud enough for me to overhear, the prosecutor rubs in how much time I'm facing.

"Judge Watson gave that Tucson drug dealer I prosecuted 200 years," her boss says, referring to my regular judge.

"Why so many?" the prosecutor asks.

"He thought he was being a smart aleck taking it to trial. He lost at trial and the judge stacked his charges." Meaning he has to serve consecutive terms for every drug crime.

"Attwood's refusing to sign a plea bargain and demanding a trial," the prosecutor says.

"How many charges?" her boss asks.

"Twenty-three I believe."

"If he loses at trial and Judge Watson aggravates his sentence and stacks his charges, Attwood could easily get 200 years."

The case they are referring to recently sent a shockwave through all of the drug dealers in the jail. In a wire-tap case like mine, Judge Watson sentenced the defendant to 200 years. I've been trying not to dwell on it, but their conversation rams the possibility of perpetual imprisonment to the forefront of my mind. For hours, I'm unable to extract my thoughts from a deep dark pit. By the time I get back to my cell, I want to smash my head against the cement-block wall until I can no longer think about it. *Do I really want to spend the rest of my life in this kind of environment sweating and itching and avoiding cockroaches and predators? Hell, no!*

Thinking about taking a razor blade to my wrists and bleeding out, I get an unexpected sense of comfort. I now have a choice. *I'll wait till a guard does a security walk, slash my wrists nice and deep and just lie here with the cockroaches. The guards won't notice until the blood starts spilling from the bunk and by then it'll be too late. I wonder how long I'll take to die.*

Before committing suicide, I want to say goodbye to my family by taking a last look at their photographs. I grab an envelope containing the maximum seven pictures permitted in my personal property. I stare at the caring and loving faces of my mum, dad, sister and Claudia. Tears pool and spill and streak down my cheeks. I close my eyes and see my mum weeping at my funeral. *She's going to get a call saying her son's slashed his wrists in an Arizona jail cell. I can't put my family through that.* Shivering and sobbing as silently as possible on my bunk, I hate myself for lacking the courage to end my life. Fretting over the man sentenced to 200 years, I imagine him in a bare suicide-watch cell – the next stop for all prisoners who receive such big sentences. *What's going through his mind?* I imagine the devastation he is feeling and that of his family. That amount of pressure would surely kill me and destroy my loved ones.

March 2004

Dear love,

I can't take it in here anymore and I can't take the uncertainty anymore, so I told Alan I'll probably sign a plea bargain. If I get the 9-year minimum sentence stipulated, I'll be out in just over 3 years. My mum and dad and Alan do not want me to risk trial and a possible 25 year + sentence.

I was moved. I am in hell again. No air is blowing. I keep passing out while reading and have to take a nap. The 101 Slayer grieved it and the jail said they are not going to fix it! Cockroaches are everywhere. We are unable to hold them at bay. This pod is the worst yet. There is a white inmate with a heavily tattooed face. It looks like war paint.

I spoke to Cody and I am happy that he got probation. He didn't buy into the BS and obviously they had no case against him. I found out that Wild Woman's mum recently died. I guess I must forgive her. It's all my own fault.

My new celly, Mark, is nice. He has conspiracy to murder charges. It sounds like BS though. He has 2 red poodles and his mum has 2.

Please write to me just one time.
Love 'n' spoonage,
Shaun XXX

Blogs:

Mar 4 04

Chicken Wing lives in cell 6. At age eleven, a car crash left him with brain damage and partial handicapping of his left side. His left arm was mangled and now sticks up uselessly in the air.

In a holding cell at Medical, he told me that a convict named Bacon had repeatedly raped him at a federal prison. Chicken Wing is institutionalised and does not have any outside support. Using the Inmate Canteen Order Form, I buy him cookies every Thursday. When he receives his cookies, he barks excitedly like a dog anticipating a walk.

On Tuesday morning, Chicken Wing had a seizure.

"Man down! Man down! Man down!" yelled Chicken Wing's cellmate, Leprechaun.

"Man down! Man down! Man down!" boomed a chorus of voices until the guards finally responded.

"He's not breathing!" screamed a female guard.

Guards swarmed the day room. They stretchered Chicken Wing to Medical.

Later in the evening, Chicken Wing returned looking somewhat better.

"Are you OK?" I asked him during my hour out.

"Am I still good for cookies?" he replied.

I laughed.

"I'm sentenced now. I got probation," he said in a sad voice.

"That's good. You'll be out of here soon."

"But where will I go? I have nowhere to stay. How will I be able to do probation?"

"You should see if Pastor Walt at Church on the Street has any beds available."

The jail's psychiatric examiner decreed that Chicken Wing has sufficient mental competency to take care of himself, so after his release he will get no help from the State of Arizona. The majority of the inmates here expect him to return soon. I doubt anyone would have cared if Chicken Wing had died last Tuesday.

Mar 11 04

The temperature suddenly rose this week. We are lounging in our cells wearing only the jail's standard-issue pink boxers. Each cell receives a trickle of swamp-cooled air, which does little to alleviate our suffering in the summer months.

On Sunday, our drinking water turned orange-brown and had particles of rust in it. The discolouration lasted for three days. I relied on the half pint of milk served with breakfast to quench my thirst.

On Tuesday, I was sitting on the toilet, about to wipe, when the door slid open.

"Get on your mattress!" said the armed member of the "goon squad" accompanying the bug-spray man.

"We'd like to refuse being sprayed," I said, waving the roll of toilet paper I was about to use at him.

"Get on your mattress!" he yelled, raising his weapon.

Suppressing the urge to pelt him with the toilet roll, I pulled up my pants and retreated to my mattress.

Our cell is sprayed every month, against our wishes, with us in it. We inevitably ingest some of the spray. We feel sick and dizzy afterwards. Spraying has zero effect on the cockroach population. Inmates have a right not to live in an environment infested with insects, but spraying enables the jail to flout the law by claiming on paper they are addressing the problem.

Mar 18 04

One of the unsettling things about cellular living is that the jail can transplant you to a new environment at any time. During my two-year stay, I've been "rolled-up" (moved) numerous times. A new cell equals a new garrison of cockroaches to battle, and I have learned to travel armed with enough AmerFresh toothpaste to block cockroach entry points effectively.

On Tuesday, our pod was moved to a different floor and I used my entire stock of AmerFresh to seal the cracks in the walls. The cell was quickly and expertly fortified against the enemy. That night, I admired the bug-free environment, relished the room's minty-fresh aroma and slept soundly. Little did I know the jail was about to sabotage my hard work.

On Wednesday, I was moved back to my original floor, into one of the most infested pods in the building. Completely unarmed with AmerFresh, I watched helplessly as the cockroaches sized me up from their launching points. I knew as soon as the lights went off I was doomed. My cellmate, Mark and I didn't get much sleep. We stayed awake watching the legions of cockroaches conquer the room. Whirling around us, they swarmed the floor. The walls. The ceiling. Our commissary bags. And finally us.

Mar 25 04

I am allowed out of my cell for one hour each day to make a phone call and to take a shower. During my first "hour out" in the new pod, I was serenaded by the inmates, who performed a husky version of "A Yellow Submarine." I was touched by their demonstration of high spirits in a part of the jail known for extreme suffering.

My new cohabitants are enduring the twin evils of a broken swamp cooler and a cockroach infestation. They are proving to be the crème de la crème of good sufferers. A neighbour who is an asthmatic happily described how he inhaled a cockroach that had crept into his inhaler during the night. When he woke up, he grabbed his inhaler and blasted the insect down his throat. Feeling the cockroach moving around inside of him, he promptly vomited his stomach contents. Unfortunately, the cockroach was not ejected, as it was lodged, he suspected, in his lung. He was subsequently awarded sufferer of the week, a title I came up with to entertain my neighbours.

Mark and I have used six tubes of AmerFresh toothpaste and six ounces of Razorless Beard Remover cementing cracks in the walls. The cockroaches still flood our cell every night and I have awoken numerous times this week to observe my hair stood on end and a cockroach crawling on my body. I previously considered my apelike fur coating as one of nature's cruel jokes, but now I have discovered it to be a useful defensive shield against verminous insects. My upright hairs must seem like an unwelcoming forest to the little foragers.

I once read about a lady in Australia whose ear was entered by a cockroach as she slept. It chose not to come out. She was hospitalised, operated on, and she successfully sued the Australian government for failing to eradicate the cockroaches from her council home. She came to mind this week when a cockroach scaled a pink flannel I had hung below our tiny steel table to dry. It gravitated toward some earwax residue on the flannel, stopped and breakfasted on it excitedly. I told my cellmate about the Australian lady and he now sleeps with his pink towel wrapped around his head.

A seventy-year old downstairs became the first victim of the soaring temperatures. He was stretchered from the pod after suffering chest pains. Before he collapsed, he became delusional and made a variety of bizarre comments that disturbed his young cellmate:

"Take me to the hospital, so I can put on my clothes."

"Take me out to the desert and shoot me."

"Let's go! Grab the key to the front door."

"I have a broken back. I can't walk!"

Chicken Wing is in a neighbouring pod and I am trying to find out if Church on the Street will accept him when he leaves.

April 2004

Claudia,

When I call you and ask you how you feel or try and get some small talk out of you, you make me feel like I am trying to pull your teeth out. I just don't get it. I understand what misery it must be to have a fiancé in jail and I sympathize with you deeply, but look at how hard it is for me as well, love. Please read my blog and you will understand more about the conditions I am in. I make every effort to be positive when talking to you because you have done so much for me. Our calls used to be the highlight of my day, and now they just seem to make me sad. I realise how stressed out you are, and that is why I never ask you for anything anymore. I am a capable person, and my family have helped me out a lot recently. I've tried so desperately hard to understand you, but no matter what I've done it just seems so difficult these days. I am a prisoner but you have put yourself in a mental prison. I love you more than anything and we can have a good life together, and children as we planned, but if you still want that, you're going to have to pull yourself together. For almost 2 years, we have had our heads above water holding each other up, but I feel that your head is slipping below water and because I am where I am I can't rescue you.

Love,

Shaun X

ps) I've had a good response to the blog and I've received letters congratulating me on a writing ability I never knew I had.

Blogs:

April Fools' Day 04

Being fairly new to this game, Mark is stuck at the unable-to-eat-the-jail-food stage. Never in trouble before, he was arrested three months ago for conspiracy to commit murder. Since then, he has shed thirty pounds and no longer resembles his booking photo. If it wasn't for the Cheez-Its, chips, granola bars and mixed nuts available from the store, he would be skeletal.

This week, more of my neighbours became ill due to the heat. On Sunday morning, a diabetic collapsed and was stretchered from the pod. As temperatures rose, so did the tempers of the inmates and guards. Two fights broke out as a result of guards shoving inmates.

Library books are delivered next week. As some of my neighbours can't read, I've purchased their allowances: three books each, payable in cookies upon delivery. An Inmate Request Form only allows topics of interest to be selected, so I requested philosophy. I am hoping for a repeat of last month's success when I received a Gandhi biography, Plato's *Republic* and the third volume of Winston Churchill's *The Second World War*, which includes the ferocious North African desert battles, in which my Grenadier Guardsman grandfather sustained life-threatening shrapnel injuries fighting the Nazis to preserve our freedom. Left for dead, he was rescued by Americans.

Apr 15 04

I received lots of eggs on Easter Sunday – cockroach eggs. I noticed what looked like a piece of a worm glued to my dictionary – it was full of cockroach larvae. I discovered two more empty egg containers and more nests in my commissary bag and legal file. In my manila envelopes, large and tiny cockroaches were running wild. I poured the contents of one envelope into the toilet, but in the time it took to press the flush button, las cucarachas had scurried out of the bowl at warp speed and were scrambling around my feet.

They were none too happy about their encampment being

besieged on a holy day, and as darkness came they began to rebel en masse. Numerous baby cockroaches, tinier than ants, started the demonstration by zigzagging on the walls like miniscule bumper cars. They were soon joined by the adult members of their community. One about the size of an almond crawled onto my foot. Some larger ones invaded the blanket near my right shoulder, and I had to sleep with a sheet wrapped around my head because I feared they had performed a reconnaissance of my orifices and intended on capturing the earwax they love so much.

The bug activity perturbed Mark. Staying awake for most of the night until his eyelids finally closed, he dreamt they were crawling all over him. He awoke in a terrible sweat, scratching his body, only to discover his dream had come true.

My new neighbour's behaviour has upset everyone. He's young and he boasts he is a rapper and a shit talka. Every day he uses his cell walls, door and table as drums. He likes to tell passers-by to fuck themselves, and he is recklessly hostile to the guards. What upsets the inmates most of all is his nighttime soliloquizing. He has received numerous threats upon his good health. Presently, he is rapping:

Da roaches,
Da roaches,
Da roaches on da wall,
We don't need no water,
Let the motherfuckers fall!

Now he's clicking his fingers and cackling to himself, "I'd have my shit on motherfuckin' billboards by now if it wasn't for these assholes! I should be a fuckin' millionaire! Please, I wanna get out of here! I wanna go home!"

I placed a green onion from my dinner into a polystyrene cup. I half filled it with water and to my delight it grew roots. Now I have a plant of my own to love and care for. I haven't seen a plant in years! Mark said I've been here for too long.

Apr 29 04

In court, I watched the sentencing hearing for fifty-four-year-old Duke. Most of the onlookers wept with him as he listed his mitigating factors. Duke had joined the military at age nineteen and was quickly dispatched to Vietnam. He served as a supply clerk in the thick of some of the goriest battles. After three years of being in hell, and watching peoples' faces getting blown off, Duke was shot in the head. Comatose for three months, his eventual survival was deemed a miracle. For serving his country, Duke was awarded the Purple Heart and Silver Star.

Duke discovered drugs in Vietnam. Upon returning home, he was prescribed painkillers, psychiatric drugs and seizure medication. He suffered from various mental problems, including PTSD. He was in and out of the Veterans' Hospital for three decades. During his most recent visit, the surgeon reattached his foot, which had been torn from his leg by a hit-and-run driver. Duke's foot is presently held on by a thirteen-inch metal rod, and he limps.

Duke shed tears as he apologized for his drug problem, which he referred to as his disease. He apologized to his children and grandchildren for letting them down. Duke's final cry for leniency was, "Please help me get help for my disease."

From Judge Watson, Duke received a four-and-a-half-year sentence for possession of .02 grams of cocaine, found on the floor of his car. His attorney said Duke's long history of drug use and the fact he owned a new car had aggravated the sentence. The prosecutor claimed Duke's car could only have been paid for by dealing drugs.

Duke was sullen as he exited the courtroom.

CHAPTER 49

In May, I go to court in two minds over whether to sign a plea bargain. Alan Simpson is one of the strongest trial attorneys in town, up against a less experienced prosecutor. If I take the case to trial and win, I'll be released right away. The police have little evidence against me. The star witness is Wild Woman, whom I don't think a jury will believe because of her harsh accent and intimidating appearance. My attorney and I joke that the court will have to hire an interpreter just for her. On the other hand, if I lose at trial, I can get up to 200 years. As much as I believe in Alan Simpson, the chance of getting 200 years is keeping me awake at night. The prospect of immediate freedom is attractive, but probably a pipe dream.

In court, my attorney presents the plea bargain to me long before the judge is due to show up.

"I don't know what to do, Alan. I've fought it for this long, maybe if I continue to hold out, I'll get a better plea."

Alan shakes his head. *He wants my case done with.* "It's your decision. The prosecutor has indicated she will be preparing for trial if you don't sign this plea bargain. I believe she's serious."

"If it goes to trial, what will the cost be to my parents?" I ask, half hoping for a large number to dissuade me.

"It's not about money. I'm defending you, so I have to represent you at trial whether they can pay or not."

"Good. They've got no money left 'cause of me."

"In that case, I'd have to do it for free."

His answer sways me from wanting to sign a plea bargain. *I can gesture that I want to take it to trial in the hope of getting a better plea bargain and if that gamble ends up in a trial, there'll be no financial burden on my parents.* "I don't think I want to sign the plea."

Alan furrows his brow. "You're taking a very big risk at this stage of the game. If the judge sentences you to somewhere around ten years, which is near the minimum stipulated in this plea bargain, with the loophole for foreign citizens, you'd be out in just over three-and-a-half. If you lose at trial, you might never get out."

The prospect of never getting out tugs me back towards signing a plea bargain, but I'm still unsure. *For the rest of my life, I'll have to live with the consequences of what I decide today.* The decision is so hard, I can't make it. *I must choose something.* I'm filled with a sense that my case is drawing to a conclusion whether I sign a plea bargain or not – a conclusion I won't like.

Ray – an attorney I'd relied on prior to my arrest – shows up, surprising me. "What's going on?" he asks.

"He doesn't want to sign the plea bargain," Alan says.

"Why?" Ray shakes his head.

"I don't think they have much of a case or they would have took me to trial already," I say. "I don't see the prosecutor wanting to go up against Alan at trial. They've got to come at me with a better plea bargain."

"No they don't!" Ray yells. "Look, you've got one of the best legal minds advising you. Why don't you just listen to him?"

"He won't listen to me," Alan says.

"Fucking listen to him or you'll be sorry!" Ray throws his hands up and marches out.

My mind is so suspicious of anything involving attorneys that I assume Alan had arranged the charade with Ray. But what Ray said is true and the forceful way he said it convinces me to go with the plea bargain. By the time the judge arrives, the pressure from what I'm about to do has me verging on a migraine. Trembling, I sign the plea bargain. I depart, praying to get the minimum sentence of nine years and not the maximum of twelve as stipulated in the agreement. *At the sentencing hearing, I must put on a good show with the help of my family. But the judge didn't pay any attention to my family at the bond hearing! Why will this be any different?*

When has a court hearing ever gone in my favour? What if he gives me the maximum sentence and doesn't allow the loophole for foreign citizens that Alan mentioned? I'll have to serve almost a decade.

May 2004

Dear Claudia,

I signed a plea bargain! If all goes well at my sentencing, I'll be out of prison in late 2007. I'm sure the time will go fast, plus we'll have a visitation relationship again. I am to be sentenced in the last week of June. I'll be meeting the presentence reporter in 1 week.

I feel that we kind of saved each other from ourselves when we first met, but unfortunately I couldn't quite kick my old lifestyle. A very expensive mistake indeed! I have learnt a lot. I will never make such mistakes again.

Sorry that I don't write to you more often, but I am trying to live off $10 a week, and I also used up all the postcards I bought from Chicken Wing. I hope that you don't think I love you any less because I am not sending you daily letters. I am also starting to feel lovesick because we haven't spoken in so long.

Forever yours,
Shaun

Mum and Dad,

I am very excited about your visit, and can't wait to see everyone. I am very nervous about speaking to the judge at the sentencing hearing, and I am currently bandying ideas around about what to say. A fellow in here recently returned from his sentencing. He'd fully expected 2 years' probation, and the judge gave him 15 years prison time because of an allegation by the prosecutor that his family members jeered at the victim in his case in the courtroom. The judge said that neither he nor his family had shown any REMORSE! The remorseless ones, especially people protesting their innocence, get hung. I also fully expect the prosecutor to paint me out to be a demon, and Detective Reid to be pushing for a harsh sentence.

Ann said that the blog about inmate sexual gratification was quite shocking and sickening, but she appreciated I was just "telling it like it is." Karen wrote that she and her friends like the more disturbing stuff. I had that in mind when I wrote about Yum-Yum. Yum-Yum brought half of the pod out of the closet. Even my anti-gay cellmate said, "I guess if I was to sleep with a guy, I'd at least want him to look like Yum-Yum." This place has a strange effect on people.

Claudia said that Karen is more than welcome to stay with her if there is overcrowding at Ann's. I'm hoping Claudia will tough it out till I'm moved to the prison system. The visits there are contact, 1 hug and kiss are allowed, and they are hours long. I think that will make a world of difference. Right now, I'm just a voice on the phone to her or a letter here and there. She told me she has to drink to get to sleep, and has uncontrollable trembling and anxiety. I feel so helpless in that I can't comfort her and help her.

I have enjoyed the Hemingway stories that I have read thus far. I was quite pleased at his ability to put someone at ease and then for something particularly nasty to happen. His short monotonous sentences lead up to enjoyable unexpected twists. It's a good style. I am guessing he was a strange man, but I know nothing about him.

Love you loads! See you soon!
Shaun

BLOGS:

May 6 04

Most inmates agree that the hardest part of incarceration is the absence of female company. There are various ways in here to address sexual frustration. The most common occurs in the shower. Some inmates even tape sexy pictures to the shower wall. Unfortunately, the shower I share with twenty-nine men drains poorly. A puddle of semen and pubic hair swirls around my feet as I wash. In the shower, I wear pink socks for protection and quickly rinse them off afterwards.

The more innovative methods of gratification are often bragged about. That's how I heard of a "fee-fee bag," a hot, wet sock, lubricated with soap or lotion. A creatively-folded towel can serve the same purpose.

I have noticed three types of gays in jail: those openly gay before and after their arrest, those who are temporarily openly gay in jail but do not tell their wives and girlfriends "gay for the stay," and those in the closet. The first two groups boast about their conquests and ultimately reveal the members of the latter.

Transsexuals, known as "cheetolins" are in high demand. Most of our resident cheetos are Native American or Mexican American. Some inmates cannot resist an opportunity to receive oral sex. Cheetos are known to convert many inmates who once thought they were straight.

A recently sentenced cheeto in our pod yelled, "I can't wait to get to prison for all that sausage!"

I could be having so much fun in here if only I were gay!

May 13 04

Frankie, a Mexican Mafia contract killer – his fee is $50,000 per hit – instigates most of the hullabaloo in our pod. He is a recent arrival from the jail's infirmary. Last month he was playing cards in a maximum-security pod when someone stuck an eight-inch shank into the back of his neck. Unfazed, he extracted the shank, and was about to return the gesture, but a guard blinded him with pepper spray. Frankie was dragged from the pod with blood gushing from the wound.

Frankie looks and acts like Joe Pesci playing Tommy DeVito in *Goodfellas*. He wears his thick, black hair slicked back, and his arms are heavily prison-tattooed. He overcompensates for his Napoleonic height with a cocksure manner, but the inmates have warmed to his lewd wittiness. During a seventeen-year sentence, he became a chess heavyweight. On my hour out, I usually play a game with him by holding the board up in front of his cell window. His piercing hazel eyes and fiendish grin animate when he attempts intimidation tactics:

"Eat dat fuckin' pawn!"

"Let me fuckin' teach ya somethin'!"

"Eat dat fuckin' bishop!"

"Watch dis! Check! Trick move! What'd I fuckin' tell ya!"

"Don't do it!"

"Move my bitch [Queen] all da way up!"

"Check-fuckin'-mate! Boo-yah!"

"Nobody fucks wiv da champ!"

Hearing my rapping neighbour whimpering to his grandmother on the phone in the day room, begging her to bail him out, the inmates lambasted him for being a cry baby. Nevertheless, his grandmother followed through and he was released.

He was replaced by Yum-Yum, an eighteen-year-old transsexual who looks like a malnourished teenage girl. Yum-Yum has black curly hair, speaks like a female, and has stirred up the love-starved inmates. Frankie is leading the pack. Every day, Frankie has offered Yum-Yum sweets to move into his cell to "make ma cell look good." Frankie complains that his eighteen-year-old cellmate, Cup Cake, will not participate in "sword fights" (sexual acts) with him. He seems confident that Yum-Yum will be more obliging. I sense a love triangle.

The heat is making it difficult to sleep. Las cucarachas are getting more adventurous. Tickling my limbs, they wake me up every night.

The inmates are speculating that the foul-smelling breakfast meat is ostrich.

My green onion, that had sprouted six inches, suddenly wilted and died.

May 20 04

The news reported a hue and cry outside of the jailhouse on Saturday morning – a public protest about the conditions. Sheriff Joe Arpaio's swift response was to have us served with tasty mashed potatoes instead of the usual rotten potato peelings. On Sunday night, we actually received a scoop of ice cream. Unfortunately, the ice cream was served on top of warm cabbage, transmuting it into cabbage soup. Anyhow, we appreciated the gesture, and we are still receiving mashed potatoes – but for how long?

The daily temperature highs are in excess of 100 °F and rising. The air is stale and debilitating. On Monday, an inmate told a guard he felt ill and requested medical treatment. The guard told him to drink plenty of water and to lie down. The inmate persisted, stating he was a diabetic and he really needed to see a doctor, but the guard continued to fob him off. On Monday night, the inmate slipped into a coma and was rushed to the hospital. He has not been seen since.

Frankie paid Yum-Yum's $225 bond. Before Yum-Yum departed, I learned he has fifty wigs at home, and that he had been arrested when the police forced their way into a hotel bathroom: "I was tweaked out o' my mind and getting fucked by my friend." Sadly, Frankie did not land a cell with Yum-Yum, but his investment will probably enhance his reputation among prison transsexuals.

I was awoken this morning by a small cockroach heading towards my face up my right arm.

Mark still refuses to eat the jail food. He had a nightmare about giant cockroaches dressed in guard uniforms chaining him to a bunk and force-feeding him red death.

May 27 04

On Sunday morning, I awoke to find two cockroach corpses crushed on my mattress. I must have rolled on top of them in my sleep.

Two more inmates collapsed and were stretchered to the Medical Unit. Including Jose from cell 1, who, during a shootout over drugs with fellow Mexican nationals, had received seventeen bullet wounds. The stitches holding his stomach in had loosened, and it appeared his internal organs were about to spill out.

Rumour has it the diabetic who entered a coma last week died, and the jail is under investigation.

We have been told for the past three months that the swamp cooler is "broken" and that a "work order" has been entered, but when the County Health Department inspected the jail on Tuesday and Wednesday, the air was blowing at gale force and the water in the shower was running hot enough to redden my skin. After the inspectors left the building someone immediately switched the air back to the broken setting. And it didn't take long for the inmates to replace the semen that had been cleaned up from the shower floor.

Frankie is always in a high state of sexual arousal. He has solicited most members of our pod, including me, to be "boned down" and "turned out." His boldness has increased due to his followers egging him on. I am convinced that if all of our cell doors were simultaneously opened, half of the inmates would form an orgy.

Frankie now proclaims, "I'm takin' us back to the fuckin' Roman days! Call me Caesar the booty teaser!" One of Frankie's new tricks is to have a neighbour throw him a "fishing line" (a long piece of string which inmates use to pass contraband from cell to cell with) so that he can tie it to his penis while his neighbour pulls on the string.

I received a large photograph in the mail. It exceeded the 4 x 6 inches allowed by the jail, so I was pleasantly surprised that it was not rejected by the mail officer. It was a picture of a bespectacled President Bush signing some documents. In the lower margin was a personalized message with my name on it: "Thank you for your support of the Republican National Committee. Grassroots leaders like you are the key to building a better, stronger, more secure future for our nation and all Americans... Best Wishes, George. W. Bush."

Now that the president has discerned my true nature, I am hopeful for a pardon!

My parents inform me that the May demonstration outside of the jail was organised by a group called Mothers Against Arpaio, whose founding members emailed that reading Jon's Jail Journal contributed to their decision to protest outside of this facility. I'm flabbergasted to learn that the son of one founder was murdered by the Aryan Brotherhood in Sheriff Joe Arpaio's Tent City jail. The brother of another founder is in this maximum-security jail in a neighbouring pod. He's been held for three years on charges of conspiring to bomb Sheriff Joe Arpaio. His sister insists that her brother is the victim of a publicity stunt orchestrated by Sheriff Joe Arpaio's office. Delighted to be linking up with fellow activists, I'm filled with a sense that the blog is gaining momentum. My excitement over what it might lead to overrides my fear of the guards trying to find out who the author is.

The weekend approaches, but I haven't received an approved property-release form back from the guards. *How am I going to get my blog entries to my aunt? Have the guards lost my paperwork?*

A sergeant appears at my cell door. "Attwood, come here."

Oh shit! Has the blog been detected? I approach the door.

The sergeant hands me the property-release form I've been waiting for. Relieved, I wonder why he's delivering it personally.

"I'm not signing off on this, Attwood."

Believing I've been discovered, I almost fall over.

"You've been requesting too many property releases."

My heart rate jumps.

"You've been submitting requests every week for two months."

The two months I've been blogging. Has he figured it out?

"You're the only inmate doing this. What's with all the property releases, Attwood?"

He's not figured it out. I need a good excuse. "I get a lot of books, which I read fast. The mail officer has been refusing to give me books because I have too many in my cell. He said I need to keep releasing them to my aunt or else he will return to sender my latest books."

He shakes his head. "I'm still not signing off on this, Attwood. You need to slow down on the property releases." He walks away.

If the blog gets discovered, what will the guards do? They might attack me or get a prisoner to do it by moving me in with a psycho or a rapist. What if the prosecutor finds out? She would surely tell the judge, who might give me a longer sentence. Should I stop blogging until after my sentencing? I'm committed now. It's already online. No point in stopping.

Having always submitted my property-release form to the day shift, I try the night shift. When it comes back signed and approved by a different sergeant, I'm relieved. The blogging resumes.

CHAPTER 50

Convinced the imminent resolution of my case has saved my relationship with Claudia, I call her. *She'll be thrilled that our visits will resume in the prison system.*

"Hey now! How're you?" I ask in my chirpiest voice.

"Hi. How're you?" she replies in a monotone.

"Your voice sounds funny. Are you OK?" I ask, disappointed.

"Not really."

Regaining my enthusiasm, I say, "Why? This is going to be over soon. We'll have visits back. Visits are much longer in prison and they let us hug and kiss."

Her humph knocks my mood down. "I don't think I can do this anymore."

A wave of heat rises through my body to the top of my skull. "Do what? What're you talking about?"

"Like this…like this relationship."

My brain explodes. Tears tumble. No one speaks.

"It's just so…" Claudia sobs. "It's just been too hard without being able to see you for a year. And you think you're getting closer to the end, but what if they keep postponing?"

Try to win her back. "I can understand this, you know, how you're feeling," I say softly, hoping no one in the cells detects I'm crying on the phone in the empty day room. "I'll accept whatever decision you want to make, but do you think it's a good idea to throw away our relationship after everything we've been through?"

"I don't. This is so hard for me, too. It's been two years of going to sleep every night thinking either you're gonna be home the next day or that this is a bad dream. And I'll wake up, and I'll be here alone, and now it's been two years, and there's not ever an end. You don't even know how long they might send you to prison for."

True. "But Claudia, I love you. I love you so much."

"Shaun, I love you, too. It's just hard. I think...what it is, I need to get my life back."

"I know you do, but this is tearing me apart."

"It's totally tearing me apart, too."

The female computerised voice comes on the line: "You have thirty seconds remaining."

"Does this mean you don't want me to call you anymore?"

"Maybe it's best not for a while."

"But what about—"

Line dead. I can't breathe. I return to my cell as dazed as during car crashes. The pressure in my head blurs my vision. Whenever I feared a break-up was coming, it never had. Now it's arrived, I can't see how I'll ever get over it. The anguish is too much. I rush to my cell and curl up on the bottom bunk. Facing the wall, I pretend to read so my cellmate can't see me crying. Occasionally turning a page that I've not read, I torture myself with images of the times we've spent together. I barely sleep. For days, I can't eat. I tell my cellmate I'm fasting. *Will this pain ever end?*

June 2004

Dearest Claudia,

Thank you for being brave enough to tell me how you feel on the phone. You are going through a lot, and my situation is too much to deal with. I am sorry so many bad things have happened because of my wrongdoing. I wish things were different, but they are not. For some reason it seems I must lose everything, and I've expected our relationship to unravel for quite some time now. I do not begrudge your decision. I'll always be your friend no matter what. I'll always remember how happy you made me for the brief time we were together. Even though I have been reduced to living like an animal, they can't take away the precious times we shared. I'll always remember singing to myself and dancing in my SUV, happy as can be driving from Tucson to see you on Bell Road. I'll always remember your pink and zebra apartment and our trips to Indian buffets and LA Fitness, and how we'd sit and drink smoothies after working out. I'm just so sad that I can't even give you a kiss goodbye. My emotional self wants me to fight to keep you. But what can I do from a jail cell? Nothing. I can't even see you. As you can gather, I am going in and out of feeling very sad as the reality of what you said sinks in. I can't even call you. There is no privacy here. I do not want to cry in front of 30 people. I don't want it to end this way. I am still the man that you fell in love with.

Shaun X

Writing the letter reduces me to tears again. I love Claudia so much that I want to keep our relationship going, but a different voice inside of me offers another angle; a voice stemming from my newfound philosophical perspective: *I must let her go because loving her means putting my needs aside and doing what's best for her.*

Blogs:

Jun 3 04

Three times a day, a crotchety nurse goes from pod to pod dispensing meds. Up to one third of the inmates are recipients of these pills. The most common are Wellbutrin, Klonapin, Prozac, Cojetin, Loxieen, Paxil, Haldol, Elovil and Seroquil.

The inmates snigger at how easy it is to obtain these free drugs. They simply tell the "psych doctor" they are hearing voices or are unable to sleep. Inmates use the pills to vary their highs, or trade for food and illegal drugs.

It's been an infernally normal week. Outdoor temperatures are approaching 110 °F. At night, I watch las cucarachas scurrying to and fro, convinced they are waiting for me to go to sleep to get my earwax. Mark and I now catch each another chasing imaginary cockroaches.

The dirty potato peelings are back in the evening chow. Dry citrus fruit are the new additions to breakfast. The stench of filth and sweat pervades the air. The bedsore on my left buttock cheek is blistered and bleeding. My mouth and tongue are ulcerated. These conditions were designed to break the human spirit. As the periodic suicides indicate, death is a more attractive place for some inmates.

Jun 10 04

Young AK was arrested after pointing an AK-47 at his stepfather. He is now my noisy neighbour. From Sinaloa, Mexico, he fancies himself as a troubadour. In Spanish, he is constantly singing romantic songs – but he ends each verse with:

Bop! Bop! Bop!

Gimme liberty or gimme death!

Bop! Bop! Bop! Bop!

His bop-bop-bopping has annoyed everyone. And usually, when everyone gets annoyed, someone gets hurt. I suspect he will be getting bopped soon.

On Saturday morning, the jail was placed on security override, and all of our cells were searched. We later found out that a drug ring was arrested here at the Madison Street jail. It included one guard, one nurse and ten inmates. Supposedly a Mexican Mafia operation. The Mexican Mafia is one of the most powerful prison gangs in Arizona.

On Tuesday morning, Frankie hollered into the vent, "Got any jelly, cell 15?"

"I do not," I said.

"Does your celly?" Frankie asked.

"I do," Mark said.

"He does," I yelled.

"Slide it under your door and I'll send Blueberry up to get it," Frankie said.

"OK," I said.

Blueberry climbed the stairs to get the jelly.

"Thanks, cell 15," Frankie shouted.

"You're welcome," I said.

"Look out of your window. Someone else wants to thank you," Frankie said.

Through the window, I saw young Blueberry bent over with his pants pulled down, his hands spreading his buttocks as wide as they'd go.

"Do you like it?" Frankie asked.

Silence.

"Do you like it?" Blueberry said, imitating a woman's voice.

"No me gusta," I responded in Spanish to Frankie, so as not to dampen Blueberry's spirit.

Frankie cackled impishly.

Jun 17 04

On Friday morning, the guards thwarted an escape attempt by two inmates, and the jail administration decided to punish everyone. We were placed on security override for four days, confined to our cells, unable to shower, make phone calls, dispose of our trash and dinner trays. Soaring temperatures and a purposefully low trickle of swamp-cooled air quickly caused us to reek like wet dogs. Our cell soon stunk like a drive-through restaurant's dumpster on a hot day. The filthy conditions were received enthusiastically by las cucarachas. They launched their most aggressive offensive yet. Around the clock, they plundered the red death Mark had left.

The lockdown and AK's bop-bop-bopping undoubtedly contributed to the nervous breakdown of Eric (AK's fifty-year-old cellmate).

Early Monday morning, Eric yelled, "Get me outta here!" repeatedly for fifteen minutes. His voice inflection ranged from that of a demonically-possessed man – worse than something from *The Exorcist* – to that of a sobbing child. The guards removed Eric from AK's cell, and after undergoing a psychiatric evaluation, he was moved in with Blueberry.

On Wednesday morning, I was summoned to the Medical Unit. I had entered a Correctional Health Services Inmate Medical Request on the 1st of June:

"Blisters have formed on the bedsore on my left buttock. Requesting cream."

Due to the amount of bedsores I've had while jailed, the medical staff regularly inspect my behind. But Wednesday morning's encounter with the new Filipino doctor was somewhat disturbing. After dropping my pants, the doctor perused my foresty posterior and stated, "You have scaling on both left and right sides."

I thought the exam was over, but the doctor said, "How about the front?"

"The front?" I asked.

"Yes, the front. Just turn around," he said, his eyes animating.

Wondering, *Who am I to question a professional?* I turned around. I was expecting a positive comment on the health of my reproductives, but he suddenly lunged forward as if to grab them. I automatically jerked backwards. To fend him off, I grabbed and raised my scrotum. Shaking it at him, I yelled, "Look! The front's fine!"

"Yes. They look quite OK to me," he replied, softening his voice.

I emerged from the doctor's with Clotrimazole Anti-Fungal Cream.

After seeing the doctor, the next patient returned to the Medical Unit holding cell and blurted out, "That doctor just grabbed my dick without any gloves on!"

"He tried to do the same to me," I said.

The rest of the inmates either sniggered or exchanged nervous looks as the prospect of receiving the same treatment dawned on them.

On Wednesday night, Frankie peeped through my cell window when I was rubbing the anti-fungal cream on my left buttock. His eyes smouldered with desire. I received a love letter from him the next morning: "...looking forward to our upcoming gay marriage in San Francisco, and shampooing your hairy ass on our honeymoon."

Frankie was delighted that the solitary witness in his double-homicide case was recently deemed "mentally incompetent" causing his proposed sentencing range to drop from twenty-five years to life, to six to ten years.

Jun 24 04

Frustration with AK climaxed on Monday morning. No one could sleep thanks to our resident cantante singing musica romantica for hours on end, interspersed with gunshot sound effects and feminine shrieks of "Sinaloa!" Enough was enough.

At the behest of the majority, Frankie implemented a plan to oust AK from our pod.

He had Cupcake borrow AK's most valuable possession: a new radio. When Cupcake refused to return it, a dispute ensued. Frankie and Cupcake cackled at AK's invective, and AK exploded. Pounding on his cell door, he yowled at the two unsympathetic guards, "They stole my fuckin' radio!"

"Why'd you lend it to 'em?" enquired Officer Bloch.

"I thought they'd give it back," AK said, emphasising each word.

"Lending your stereo to other inmates is against the Inmate Rules and Regulations!"

"Roll your stuff up! You're being moved!" Officer Perez ordered.

Walking towards the pod door, AK suddenly dropped his mattress. Before the guards could stop him, he dashed to Cupcake's cell and yelled, "Gimme my fuckin' stereo back, you scheming fuckers!"

The guards restrained him. As they briskly steered AK out of the pod, applause from the cells increased.

My right shin looks like I spilled battery acid on it. A cluster of thirty or so red sores emerged last week when we were denied showers for four days. Some are bleeding, but I'm reluctant to make an appointment with the penis-grabbing Filipino doctor.

Half of the shower area is refusing to drain. Hair matted with semen has clogged it up. To shower, I had to step into the puddle of scum. This disturbed the multitude of tiny black flies ensconced on the white clumps and they formed a cloud around my head. Fortunately, they bolted when the shower was turned on and migrated to the dried fruit peel in the trashcan. When the water was turned off, they abandoned the fruit peel and returned to the shower. The flies prefer the semen.

CHAPTER 51

The night before my sentencing I can't sleep. I rest on my bunk, stuck to the towel I've put down to absorb my sweat, worrying about the effect of the hearing on my parents, sister and Aunt Mo, who's also flown from England. (Aunt Mo moved back in 1992.) Over the past two years, I've put my family through so much. I hate the idea of them grovelling for leniency in the sterile atmosphere of the courtroom. I also wonder if Claudia and her family will show up. I haven't called her since the break-up, but her father, Barry, assured me he'll come to the sentencing even though he's had brain surgery and is suffering seizures. Watching the cockroaches climb the walls, I pray the judge will give me the minimum sentence in my plea bargain: nine years. *If I get the aggravated maximum without the half-time release loophole, I'll serve almost a decade and end up institutionalised.* It's hard to believe I'll be out of the jail and on my way to the prison system in a few weeks. I wonder how the prisoners will receive me and if I'll meet anyone I know such as Little Italy.

Daybreak: retreating cockroaches.

"Get up for court, Attwood!"

Suffering anxiety constipation, I strain on the toilet. No result. The cheap plastic shaver cuts my chin as my trembling hand rushes to remove a week's stubble in the ten minutes permitted to shave. I shower fast and put on a set of clothes provided by a guard. Each act I complete reminds me that I'm a step closer to court. Leaving the day room, I again pray for nine years.

Hours later, sitting alone in cuffs and leg chains in a holding cell outside of the courtroom, I imagine my family in the public gallery. *What are they thinking? Are they as nervous as me?* By the time I hear the jingling keys and boot steps of the guard coming to fetch me, my hunched shoulders are aching from the build-up of tension. Standing up, I feel the blood drain from my face. In the corridor, I have a sense of disembodiment, as if I'm floating alongside the guard like a ghost.

We enter the courtroom. The stenographer is a young woman, around thirty, my sister's age. She appears passive. The clerk of the court is a stern-faced woman, around fifty. No judge. I pass the prosecutor, dressed smart in a light-coloured suit. *Today she hopes to make her name on the back of my case.* Detective Reid, with his thick dark hair trimmed and slicked back, has an intense expression as if he's in a hospital, waiting to find out whether a family member is dead or alive. The guard instructs me to sit on one of the benches at the side and to not so much as even smile at my family and Claudia's, who are about twenty strong, two rows of sombre faces. I can see in their eyes that they are shocked by my gaunt appearance. Pleased and thankful to see them, I'm too nervous to smile. My jaw is trembling, my face contorting.

Alan Simpson approaches me. "How're you feeling?"

"Terrified."

The sentencing judge enters, a narrow-faced man with greying hair, large protruding eyes and the air of someone who presides over matters of great importance. Everyone rises. Even though the court is the biggest room I've experienced in two years, my claustrophobia peaks as the proceedings start. When we are seated, he announces my case number. "Is the State ready for sentencing?"

"Yes, Judge," the prosecutor says. "Gloria Olivia Davis on behalf of the Attorney General's Office."

"Alan Simpson on behalf of Mr Attwood, who is present in custody, and we are ready to proceed."

"It is my understanding that several family members would like to speak on behalf of Mr Attwood before I pronounce sentence…"

My involuntary movements are most noticeable in my legs, which won't stop shaking. As if trying to exit the situation, my mind keeps going blank and snapping back to the courtroom.

My mother, wearing a black shirt, dress and jacket – funeral clothes – rises to speak. That my actions have brought her here adds to my humiliation. "Shaun is my son and I love him very much. I know he has done wrong and we are sorry for that, but there's so much good in him. It's been so difficult living so far away and not being able to visit him. Without Ann, my husband's sister who visits him every week, I don't know what we would have done."

Crushed by the shame in my mother's trembling voice, I almost cry.

"Shaun's a very special person. He's a kind, loving and generous person who always wants to help people. He naïvely believed that by making loads of money you could make things right for people. He was a beautiful baby and an energetic child. Shaun has always had this amazing energy bordering on manic, but I somehow managed to channel that energy into his studies. All through his childhood there were never any complaints about fighting or aggression, and he was successful, eventually getting a place at university and an honours degree." She looks proud. *I've let her down so badly.* "Shaun has a charismatic personality, and from an early age he has always attracted people." She pauses. "Your Honour, can I say something about Shaun's relationship with Peter?" she asks, referring to Wild Man. In previous court hearings the prosecutor portrayed Wild Man as a Frankenstein's monster I'd unleashed on American society, so my mother wants to provide some background.

Detective Reid is shaking his head. The judge nods sympathetically, encouraging her to continue.

"Shaun has a bond with Peter I never understood. Peter was a problem child who grew into an aggressive teenager. At sixteen, he tried to commit suicide, but instead of contacting his parents, he asked Shaun for help. That shows the strength of the bond between them. Shaun had a tree, which he and his friends called the Thinking Tree. It overlooked a deep quarry in a woodland, where the boys used to play. Shaun would sit in the Thinking Tree, and he knew then that he would be successful, and he promised his friends, including Peter, he would make everything right for them. Shaun used to believe that Peter would make good if given the chance. It was in keeping this promise that he brought Peter to America."

She says I hadn't meant to hurt people, but had tried to make them happy in a misguided way. "He became very successful as a stockbroker and later on as a day trader, and we visited him regularly. When he told us about promoting rave parties, we didn't worry. Perhaps we were naïve. Shaun's a natural entrepreneur. But I think it all just escalated. He gained a kind of rock-star status and attracted a following of young women.

"I don't know about the drug-taking. Perhaps it was his way of self-medicating his depressions. I feel guilty in a way. Perhaps I should have got him anti-depressants in England. I've suffered from depression myself over the years, but have always been reluctant to take medication," she pauses, "until now. That's what's helping me get through this without crying. I just want to take him home with me." Feeling her anguish, I briefly close my eyes and exhale loudly through my mouth. "I love him so much, and it's so difficult living so far away. I know that's not possible, but once he's back in England with the support of our family, which is very close and loving, nothing like this will ever happen again." She emphasises the last line as if it's her final plea to convince him. She returns to her seat next to my father, who puts his arm around her shoulder and hugs her tightly.

Detective Reid – who shifted in his seat throughout her speech – seems agitated. The prosecutor has a ready-to-do-battle expression.

My aunt Ann is up next. In contrast with my mother, she has on casual American clothes. She didn't write anything down in advance as she feels she'll find the right words to say. Speaking from the heart, she says how she visits me weekly without fail, and of the changes in my character she's witnessed and the subtlety of those changes that others who don't know me like she does may not have noticed. She's so kind, I'm grateful.

Alan calls Karen up next. My tall elegant sister takes the podium, forcing a smile that betrays how nervous she is. Despite our childhood squabbles, she's stood by me, and I admire that. Gulping for breath, she tells the judge how proud she's always been of her big brother. How proud she is of me now. She starts to cry, but still manages to make herself heard as she recounts childhood anecdotes. Hearing Karen's words, I again fight back tears.

In a business suit, my aunt Mo, who helped launch my stockbroking career, stands next. Nervous, she charges into her speech. The judge asks her to slow down. Taking deep breaths, she describes our strong bond. She apologises as she feels she's failed me, her godson, in some way, and must bear some responsibility. She concludes that she and all of our family will always provide a strong platform of support. She sits, relieved to have got through it.

My father gets up next, the pressure apparent in lines on his face. "Your Honour, it is true to say that my family and I have been in a state of shock since Shaun's arrest in May 2002. The situation has seemed so unreal, compounded by the 5000 mile distance between us and our son. But of course the situation is very real, and frightening, and here I am today talking to a superior-court judge just a few yards from the son that I love who is attired in jail stripes and shackles." He glances at me. "A son who I played with and introduced, along with his sister, Karen, to the beauties of the English countryside, to the birds and the wild flowers and trees. Shaun developed a passion for ornithology, and I remember him when he was aged around ten or eleven dragging a young ten-foot elderberry, complete with roots, into our back garden, which he insisted on planting in order to attract wild birds, which he could watch from his bedroom window."

As my father reminisces, I break down. His gentle loving voice penetrates my soul. I'm appalled at myself for letting him down, for letting them all down. I curse my existence and feel deep regret for what I've done. The tears start. As much as I try to withhold them, they gush. I can only cry. I'm all tears and heartbeat and twitching nerves. My father pauses to give me a look willing me to be strong. My attorney takes my shoulder and hands me a tissue.

"I also taught Shaun to play chess, a game at which I believe he has become something of a legend while in jail. I believe that my son has suffered enough. I can tell you that, as a father, if I could step inside his shoes, I would gladly serve the rest of his time in prison. I realise that this is not possible, so all I can do is respectfully ask Your Honour to show mercy in the sentencing of my son today."

The courtroom is silent for a long time. Even the stenographer wipes away tears.

It's my turn to speak. In leg chains, I shuffle towards the podium. My eyes meet Detective Reid's, who scowls as if trying to psych me out. Our brief eye contact tells me we are both thinking the same thing: our personal battle is almost over. Motivated in part by his attitude, I focus on gathering myself back together. Having stopped crying, I feel embarrassed, ashamed and queasy. Tremors are running through my body. I try to ground myself with yogic breathing. Approaching the judge, conscious of the spasms in my face, I clench my teeth. I gaze up at the judge. He leans forward, his unblinking eyes studying my face. Up close, his eyes are more unnerving than Detective Reid's. He has the look of a hawk about to swoop on a mouse. My anxiety keeps spiking, forcing me to avert my eyes from his gaze.

"Mr Attwood," says the judge, "I know your name is Shaun Patrick Attwood, and based upon a determination made previously, it is the judgement of the court that you are guilty of money laundering, a Class 3 non-dangerous non-repetitive felony, attempting to commit a dangerous drug violation, a Class 3 non-dangerous non-repetitive felony, and use of wire or electronic communication to facilitate a drug transaction, a Class 4 non-dangerous non-repetitive felony. I read your presentence report and all of the attachments, letters of support, and also the prosecutor's aggravation memorandum. I have also considered the fact that as of today, you have done 775 days of presentence incarceration. Does that sound right, Mr Simpson?"

"Yes, Judge."

"Mr Attwood, is there anything you would like to tell me before I pronounce sentence?"

"Yes, Your Honour. Thanks for the opportunity to address the court." Trembling, I can only stammer. "I came to America to be a stockbroker, and America was good to me." Congested from crying, I keep pausing to sniff. "I made lots of money while still young, and after years of hard work and study, I stupidly got off track. I ended up throwing wild parties and taking drugs, which led to the commission of these crimes. I have no excuses, Your Honour. I am deeply sorry for the effects on society my mistakes have caused.

"Despite the hardships of jail, I've made the most of the last two years by studying. I hope the résumé of my achievements shows my sincere desire to return to university in England. While in jail, I've developed writing skills, and my recommendation to buy gold was published in *Investor's Business Daily*." Hoping my words are having a positive effect, I try to read his body language, but his fixed look of contempt increases my fear. "Recidivism is not an option, and in the hundreds of letters of support, my family and friends have expressed their confidence in my future behaviour.

"I invested in drugs out of greed and hedonism. I wish to apologise to the State of Arizona, society, and my family for the harm my actions have caused. I am a first-time offender who has sincerely learnt from his mistakes." I hesitate over using a quote, but it just comes out. "Mahatma Gandhi once said that the law should be used to change men's hearts. Well now that I've gone through this, my heart is in the right place. I humbly ask for your leniency this day." *If the hearing is going well, surely he'd be showing some sympathy.*

"Remain where you are, Mr Attwood. OK, Miss Davis."

The prosecutor stands to take her turn but seems at a loss for words. *Is it part of an act or has she been caught off guard by the emotional atmosphere?* The warmth and sincerity of the speeches have surprised everyone. After an expression of deep thought, she begins, "Mr Attwood, you are extremely lucky to have such a loving and caring family. How could you do this to them?" She looks around the court as if expecting everyone to side with her. "Your family came here today, some from England even, and spoke so eloquently on your behalf. The only way you could do this to them and the only explanation I can think of for your family's kind words is that you have a Jekyll and Hyde personality."

Detective Reid smirks. I feel the good will the previous speeches generated start to dissolve.

"It seems you managed to keep your family charmed while you committed a pattern of serious drug crimes over a number of years because your parents live in England and had no clue what was going on here in Arizona. Mr Attwood, have you any idea of the deaths drug dealers cause? Although you were never charged with any violent crimes, isn't it true that your chief enforcer, Mr Peter Mahoney, committed acts of violence?"

Detective Reid is nodding, his face animating.

"Judge, I filed the submission of the documents for aggravation of Mr Attwood's sentence. In summary, what this all shows is that the information that the State and law enforcement had prior to going up on the wire showed Mr Attwood was the head of a criminal organisation employing hundreds of people over six years, involved in the sale and distribution of millions of dollars of drugs at street value for his own personal gain. That Mr Attwood is an educated man who can make eloquent speeches to the court like you heard today makes his crimes all the more inexcusable. He should have known better. If you look at the volume of drugs dealt, his lead role in the organisation, the State would ask you that this court impose the maximum aggravated sentence, given that the aggravated circumstances far outweigh the mitigated circumstances in this particular case. Thank you."

With all of the speeches at an end, the judge shuffles his papers while I exchange worried glances with my family. Aching with guilt, I pray the judge shows mercy.

"I have considered all the circumstances presented to me," the judge says. "I have considered the mitigating circumstances which are that Mr Attwood avows no prior felony convictions in any jurisdiction, he has a diagnosis of bipolar disorder as indicated in the psychological evaluation, and that rather than just sitting on his rear in the jail, Mr Attwood took all the classes and his behaviour was exemplary. Also, he has accepted full responsibility for what he did and shown remorse. I have also considered the strong family support that he has in England."

My hopes rise.

"I have also considered the aggravating circumstances, which are your repetitive involvement in the transportation and sales of large quantities of illegal drugs, the negative impact on the community, and your lack of moral concern for others in society. As if you were unable to ascertain an ethical difference, you traded drugs like you traded the stock market until you were forced to face the consequences."

It's all going against me. I brace for the maximum sentence.

"The picture that's painted throughout all this, and also in some of the aggravating-circumstance documents that Miss Davis prepared for me, conflict with your family's view of you. Obviously, they have a lot of love for you as shown today. But at the same time, they say this is all out of character. Well, it's out of character, but only to the extent that this has been going on for six years. I also considered the statutory aggravating factors. The fact that this was committed for personal gain and that there were so many accomplices involved. Based on all that, it is ordered the defendant be sentenced to a term of–"

I feel as if I'm stood in front of a train.

"–9½ years in the Department of Corrections to date from today but with full credit for 775 days of presentence incarceration."

My relief begins with a long exhale – until my attorney springs up. "I'd just like to seek clarification from the court that as stipulated in the plea bargain, Mr Attwood is eligible for a half-time release on the balance of the sentence under the terms of Arizona Revised Statutes 41-1604.14: Release of prisoners with detainers; eligibility; revocation of release." He's referring to the loophole.

"Miss Davis?" the judge says.

"I don't know anything about this," the prosecutor says. "Mr Attwood must serve 85 percent of the sentence in accordance with Arizona's laws."

That's not what I'd agreed to in the plea bargain! I'm shocked. Alan said the prosecutor had agreed to the half-time release, which would get me out in three and a half years. *Have I signed under false pretences? Was I tricked? It would have been better to risk a trial.*

"Here is the plea agreement," my attorney says, "specifying that Mr Attwood is eligible to be deported back to England when he has served at least one half of the balance of the sentence imposed by the court."

"Let me see that." The judge seems confused, but after reading the paperwork more thoroughly, he says, "Yes, it says here that Mr Attwood is eligible for the half-time release."

Has Alan tricked the prosecutor into agreeing to a longer sentence knowing he could reduce it through a loophole at the last minute? Or is the prosecutor simply feigning ignorance for the benefit of Detective Reid who wants me to get a life sentence?

"As far as the Attorney General's Office is concerned," the prosecutor says, "Mr Attwood must serve 85 percent of his sentence. If he is deported back to England, then he would have to serve the balance of his sentence there, too."

"That's not what the plea says," my attorney says.

"Then I'm left with no choice but to revoke the plea agreement," the judge says.

His words are like a punch to the head that hasn't quite knocked me out. Stunned, I can't believe my sentencing is getting cancelled. *I've never heard of such a thing happening to any other prisoners. I'll have to start all over again. More months or years fighting my case, while rotting away in the jail. If a guard tries to take me away, I'm going to yell at the judge.*

"Is the plea agreement you are holding, Judge, the same as the one in Miss Davis's possession?" my attorney asks, urgency in his voice.

After pausing for a few seconds, the judge says, "This is most unusual. I'd like to see you both, Miss Davis and Mr Simpson, in my chambers."

Watching them leave the courtroom, taking my future with them, I burn with outrage. I want to burst out of my chains and bolt out of there. If I go down in a hail of bullets, so be it. Awaiting the judge's return, my family members' faces turn ashen. My dad is supporting my mum as if to prevent her from collapsing. Claudia's father, Barry, looks as if he's in the disorientation stage of a tropical illness – unknown to me he had a mini-seizure upon entering the building but in spite of that had insisted on staying. Barry is sweating, swaying, unfocussed, his mouth moving as if he's trying to garble something that won't come out. *My sentencing hearing is falling through after my family just flew 5000 miles. Fuck the whole judicial process! Alan is going to tell me that I just need to tough the jail out for another year while he continues to fight the case.* I can see in the eyes of my parents, sister and Aunt Mo that they think they've flown over for nothing. That they've been had. Detective Reid's eyes are saying, *Gotcha!* I'm ready to explode in a rage and curse the judge, the prosecutor and my lawyer right here in the courtroom. Awaiting the decision, I flex my body against my chains. I ball my hands into fists and unclench them over and over again. These are the longest most agonising moments of my life.

Eventually, the judge, Alan and the prosecutor return with blank faces. Everyone else seems apprehensive. My fingers are tingling, my heart about to pop one of its chambers. But for the handcuffs, I'd be clutching my chest.

The judge's hawkish gaze unsettles me further. I sway as if

about to faint. "Based on my conversation with Miss Davis and Mr Simpson, it is the recommendation of this court that the defendant be eligible for the half-time release on the balance of his sentence and be deported back to England at that time."

Twenty-six months of uncertainty lifts like a tombstone. Detective Reid stands and curses. My loved ones cheer and throw up their arms. The prosecutor gathers her paperwork as if in a hurry to leave. The escorting guard smiles in my direction. My attorney shakes my hand, proud of the outcome.

"You did it, Alan," I say, wishing I could hug him and all of my supporters. "Thanks so much."

I'm surging with relief and smiling bizarrely, like a lone survivor of a natural disaster. Electrified by a strange sense of release, my body feels lighter. My future is no longer up in the air and that's all that matters. I can see an end to it. I can see when I'm getting out. Even though I've just received a nine-and-a-half-year sentence, it's one of the happiest days of my life.

CHAPTER 52

I receive a note from Frankie:

Englandman, my friend and wife to be. I know you'll be leaving soon. I'm giving you some secret info. Use my name in prison. It's like a gold card. Keep in touch and when you get to prison, let me know who's around you, people with older prison numbers or ex-gangsters. I will send word and make sure you are well looked after. Good luck my friend, and don't be crying 'cause you miss me. Kiss! Kiss!

Blogs:

Jul 2 04

Periplaneta Americana, more commonly known as the American cockroach, has an average lifespan of 440 days. As of today, I have been a resident of this crowbar motel for almost two cockroach lifespans. I have endured enough. It is time for me to move on, so I have signed myself over to the Arizona Department of Corrections.

Parents of inmates, horrified by the conditions in the jail, have directed this blog to local groups such as Mothers Against Arpaio who are working to get changes made. Although I shall soon be free of this place, I hope that changes are made so that other un-sentenced inmates – who are supposed to be presumed innocent until proven guilty – do not have to be warehoused like animals. When a society treats its prisoners like animals some will behave like animals when they return to society.

Epicurus, as quoted by Marcus Aurelius: "Pain is neither intolerable nor continuing, provided you remember its limits and do not let your imagination add to it." Marcus Aurelius: "Delve within;

within is the fountain of good, and it is always ready to bubble up, if you always delve."

Jul 13 04

I am still at the jail. A sudden spate of tragedies has compelled me to write this entry. At the weekend, two inmates on my floor attempted to commit suicide. One threw himself off the balcony and survived. The other was discovered trying to hang himself. Sadder still, an inmate housed in a medium-security pod was found dead in the shower. Inmates are often "smashed" in the shower area because it is out of view of the cameras. The jail has refused to release the cause of his death.

The temperature outside is 114 °F. The trickle of air into our cells feels like hot air blowing from a hairdryer. We are soaked in sweat all day and night. It is difficult to write on this sweat-moist-ened paper. The majority now have skin infections and rashes, which persistently itch. Between the sweat trickling down my body and the cockroaches tickling my limbs, it is impossible to sleep properly. Last night, while sleeping on my side, my ear filled up with sweat, and when I moved my head, the sweat spilled onto my face. I woke up, startled. It felt like someone was touching my cheek.

When I was a small child, I imagined hell consisted of caves in which the damned were trapped, tortured and burnt. I imagined serpents and indescribable creepy crawlies tormenting the cap-tives. I never imagined man's nature could be so hateful as to recreate these conditions on earth.

SHAUN'S JOURNEY CONTINUES IN CHAPTER 1 OF PRISON TIME

"I've got a padlock in a sock. I can smash your brains in while you're asleep. I can kill you whenever I want." My new cellmate sizes me up with no trace of human feeling in his eyes. Muscular and pot-bellied, he's caked in prison ink, including six snakes on his skull, slithering side by side. The top of his right ear is missing in a semi-circle.

The waves of fear are overwhelming. After being in transportation all day, I can feel my bladder hurting. "I'm not looking to cause any trouble. I'm the quietest cellmate you'll ever have. All I do is read and write."

Scowling, he shakes his head. "Why've they put a fish in with me?" He swaggers close enough for me to smell his cigarette breath. "Us convicts don't get along with fresh fish."

"Should I ask to move then?" I say, hoping he'll agree if he hates new prisoners so much.

"No! They'll think I threatened you!"

In the eight by twelve feet slab of space, I swerve around him and place my property box on the top bunk.

He pushes me aside and grabs the box. "You just put that on my artwork! I ought to fucking smash you, fish!"

"Sorry, I didn't see it."

"You need to be more aware of your fucking surroundings! What you in for anyway, fish?"

I explain my charges, Ecstasy dealing and how I spent twenty-six months fighting my case.

"How come the cops were so hard-core after you?" he asks,

squinting.

"It was a big case, a multi-million dollar investigation. They raided over a hundred people and didn't find any drugs. They were pretty pissed off. I'd stopped dealing by the time they caught up with me, but I'd done plenty over the years, so I accept my punishment."

"Throwing raves," he says, staring at the ceiling as if remembering something. "Were you partying with underage girls?" he asks, his voice slow, coaxing.

Being called a sex offender is the worst insult in prison. Into my third year of incarceration, I'm conditioned to react. "What you trying to say?" I yell angrily, brow clenched.

"Were you fucking underage girls?" Flexing his body, he shakes both fists as if about to punch me.

"Hey, I'm no child molester, and I'd prefer you didn't say shit like that!"

"My buddy next door is doing twenty-five to life for murdering a child molester. How do I know Ecstasy dealing ain't your cover story?" He inhales loudly, nostrils flaring.

"You want to see my fucking paperwork?"

A stocky prisoner walks in. Short hair. Dark eyes. Powerful neck. On one arm: a tattoo of a man in handcuffs above the word OMERTA – the Mafia code of silence towards law enforcement. "What the fuck's going on in here, Bud?" asks Junior Bull – the son of "Sammy the Bull" Gravano, the Mafia mass murderer who was my biggest competitor in the Ecstasy market.

Relieved to see a familiar face, I say, "How're you doing?"

Shaking my hand, he says in a New York Italian accent, "I'm doing alright. I read that shit in the newspaper about you starting a blog in Sheriff Joe Arpaio's jail."

"The blog's been bringing media heat on the conditions."

"You know him?" Bud asks.

"Yeah, from Towers jail. He's a good dude. He's in for dealing Ecstasy like me."

"It's a good job you said that 'cause I was about to smash his ass," Bud says.

"It's a good job Wild Man ain't here 'cause you'd a got your ass thrown off the balcony," Junior Bull says.

I laugh. The presence of my best friend, Wild Man, was partly the reason I never took a beating at the county jail, but with Wild Man in a different prison, I feel vulnerable. When Bud casts a death stare on me, my smile fades.

"What the fuck you guys on about?" Bud asks.

"Let's go talk downstairs." Junior Bull leads Bud out.

I rush to a stainless steel sink/toilet bolted to a cement-block wall by the front of the cell, unbutton my orange jumpsuit and crane my neck to watch the upper-tier walkway in case Bud returns. I bask in relief as my bladder deflates. After flushing, I take stock of my new home, grateful for the slight improvement in the conditions versus what I'd grown accustomed to in Sheriff Joe Arpaio's jail. No cockroaches. No blood stains. A working swamp cooler. Something I've never seen in a cell before: shelves. The steel table bolted to the wall is slightly larger, too. *But how will I concentrate on writing with Bud around?* There's a mixture of smells in the room. Cleaning chemicals. Aftershave. Tobacco. A vinegar-like odour. The slit of a window at the back overlooks gravel in a no-man's-land before the next building with gleaming curls of razor wire around its roof.

From the doorway upstairs, I'm facing two storeys of cells overlooking a day room with shower cubicles at the end of both tiers. At two white plastic circular tables, prisoners are playing dominoes, cards, chess and Scrabble, some concentrating, others yelling obscenities, contributing to a brain-scraping din that I hope to block out by purchasing a Walkman. In a raised box-shaped Plexiglas control tower, two guards are monitoring the prisoners.

Bud returns. My pulse jumps. Not wanting to feel like I'm stuck in a kennel with a rabid dog, I grab a notepad and pen and head for the day room.

Focussed on my body language, not wanting to signal any

weakness, I'm striding along the upper tier, head and chest elevated, when two hands appear from a doorway and grab me. I drop the pad. The pen clinks against grid-metal and tumbles to the day room as I'm pulled into a cell reeking of backside sweat and masturbation, a cheese-tinted funk.

"I'm Booga. Let's fuck," says a squat man in urine-stained boxers, with WHITE TRASH tattooed on his torso below a mobile home, and an arm sleeved with the Virgin Mary.

Shocked, I brace to flee or fight to preserve my anal virginity. I can't believe my eyes when he drops his boxers and waggles his penis.

Dancing to music playing through a speaker he has rigged up, Booga smiles in a sexy way. "Come on," he says in a husky voice. "Drop your pants. Let's fuck." He pulls pornography faces. I question his sanity. He moves closer. "If I let you fart in my mouth, can I fart in yours?"

"You can fuck off," I say, springing towards the doorway.

He grabs me. We scuffle. Every time I make progress towards the doorway, he clings to my clothes, dragging me back in. When I feel his penis rub against my leg, my adrenalin kicks in so forcefully I experience a burst of strength and wriggle free. I bolt out as fast as my shower sandals will allow, and snatch my pad. Looking over my shoulder, I see him stood calmly in the doorway, smiling. He points at me. "You have to walk past my door every day. We're gonna get together. I'll lick your ass and you can fart in my mouth." Booga blows a kiss and disappears.

I rush downstairs. With my back to a wall, I pause to steady my thoughts and breathing. In survival mode, I think, *What's going to come at me next?* In the hope of reducing my tension, I borrow a pen to do what helps me stay sane: writing. With the details fresh in my mind, I document my journey to the prison for my blog readers, keeping an eye out in case anyone else wants to test the new prisoner. The more I write, the more I fill with a sense of purpose. Jon's Jail Journal is a connection to the outside world that I cherish.

Someone yells, "One time!" The din lowers. A door rumbles open. A guard does a security walk, his every move scrutinised by dozens of scornful eyes staring from cells. When he exits, the din resumes, and the prisoners return to injecting drugs to escape from reality, including the length of their sentences. This continues all day with "Two times!" signifying two approaching guards, and "Three times!" three and so on. Every now and then an announcement by a guard over the speakers briefly lowers the din.

Before lockdown, I join the line for a shower, holding bars of soap in a towel that I aim to swing at the head of the next person to try me. With boisterous inmates a few feet away, yelling at the men in the showers to "Stop jerking off," and "Hurry the fuck up," I get in a cubicle that reeks of bleach and mildew. With every nerve strained, I undress and rinse fast.

At night, despite the desert heat, I cocoon myself in a blanket from head to toe and turn towards the wall, making my face more difficult to strike. I leave a hole for air, but the warm cement block inches from my mouth returns each exhalation to my face as if it's breathing on me, creating a feeling of suffocation. For hours, my heart drums so hard against the thin mattress I feel as if I'm moving even though I'm still. I try to sleep, but my eyes keep springing open and my head turning towards the cell as I try to penetrate the darkness, searching for Bud swinging a padlock in a sock at my head.

SHAUN'S STORY STARTS IN CHAPTER 1 OF PARTY TIME

We approach two drug dealers, lads about our age, twenty, skulking in a corner of a dark nightclub, skulls shaved.

"Can we get two hits of Ecstasy and two grams of speed?" my friend asks.

My fingers and legs start to shake.

"E's twenty quid. Tenner a wrap of Billy Whizz."

"Here you go." My friend offers our money.

The dealers exchange looks as if pondering whether to rob us. My body stiffens like plaster setting in a cast. The biggest snatches our cash. The other passes the drugs imperceptibly. They vanish. I worry about getting arrested for possession. It's 1989, and drug deals rarely end happily on my TV. Bracing for undercover cops to grab us, I spin my eyes around the room.

My friend yanks my arm, rushes us to the toilets, locks us in a stall. He reveals two white pills and speed meticulously wrapped in little paper rectangles. "You put the Billy Whizz in your drink," he whispers, tipping white powder into a bottle, "and neck the White Dove."

Committing to do drugs is one thing, taking them another. *Will I be hooked for the rest of my life?* My fear of ending up in an ambulance and my parents finding out recedes as the thrill rises. *I can experiment a few times, have fun, quit whenever I want…*

"Come on, get on with it," he says, having taken his.

I dump the speed into a bottle of Lucozade, pop the pill, take a swig, and gag on the chemical aftertaste. *Oh my God! What happens now?* I turn to my friend. "How long before I feel it?"

"Within the hour."

My friend is a fellow Economics student at Liverpool University. Raves are making headline news, so I'm at The Thunderdome in Manchester to find out what all the fuss is about. The bare square room with a stage at the front is unimpressive. Only a few people are dancing to music that makes no sense. Repetitive beats and beeps like signals from outer space. Most of the ravers are stood by the walls, gazing at the dance floor as if expecting an elephant to materialise. Nightclubs intimidate me. I feel shy in them. I don't dare talk to anyone other than my friend. Convinced I'm about to overdose – die even – I spend the next half-hour checking my pulse, timing the beats per minute.

An expression blossoms on my friend's face as if he's having an orgasm. Exuding the kind of bliss seen on angels in medieval paintings, he can't stop smiling or stand still. He asks me to dance. I haven't enjoyed dancing since the days of punk rock. I say no. He bounces off. I regret letting him down. Frustrated at the drugs for not affecting me, I finish my drink. I walk towards the bar. My knees buckle and the strength drains from my legs. I try to soldier on but wobble as if on sinking sand and have to sit down.

Someone kicks me. "Sorry, mate."

Staring up at a happy raver in baggy jeans, I break into a smile that wraps around my face and refuses to go away. There's a strange feeling on my back. *Has a bug landed there?* I reach over my shoulder to slap it off. *No bug.* It's the sensation of my T-shirt against my skin. Running my fingertips up and down the nape of my neck feels like feathers are tickling my skin. *Or are my fingers melting into my skin?* A sensation so pleasurable, I massage myself. Breathing feels different, too. Each inhale pulses pleasure through my body as if I'm getting fondled by an invisible woman. Smiling at the forest of legs growing around me, I remember going to the bar – but that doesn't matter anymore, nor does losing my girlfriend, the engine problems with my car, the calculus-heavy five-thousand-word balance-of-payments essay due on Monday morning… The high is demolishing every worry in my life, leaving me no choice but to be happy with the way things are.

The club fills. Time is irrelevant. Ravers are everywhere, a

kaleidoscope of coloured clothing. Hugging, grinning, groov-
ing, jumping happiness machines, raising the temperature with
their body heat. My desire to join them gains strength – it's just
a matter of time. My high keeps rising, interrupting the flow of
my thoughts, making my eyeballs flutter upwards as if under the
influence of the moon's magnetic pull. Hot, I want to take my
T-shirt off – pondering the urge melts it away. The music and
beeping noises are making sense now. They're saying, *Get off your
arse and dance!*

I'm bobbing my head, playing the piano on my thighs when
my friend finds me. He smiles. Our eyes sparkle in recognition of
each other's highs.

"Come on," he says.

I follow him into the thicket of bodies. He starts to dance.
I jump from side to side, trying to find my groove, and settle into the same rocking motion as everyone else. I'm dancing,
loving dancing, surprised by how natural it feels, experimenting
with moves copied from those around me. My heart is beating
hard and in time with the *boom-boom-boom* blasting from giant
black speakers. My arms are jerking up and down as if throwing
boulders at the ceiling when everyone stops dancing. *Has someone turned the music off? No.* Only the beat has stopped, leaving
a soothing sound. Hands shoot up. Whistles blow. A machine
hisses out smoke. A black woman sings with beauty bordering
on spiritual, tingling my skin all over. Piano notes are struck. We
sway, our fingers reaching into the beams of the sun laser. An air
horn sounds. Bracing for a lorry to plough through the club, I
jump. Such an absurd notion makes me laugh aloud. The soulful
woman's voice fades as DJ Jay Wearden mixes in a Guru Josh
track: *1990's... Time for the Guru...* A saxophone solo sends a
tremor through my body. My eyeballs shiver. In the square room
that had bored me earlier, I feel as if I'm at one with God. I never
want the party to end.

MY SOCIAL-MEDIA LINKS

Email: attwood.shaun@hotmail.co.uk
Blog: Jon's Jail Journal
Website: shaunattwood.com
Twitter: @shaunattwood
YouTube: Shaun Attwood
LinkedIn: Shaun Attwood
Goodreads: Shaun Attwood
Facebook pages: Shaun Attwood, Jon's Jail Journal, T-Bone
Appreciation Society

I welcome your questions, comments and
feedback on any of my books:
Party Time
Hard Time
Prison Time
Lessons
Two Tonys (Expected 2015-2016)
We Are Being Lied To (Expected 2015-2016)
T-Bone (Expected 2017)

Thank you for the hundreds of great reviews on
Amazon and Goodreads!

PARTY TIME

In *Party Time*, Shaun Attwood arrives in Phoenix, Arizona a penniless business graduate from a small industrial town in England. Within a decade, he becomes a stock-market millionaire.

But he is leading a double life.

After taking his first Ecstasy pill at a rave in Manchester as a shy student, Shaun becomes intoxicated by the party lifestyle that changes his fortune. Making it his personal mission to bring the English rave scene to the Arizona desert, Shaun becomes submerged in a criminal underworld, throwing parties for thousands of ravers and running an Ecstasy ring in competition with the Mafia mass murderer "Sammy the Bull" Gravano.

As greed and excess tear through his life, Shaun experiences eye-watering encounters with Mafia hit men and crystal-meth addicts, extravagant debaucheries with superstar DJs and glitter girls, and ingests enough drugs to kill a herd of elephants. This is his story.

PRISON TIME

Sentenced to 9½ years in Arizona's state prison for distributing Ecstasy, Shaun finds himself living among gang members, sexual predators and drug-crazed psychopaths. After being attacked by a Californian biker in for stabbing a girlfriend, Shaun writes about the prisoners who befriend, protect and inspire him. They include T-Bone, a massive African American ex-Marine who risks his life saving vulnerable inmates from rape, and Two Tonys, an old-school Mafia murderer who left the corpses of his rivals from Arizona to Alaska. They teach Shaun how to turn incarceration to his advantage, and to learn from his mistakes.

Shaun is no stranger to love and lust in the heterosexual world, but the tables are turned on him inside. Sexual advances come at him from all directions, some cleverly disguised, others more sinister – making Shaun question his sexual identity. *Prison Time* is the first ever book to detail the sex lives of prisoners.

Resigned to living alongside violent, mentally-ill and drug-addicted inmates, Shaun immerses himself in psychology and philosophy to try to make sense of his past behaviour, and begins applying what he learns as he adapts to prison life. Encouraged by Two Tonys to explore fiction as well, Shaun reads over 1000 books which, with support from a brilliant psychotherapist, Dr Owen, speed along his personal development. As his ability to deflect daily threats improves, Shaun begins to look forward to his release with optimism and a new love waiting for him. Yet the words of Aristotle from one of Shaun's books will prove prophetic: "We cannot learn without pain."

LESSONS

A self-help book like no other, *Lessons* includes what Shaun learned when he was forced to reappraise his life in the harsh reality of Arizona's penal system, including supermaximum-security prison. The people imparting wisdom to Shaun range from his psychotherapist, Dr Owen, and his meditation master, Andrew, to Two Tonys, a Mafia mass murderer serving 112 years for killing rival gangsters, and T-Bone, an ex-Marine using formidable fighting skills to stop prison rape.

These lessons – told via anecdotes and Socratic dialogue – will force you to re-examine your life and what is truly important. They include:

• Love the Right Person: a dysfunctional relationship can derail everything you have worked for

• Take Time for Introspection: the foundation for personal development is self-knowledge

• Identify and Overcome Addictions: unacknowledged addictions can creep out of control and devastate your life

• Value Your Family: make time for the people who love you unconditionally

NEW TITLES EXPECTED 2015–2017

Two Tonys
The biography of Two Tonys, an old-school Mafia mass murderer, sentenced to 112 years. He left the corpses of rival gangsters from Arizona to Alaska.

T-Bone
The biography of T-Bone, a deeply spiritual massive African American covered in scars who used formidable fighting skills acquired as a Marine to stop prison rape. After serving in the army, T-Bone entered the equally violent world of being a bodyguard and a cocaine dealer, which landed him in Arizona's deadliest prisons.

We Are Being Lied To
?

ABOUT SHAUN ATTWOOD

Shaun Attwood is a former stock-market millionaire and Ecstasy supplier turned public speaker, author and activist, who is banned from America for life. His story was featured worldwide on National Geographic Channel as an episode of Locked Up/Banged Up Abroad called Raving Arizona (available on YouTube).

Shaun's writing – smuggled out of the jail with the highest death rate in America run by Sheriff Joe Arpaio – attracted international media attention to the human rights violations: murders by guards and gang members, dead rats in the food, cockroach infestations…

While incarcerated, Shaun was forced to reappraise his life. He read over 1000 books in just under six years. By studying original texts in psychology and philosophy, he sought to better understand himself and his past behaviour. He credits books as being the lifeblood of his rehabilitation.

Shaun now tells his story to schools to put young people off drugs and crime. He campaigns against injustice via his books and blog, Jon's Jail Journal. He has appeared on the BBC, Sky News and TV worldwide to talk about issues affecting prisoners' rights.